10-31

An Atheling Book

*A Study in the History
of Social Theory*

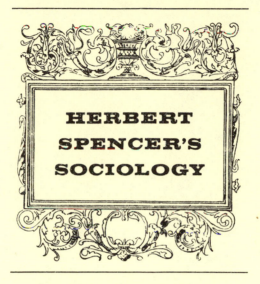

**HERBERT
SPENCER'S
SOCIOLOGY**

by Jay Rumney

An Atheling Book

ATHERTON PRESS · NEW YORK · 1966

The occasional uneven impression of the type in this book was unavoidable. It occurred in the original work from which this volume was reproduced by photo-offset.

HM
51
57
.R8

Published by arrangement with The Rationalist Press
Association, Ltd.

Foreword Copyright © 1965 by Atherton Press

Manufactured in the United States of America
Cover design by Mel Byars

FIRST ATHELING EDITION, 1965

Atheling Books are published by
Atherton Press
70 Fifth Avenue
New York 10011

Foreword

The republication of this book is eminently fitting at this time. It is a valuable, and most readable, contribution to a subject meriting renewed reflection.

Jay Rumney's HERBERT SPENCER'S SOCIOLOGY first appeared in 1937. In that year Talcott Parsons, citing Crane Brinton, declared: "Spencer is dead. But who killed him and how?" It was the thesis of Parsons' famous THE STRUCTURE OF SOCIAL ACTION that the evolution of scientific theory had put an end to Spencer. And for more than a generation the man whose name had been synonymous with sociology was, or so it seemed, repressed and forgotten.

Of late there has been a notable revival of interest in Herbert Spencer. Summary rejection of his ideas has yielded to a more judicious appreciation of his contribution to sociological thought. To be sure, social evolutionism in its classic form has passed from the scene. No one today considers society a biological organism. No longer does anyone believe in an iron or cosmological law of Evolution guaranteeing the unilinear development of human society to perfection. But while it was fashionable at one time to dwell upon those aspects of Spencer's work that have since met an honorable demise, there is now undoubtedly a general agreement with Talcott Parsons' more recent statement that Spencer's thinking about society was informed with three main positive ideas: that of society as a self-regulating system, that of differentiation and function, and that of evolution—all of which remain as important today as they were when he wrote.

Indeed, the sociological work of Spencer is rich in passages that have the ring of contemporaneity. On the level of "approach," they might serve as veritable models of the modern structural-functional mode of analysis. Even in regard to the principal assumptions of evolutionism, not a few sociologists —and most anthropologists—today profess a "neo-evolutionism," however modified. They still insist on the usefulness of the concept of stages, and they would agree with Malinowski that

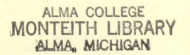

"certain forms definitely precede others: a technological setting such as expressed in the terms *stone age, bronze age, iron age,* or the levels of clan or gentile organization, of numerically small groups thinly scattered, as against urban or semiurban settlements, have to be viewed from the evolutionary point of view."*

In the re-examination of the sociological writings of Herbert Spencer, in the sifting of what is alive and relevant from what is dated and irrelevant in his thought, in the determination of the extent to which both the originality and the inadequacy of his views have stimulated scientific inquiry, I know of no better and more lucid guide than the present book by Professor Rumney. Its reissuance also affords me an opportunity to acknowledge my continued indebtedness to the man who, until his untimely death in 1957, was my friend and mentor throughout the many years of our association in the Department of Sociology at Rutgers University.

Joseph Maier

*T. Parsons, Introduction to H. Spencer, *The Study of Sociology* (Ann Arbor: University of Michigan Press), 1961.

INTRODUCTION.

THE present volume is designed by the trustees appointed under Herbert Spencer's will to form the final volume of a series of works begun by him nearly seventy years ago, but which he did not live to complete himself. It may therefore be desirable to recapitulate the circumstances in which the work was conceived and to relate how it has been carried through.

In 1867, to assist him in the preparation of the book he was then writing, *The Principles of Sociology*, Spencer devised a system of collecting and classifying large numbers of facts relating to societies of different types, ancient and modern, in order to draw from them inferences and generalizations.

Spencer conceived the social organization of mankind to be evolutionary, " and excludes the notion of manufacture or artificial arrangement, while it implies natural development " (*Autobiography*, chap. xxxvi). " A social organism is like an individual organism, it grows ; in growing it becomes more complex ; its parts acquire increasing dependence ; its life is immense in length compared with the lives of its component units. Increasing integration is accompanied by increasing heterogeneity and increasing definiteness " (*ibid.*).

From this scheme for the collection of materials by other hands than his own sprang the great series of volumes known as *Descriptive Sociology*. He found the results so obtained of so much interest in themselves and of such value apart from their use in connexion with *The Principles of Sociology*, that he decided to extend their scope and to issue them as a contribution to general knowledge.

He says in the Provisional Preface to some of the earlier volumes of the series : " This classified compilation was entered upon solely to facilitate my own work ; yet after having brought the mode of classification to a satisfactory form . . . I decided to have the undertaking executed with a view to publication ; the facts collected and arranged . . . being so presented, apart from hypotheses, as to aid all students of social science in testing such conclusions as they have drawn, and in drawing others, uninfluenced by the hypotheses or prejudices of others."

The " satisfactory form " of the classification of societies consists of three large divisions, comprehending these groups : 1. Uncivilized Societies ; 2. Civilized Societies, extinct or decayed ; 3. Civilized Societies, recent or still flourishing.

Spencer pursued his work on the assumption that the entire social fabric of any race could be set forth in tabular form (short generalizations founded on the detailed information supplied by the extracts), and on account of the size of these tabular statements he found it necessary to use an exceptionally large format (royal folio) so that the tables could be opened out to display in a sort of literary map the information they contained.

The tables thus constitute a conspectus, for each society treated, " of its morphology, its physiology and its development " (*see* Provisional Preface, 1873). Each part of the *Descriptive Sociology* therefore, opens with the tables arranged in columns with headings in accordance with the classification Spencer devised.

(The arrangement of the headings is here placed vertically instead of horizontally, for convenience of printing) :

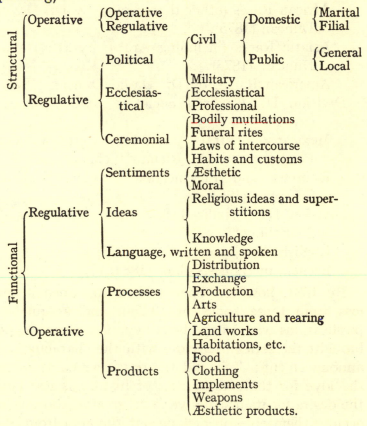

At the head of the tables are summarized particulars as under:

1. Inorganic environment
2. Organic environment
3. Sociological environment
4. Physical characters
5. Emotional characters
6. Intellectual characters.

From the year 1867 to 1881 Spencer had prepared and published eight parts, namely :—

Division I. Uncivilized Societies :

Lowest Races, Negrito Races and Malayo-Polynesian Races, by Dr. David Duncan (1874).

African Races (other than Arab), by Dr. David Duncan (1875).

Asiatic Races (including Arab), by Dr. David Duncan (1876).

American Races, by Dr. David Duncan (1878)

Division II. Civilized Societies, extinct or decayed :

Mexicans, Central Americans, Chibchas and Peruvians, by Dr. Richard Scheppig (1874).

Hebrews and Phœnicians, by Dr. Richard Scheppig (1880).

Division III. Civilized Societies, recent or still flourishing :

English, by James Collier (1873).

French, by James Collier (1881).

By 1881, however, Spencer had sustained a net loss from these books of £3,250, and as further publications would have been beyond his means, he brought the series to a close with the characteristic announcement : " Should the day ever come when the love for the personalities of history is less and the desire for its instructive facts greater, those who occupy themselves in picking out the gold from the dross will, perhaps, be able to publish their results without inflicting on themselves losses too grievous to be borne." (*Notice of Cessation*, issued with Part VIII, French, 1881.)

Yet, in spite of his own inability to continue the

preparation of the *Descriptive Sociology*, Spencer was so convinced of its usefulness that he resolved to devote, after his death, the residuum of his estate to the completion of the work upon the plan he had laid down, and by his will appointed three trustees to carry out his wishes. The successive trustees up to the present time have been : the Hon. Auberon Herbert ; Dr. H. Charlton Bastian, F.R.S. ; Dr. David Duncan ; Prof. Sir Arthur Keith, F.R.S. ; Major Leonard Darwin, Sc.D. ; and Lieut.-Col. Sir David Prain, F.R.S.—the three last named forming the present acting body of the Trust.

The trustees had, of course, other work to accomplish in connexion with the instructions conveyed in Spencer's will, but the particular part of their activities with which the *Descriptive Sociology* deals has resulted in the issue of the following parts :

Division I. Uncivilized Societies :

> Lowest Races, a new edition brought up to date by the original compiler, Dr. Duncan (1925).

> African Races, a new edition, practically re-written and greatly enlarged, by Emil Torday (1930).

Division II. Civilized Societies, extinct or decayed :

> Greeks, Hellenic Period, by Sir J. P. Mahaffy and Prof. W. A. Goligher, LL.D. (1910).

> Ancient Egyptians, by Sir W. Flinders Petrie (1925).

> Greeks, Hellenistic Period, by Prof. W. A. Goligher, LL.D. (1928).

> Mesopotamia, by Reuben Levy, Litt.D. (1929).

Division III. Civilized Societies, recent or still flourishing :

Chinese, by E. T. C. Werner (1910).

Islam, by Reuben Levy, 2 vols. (1933).

Besides the above completed parts, there are still in course of preparation (1934) :

Division I.   Uncivilized Societies :

The Heritage of Solomon (Ancient Palestine), by Prof. John Garstang, LL.D.

Division II. Civilized Societies, extinct or decayed :

Ancient Romans, by Prof. W. A. Goligher and Dr. E. H. Alton.

This list of titles shows that the books published by Spencer in his lifetime and those issued by the trustees in his name since his death, cover most of the representative races and civilizations from prehistoric times to the present.

Spencer's own methods of work were always meticulous. He carried into all his literary output the same desire for perfection of detail that he exhibited in his ordinary mode of life, whether in his domestic arrangements or in his contacts with the outside world.   In order to secure that accuracy of detail which was a part of his nature, he left for the scholars to be employed by the trustees after his death, very definite instructions as to the way in which they were to pursue their labours in compiling the successive parts of the *Descriptive Sociology*.   Here are a few of these directions :

Before the commencement of the work the Compiler shall submit to the Editor a list of the books and authorities he proposes to use.

The Compiler is to go through the whole book and tick lightly in pencil such passages as are to be copied   . . .   to avoid unnecessary duplication.

The Compiler when copying extracts is to use as a guide to the eye a heavy strip of lead or brass with a bevelled edge, which will be moved down line by line as the extract is copied. For copying from an inclined book a mechanical implement should be used.

The extracts are to be copied into copybooks approved by the Editor, in the order in which they appear in the books from which they are taken.

Proper names are to be copied in ROMAN LETTERS. In copying extracts, etc., the titles of books are to be underscored so as to appear in the proof as *italics*, not in quotation marks. The diphthong æ is not to be rendered as " a e " but always " æ."

The Compiler should see his work through the press and read each revise. All quotations and references must be carefully verified by the Compiler when the volume is in proof.

The somewhat cumbersome format in which Spencer had originally decided to issue these books militated against their extensive use by students, as few people have the space necessary to accommodate or store, where they can be easily available for use, books 20 inches in height and 13 inches in width. The trustees applied to the High Court in 1928 and obtained a judge's order to vary the shape of the books and to issue volumes ranging in size with Spencer's own works in the Synthetic Philosophy, that is, demy octavo. The Judge also authorized the adoption, in preference to the presentation of tables and extracts, of a narrative style of composition supplemented by full bibliographies.

The work on the Sociology of Islam mentioned in the list on page 201 has, accordingly, appeared in octavo, and the book on Palestine will also appear as an octavo volume.

There was, however, in Spencer's mind from the very outset an addition to this scheme. He had written his *Principles of Sociology* largely from the generalizations he had formed from the materials accumulated for him up to the date of that work. He foresaw the time when the series must be finished, and therefore left instructions, written after he had prepared his will, that the whole work, including those parts already published up to 1881 (the date he issued the Notice of Cessation), was to be revised and rearranged, involving " not merely correction of the text, but revision and amplification of the matter, the whole work being brought up to date " (Memorandum prepared August 12, 1899).

This instruction, construed in its widest sense, clearly implies co-ordination of the material included in the eighteen volumes of the complete series.

As the Trust set up by Herbert Spencer's Will was due to expire in December, 1934, in 1933, the Trustees began to make preparations for the compilation of a final volume on the Descriptive Sociology on the lines laid down by Spencer himself in the Memorandum quoted above.

After serious thought, it was decided to entrust the work to Dr. Morris Ginsberg, Martin White Professor of Sociology in the University of London. Professor Ginsberg prepared a scheme,' but unfortunately, however, found himself unable to undertake the work. He commended to the Trustees Dr. Rumney, whose studies in Sociology had been guided by himself and who had held a Rockefeller Travelling Fellowship. Dr. Rumney undertook the task, albeit the limit of time imposed upon him made the work a difficult one. He indicates in this book the enormous advances that have been made in the study of sociology since Spencer laid down his pen, and shows that, in spite of the investigations and conclusions of modern sociologists, the eminence of Herbert Spencer remains.

The Trustees are gratified to state that Professor Ginsberg has shown personal interest in the pages of Dr. Rumney's work and he has furnished a stimulating preface.

Spencer's concepts as noted on page 288, cannot be entirely reconciled with the conclusions of modern sociologists, but the present book will show how much modern sociology owes to the work done by Spencer. Dr. Rumney in this book discusses the changes that have occurred in the outlook of sociologists since Spencer began his studies more than half a century ago. He emphasizes the lines on which modern sociologists have made a real advance. At the same time, he has compared the Spencerian deductions with the results of modern research. Hence the title chosen for this book.

The classification devised by Spencer for the study of sociology is still retained. The one conception which modern sociologists have modified in Spencer's scheme is his attempt to trace all progress in sociology to evolution. The present book shows how, in detail, many of Spencer's conclusions have had to be modified, although the framework which he built is still the framework for later inquiries.

The opinions expressed by Dr. Rumney in the course of his Treatise are, of course, his own and the Trustees are not in any way responsible for them. The Trustees are confident that in commissioning Dr. Rumney to undertake the present volume, they have brought to a fitting conclusion their efforts to carry out the task entrusted to them by the Will of Herbert Spencer.

In order to make this book the final work of the Trust, the Trustees have thought it desirable to issue a complete Bibliography on Spencer and his writings, not only on the Descriptive Sociology, but on the whole of the Synthetic Philosophy and his other contributions to scientific thought. It was originally intended to issue this Bibliography in separate book form, but for the reason mentioned above, it has been decided to append it in the present work. For this reason, Spencer's own Prospectus of a System of Philosophy, dated 1858, is reprinted on pages 297 to 303, and this is followed by the Bibliography specially prepared by Dr. Rumney, who has consulted the original editions of many of the books mentioned, some of which are unobtainable in this country.

CONTENTS.

PREFACE.

DESPITE the very great influence exerted by Herbert Spencer upon the development of sociology, there exists, so far as I am aware, no comprehensive exposition in English of his sociological teaching. It is therefore a matter for congratulation that the Herbert Spencer Trust has decided to add to the series of volumes on Descriptive Sociology which they have been publishing in accordance with the terms of his will a volume summarizing his achievements, and reviewing his principal conclusions in the light of the developments which have occurred in sociology since his death. They have found in Dr. Rumney a scholar peculiarly well fitted by his wide knowledge of sociology, and of the related social sciences, to carry out this important task. He has produced a work which will be of value not only for the light it throws on Spencer's teaching, but also as a guide to contemporary sociological theory in England and abroad.

Sociology does not now stand in need of the elaborate defence which Spencer found it necessary to make in his still suggestive and important work on *The Study of Sociology*. Sociology has won for itself a place among the social sciences, and there is increasing recognition of its importance in the understanding and control of social life. Yet the fundamental problems raised by Spencer still demand a solution, and in some ways they appear now in a more acute form than in his time. The unification

of all knowledge, which Spencer took to be the
ultimate aim of philosophy, now seems more than
ever difficult of achievement owing to the growing
specialization of the sciences, and there are few, if
any, philosophers who would now venture on an
ambitious synthesis of all knowledge on the scale
attempted by Spencer. A grasp of broad generic
truths is, however, of the greatest importance in the
interpretation of human life, and the lack of
agreement in regard to them, together with the
enormous specialization which has occurred both in
the natural and the social sciences, constitute the
chief obstacles in the way of utilizing the methods and
the results of science in the reorganization of social life.
The general law of evolution which was the basis of
Spencer's vast synthesis has been subjected to much
criticism, and here, again, few philosophers or men
of science would now be ready to accept the formula
which he suggested, or to regard it as applicable in
the same sense to the various spheres of reality,
matter, life, mind and society. In the field of
sociology itself the value of the concept of evolution
has recently been seriously questioned. The com-
plaint is especially made that sociologists have
concerned themselves too much with problems of
origins, and have neglected inquiry into processes
and functions. But here Spencer is on stronger
ground. Despite all criticism, the notion of evolution or development remains integral to sociology.
We must still say with Spencer : " on comparing
rudimentary societies with one another and with
societies in different stages of progress that they *do*
present certain common traits of structure and
function, as well as certain common traits of develop-

ment " (*Study of Sociology*, p. 386), and that to discover the conditions of social growth, arrest and decay is one of the principal tasks of sociology. It is to be noted that Spencer's use of the word evolution does not imply that every people necessarily goes through the same stages in regular and progressive order. " There is no uniform ascent from lower to higher, but only an occasional production of a form which, in virtue of greater fitness for more complex conditions, becomes capable of a longer life of a more varied kind " . . . and it is only by taking into consideration the " entire assemblage of societies " that the law of evolution can be shown to be at work in humanity (*Principles*, III, 598, *seq.*). It is further important to point out that in applying the idea of evolution sociologists are not in any way bound to start by assuming a hypothetical original form of society, and then deduce existing types therefrom. The real object of evolutionary procedure is to discover by wide comparative study the various ways in which societies adapt themselves to changing conditions, and to distinguish between what is fundamental and permanent and what accidental and modifiable. If the conditions under which societies arise or change were known, we might perhaps be able to reconstruct the type of society likely to have existed under conditions more primitive than any of which we have a record. Such reconstructions, however, should not be used as the starting point for a theory of society. They would be rather conclusions, and very doubtful conclusions, of a theory already formed. In short, the theory of social evolution does not rest upon an imaginary reconstruction of the

" first stages " of institutions, but upon a comparative study of the forms of social life designed to
bring out the factors which make for permanence
or change, for arrest, decay or development.

Spencer recognized very clearly the importance
of the comparative method, and the volumes on
Descriptive Sociology which he planned were
designed to facilitate its application. In this
emphasis on comparative study he has been followed
by many distinguished sociologists, notably,
Durkheim, Westermarck and Hobhouse. By other
sociologists the method has been severely criticized.
It has been argued, for instance, that the institutions
of a particular area can only be properly understood
in their full cultural and social setting, and that to
compare them with " similar " institutions elsewhere
can only lead to superficial generalizations. This
objection has point, and may serve to check abuses ;
but it can be carried too far. All scientific work
involves abstraction and isolation, and in the social
sciences, where experiment is difficult, we can very
often discover what is essential and what accidental
in an institution only by observing it at work in
different historical and social conditions. Needless
to say, comparative study cannot dispense with,
but on the contrary depends upon, accurate intensive
studies of particular areas or periods. In this respect
the sociologist of to-day has available a far richer
and more reliable supply of both anthropological
and historical data than Spencer had at his disposal.
A more serious objection to the comparative method,
and one that has often been raised against the use
Spencer made of it, is that it lends itself too readily
to the establishment of preconceived hypotheses.
The data of history and anthropology are so various

and so vast that, by judicious selection, a plausible case can be made out in support of almost any general theory of human evolution. It must be conceded that no science is so full of ambitious theories easily established and as easily confuted as sociology. But here, again, the fault lies not in the method as such, but in its abuse, and the remedy lies not in avoiding comparisons but in making them more complete, and particularly in giving scrupulous attention to negative instances. To this end, it may be remarked, the tabulations in the Descriptive Sociology ought to be of great service.

It is perhaps to be regretted that Spencer, like so many other distinguished sociologists, concentrated his attention on anthropological data, and tended to neglect the richer field of the history of civilization. But this was natural in the early stages of sociology. The life of savage peoples had a peculiar power of attraction. The data appeared to be easily manageable, and their interpretation simple. The more intensive work of modern field workers has shown this simplicity to be illusory. It is now realized that the understanding of savage life presents difficulties often as great as those which confront the student of modern societies, and more particularly that the interpretations given by anthropologists are liable to be coloured by theories of society and social evolution which they have imbibed from their own surroundings in their own society Modern sociologists are therefore turning increasingly to the comparative study of civilizations, ancient and modern, and especially of contemporary civilizations. It should be noted that although in the *Principles of Sociology* Spencer relied mostly on data derived from anthropology, he was perfectly well aware of the importance of historical and contemporary data, and the scheme of publications under his will includes many important volumes devoted to civilized societies. It is very much to be hoped that the efforts of the Trustees in this direction will inspire others to continue the work, and to devise new schemes of compilation and classification adapted to the rich variety of material now available.

There is another point in Spencer's methodology to which brief reference must here be made. He saw clearly that the inductions arrived at by means of the comparative method did not suffice to establish sociological laws. They needed to be verified by being shown to follow deductively from more general laws. The laws to which he appealed in this connection were his general law of evolution, especially in the form which it takes in biology, and also the laws of psychology. Psychology, indeed, does not loom large in his sociological work. This is due probably not to a failure on his part to recognize its importance, but to the rudimentary condition of psychology, and especially of social psychology, in his time. In his use of biological laws a very striking feature is his belief in the inheritance of acquired characters. This enabled him to regard human nature as more plastic and modifiable than would be admitted by many biological sociologists who followed in his wake. It is also important to remember that whilst the notion of struggle and the survival of the fittest is regarded by him as fundamental in sociology, he did not think of selection as operation automatically in human societies, or as not subject to control. Thus, although he was opposed to many forms of state control within any given society, he certainly thought that war, or the conflict between societies, should be forbidden. In the past, indeed, war played an important role by bringing about social integration and the extension of the more powerful and intelligent races over the earth. But he adds: "from war has been gained all that it had to give" (*Principles*, II, 664), and he looked forward to a time when an end would be put to "the re-barbarization which is continually undoing civilization" (*Principles*, III, 600). How far this restriction of struggle between communities is consistent with the use that Spencer makes of the notion of the survival of the fittest, in its application to individuals within the community, I do not now inquire. The difficulty here involved serves to emphasize the need of caution in applying biological principles to social phenomena, and the importance of a direct study of the facts of social life.

In England, Spencer's influence on sociology has not been so strong as on the Continent and in America. Here his work did much to encourage the tendency to subordinate sociology to biology, often in a manner not really consistent with his teaching. On the other hand, it has also led, by way of reaction, to a deeper analysis of the significance of the organic principle in social life, and of the relation between evolution and progress. A knowledge of his work is essential to an understanding of the history of sociology in England. Such an understanding will be facilitated by Dr. Rumney's admirable study.

MORRIS GINSBERG.

University of London,
London School of Economics.

ACKNOWLEDGMENT.

THIS work would never have been completed in the short time I had at my disposal had it not been for the untiring and unfailing assistance of Professor Morris Ginsberg, with whom I have worked for many years. He has been kind enough to read the proof sheets, and the impress of his teaching and guidance is evident throughout the book.

I am also indebted to the Trustees of the Herbert Spencer Trust for many helpful suggestions. I need hardly add that all expressions of opinion are mine only for which the Trustees have no responsibility.

And finally, my very sincere thanks are due to Mr. T. W. Hill, the Editor of the series, whose meticulous editorship and scholarship have been freely given and who has seen the book through to press for me.

J. RUMNEY.

INSTITUTE OF SOCIAL RESEARCH,
        LONDON, W.C.1.

October 1st, 1934.

CHAPTER I.

The Scope of Sociology.

THAT imposing edifice, *The Principles of Sociology*,[1] whose construction took two decades to complete, incorporated many architectural features, the design of which Spencer had adumbrated many years before. In a series of letters on the Proper Sphere of Government, published in the *Nonconformist* newspaper in 1842, and republished as a pamphlet in 1843, Spencer expressed a belief in the conformity of social phenomena to invariable laws—in human progression as determined by such laws—in the moral modification of man as caused by social discipline—in the tendency of social arrangements of themselves to assume a stable equilibrium—in the repudiation of State control over various departments of social life—and in the limitation of State action to the maintenance of equitable relations among citizens.[2] In *Social Statics*, 1850, there is everywhere manifested a recognition of the evolution of man and of society, as in both cases determined by the incidence of conditions—the actions of circumstances, and of the fact that organic and social

---

[1] Vol. i, first edition appeared in 1876 ; second edition, 1877 ; third and enlarged edition, 1885. Vol. ii, Part IV, 1879 ; Part V, 1882. Vol. iii, Part VI, 1885 ; Parts VII and VIII, 1896.

[2] *Reasons for Dissenting from the Philosophy of M. Comte. Essays*, Vol. i, p. 137, note.

evolution are expressions of the same law. It is further maintained that the essence of the social process is the interaction between individuals and society, between the units and the mass, and their adaptation as a result of the adjustment of the natures of men to society and of the social organization to the nature of its constituent units. Where adaptation is incomplete, and the machinery of society is disjointed and creaking, social evils and imperfections will necessarily result. Fortunately, there is always available the lubricating oil of Evolution to minimize and ultimately to abolish all social friction. The universal tendency is towards harmonious adaptation, perfect equilibrium. In support of this argument, Spencer adduces two biological laws. The first will ruthlessly exterminate individuals who cannot adapt themselves—the survival of the fittest—a dogma that Spencer had arrived at before Darwin. The second will favour individuals whose natures have become adapted to social life, and transmit their acquired modifications to a next generation—a Lamarckian dogma which Spencer accepted. This more perfect adaptation is a phase in a process of universal development that is ever tending towards the creation of higher and still higher types of being. Throughout nature there runs a transcendental and spiritual force in virtue of which nature, and society as part of nature, evolve according to immanent laws towards a final " individuation." Coleridge and Schelling, biology and physics, Idealism and Materialism are inextricably interwoven.

Between 1850 and 1860, Spencer clarified and elaborated these views and shaped them into a system of philosophy. In the *Development Hypothesis*,

1852, the law of evolution or development as against the special-creation interpretation of the universe is presented with great skill. Another influence— that of Malthus, is evident in the *Theory of Population*, 1852, where it is argued that owing to excessive reproduction and the continual pressure of rapidly multiplying organisms upon the slowly increasing means of support there is struggle and selection and the evolution of higher types. In the *Theory of Style*, 1852, the view is put forward that development in literary style is analogous to development in society in that it implies not " a series of like parts simply placed in juxtaposition, but one whole made up of unlike parts that are mutually dependent." In the *Art of Education*, 1854, it is claimed that true methods of education consist in the gradual unfolding of the mental faculties and in a progression from the simple to the complex and from the indefinite to the definite. His *Essay on Manners and Fashions*, 1854, shows that ecclesiastical, political and ceremonial restraints trace back to one primitive form " in conformity with the laws of evolution and of all organized bodies." It maintains that " government originally one and afterwards subdivided for better fulfilment of its function must be considered as having been in all its branches, political, religious and ceremonial—beneficial ; and indeed absolutely necessary. Government " must be regarded as subserving an office made needful by the unfitness of aboriginal humanity for social life ; and the successive diminutions of its coerciveness in State, in Church and in Custom, must be looked upon as accompanying the increasing adaptation of humanity to its conditions." And, finally, " there requires to be borne in mind the third fact that the genesis, the maintenance and the decline of all governments, however named, are alike brought about by the humanity to be controlled ; from which may be drawn the inference that on the average, restrictions of every kind cannot last much longer than they are wanted, and cannot be destroyed much faster than they ought to be."[1]

Spencer was the first to apply Evolution to the study of Sociology, and on Evolution, together with development and progress, depends the architecture of his synthetic system. Spencer has now a formula with which he explains the *Genesis of Science*, 1854, the *Origin and Function of Music*, 1857, and, finally, the Cosmos and everything in it. In *Progress : Its Law and Cause*, Spencer delivers his credo. It is " that the law of organic progress is the law of all progress. Whether it be in the development of the Earth, in the development of Life upon its surface, in the development of Society, of Government, of Manufacture, of Commerce, of Language, Literature, Science, Art, this same evolution of the simple into the complex through successive differentiations holds throughout. From the earliest traceable cosmical changes down to the latest results of civilization, we shall find that the transformation of the homogeneous into the heterogeneous is that in which progress essentially consists."[2] Later on Spencer added another factor, increase in coherence, and evolution connoted that a change must show increasing heterogeneity, together with increasing coherence.

---

[1] *Manners and Fashions*, Essays, Vol. iii, p. 50.
[2] *Progress : Its Law and Cause.* Essays, Vol. i, p. 10.

A few other essays of this period are important for the bearing they have on Spencer's sociological thought. *Transcendental Physiology*, 1857, collates those laws of development and function which apply to all organisms. *Representative Government— What is it Good For?* 1857, presents the thesis that " representative government is best for securing justice, but is the worst for all other purposes." In the *Social Organism*, 1860, two points are made, that society is a growth and that it is a social organism. Spencer's Sociology may be regarded as a detailed expansion of these statements, and a skilful application of those mentioned above.

But it is important to remember that this sociological structure was one among many edifices reared by Spencer ; it may even be regarded as one storey of his intellectual building. To understand the *Principles of Sociology*, therefore, it is necessary to know something about the elaborate architectural plan Spencer had conceived. In brief, this was the construction of the complete history of the knowable universe on the broad and wide foundation of Evolution, and the fitting together of every department of inorganic and organic nature into one connected whole. The plan was adhered to closely (although inorganic nature had to be omitted) and Spencer devoted his life to its execution. *First Principles*, the *Principles of Biology*, the *Principles of Psychology*, the *Principles of Sociology*, and the *Principles of Morality* were the fruits of his labour and constitute his *System of Synthetic Philosophy*.[1]

This vast undertaking influenced to a considerable

---

[1] See Appendix A, giving the prospectus of the *Synthetic Philosophy* which Spencer issued in 1859.

extent the construction of Spencer's Sociology. The *First Principles*, his *Biology* and *Psychology* were apt to become the framework of the Sociology, often determining unconsciously both the selection and the brickwork of facts. They are in a sense the *a priori* elements of whose truth Spencer was already certain when applying them towards the elucidation of sociological problems. It is thus necessary to outline in brief Spencer's main philosophical doctrines. These were as follows[1] :—

1. Throughout the universe, in general and in detail, there is an unceasing redistribution of matter and motion.

2. This redistribution constitutes evolution where there is a predominant integration of matter and dissipation of motion, and constitutes dissolution where there is a predominant absorption of motion and disintegration of matter.

3. Evolution is simple when the process of integration, or the formation of a coherent aggregate, proceeds uncomplicated by other processes.

4. Evolution is compound when along with this primary change from an incoherent to a coherent state there go on secondary changes, due to differences in the circumstances of the different parts of the aggregate.

5. These secondary changes constitute a transformation of the homogeneous into the heterogeneous—a transformation which, like the first, is exhibited in the universe as a whole and in all (or

---

[1] See *First Principles*. This summary was made by Spencer himself for publication in Appleton's *American Cyclopædia*. See also *An Introduction to the Philosophy of Herbert Spencer*, by W. H. Hudson, 1897, pp. 94–98.

nearly all) its details—in the aggregate of stars and nebulæ ; in the planetary system ; in the earth as an organic mass ; *in each organism vegetal or animal* (Von Baer's law) ; in the aggregate of organisms throughout geologic time ; in the mind ; in society ; in all products of social activity.

6. The process of integration, acting locally as well as generally, combines with the process of differentiation to render this change, not simply from homogeneity to heterogeneity, but from an indefinite homogeneity to a definite heterogeneity; and this trait of increasing definiteness, which accompanies the trait of increasing heterogeneity is, like it, exhibited in the totality of things, and in all its divisions and subdivisions down to the minutest.

7. Along with this redistribution of the matter composing any evolving aggregate, there goes on a redistribution of the retained motion of its components in relation to one another ; this also becomes, step by step, more definitely heterogeneous.

8. In the absence of a homogeneity that is infinite and absolute, this redistribution, of which evolution is one phase, is inevitable. The causes which necessitate it are :

9. The instability of the homogeneous, which is consequent upon the different exposure of the different parts of any limited aggregate to incident forces. The transformations hence resulting are complicated by—

10. The multiplication of effects : every mass, and part of a mass on which a force falls subdivides and differentiates that force, which thereupon proceeds to work a variety of changes ; and each of these becomes the parent of similarly multiplying changes :

the multiplication of these becoming greater in proportion as the aggregate becomes more heterogeneous. And these two causes of increasing differentiations are furthered by —

11. Segregation, which is a process tending ever to separate unlike units, and to bring together like units, so serving continually to sharpen or make definite differentiations otherwise caused.

12. Equilibration is the final result of these transformations which an evolving aggregate undergoes. The changes go on until there is reached an equilibrium between the forces which all parts of the aggregate are exposed to, and the forces these parts oppose to them. Equilibration may pass through a transition stage of balanced motions (as in a planetary system) or of balanced functions (as in a living body), on the way to ultimate equilibrium ; but the state of rest in inorganic bodies, or death in organic bodies, is the necessary limit of the changes constituting evolution.

13. Dissolution is the counterchange which sooner or later every evolved aggregate undergoes. Remaining exposed to surrounding forces that are unequilibrated, each aggregate is ever liable to be dissipated by the increase, gradual or sudden, of its contained motion ; and its dissipation, quickly undergone by bodies lately animate, and slowly undergone by inanimate masses, remains to be undergone at an indefinitely remote period by each planetary and stellar mass which, since an indefinitely remote period in the past, has been slowly evolving : the cycle of its transformations being thus completed.

14. This rhythm of evolution and dissolution, completing itself during short periods in small aggre-

gates, and in vast aggregates distributed through space completing itself in periods which are immeasurable by human thought, is, so far as we can see, universal and eternal : each alternating phase of the process predominating—now in this region of space, and now in that—as local conditions determine.

15. All these phenomena, from their great features down to their minutest details, are necessary results of the persistence of force under its forms of matter and motion. Given these in their known distributions through space, and, their quantities being unchangeable either by increase or decrease, there inevitably result the continuous redistributions distinguishable as evolution and dissolution, as well as all those special traits above enumerated.

16. That which persists, unchanging in quantity but ever changing in form, under these sensible appearances which the universe presents to us, transcends human knowledge and conception ; is an unknown and unknowable power, which, we are obliged to recognize as without limit in space, and without beginning or end in time.

The metaphysical basis of the foregoing conceptions and the implications of such an eschatological law of evolution do not concern us here. Their importance lies, as we shall see later, in the way they influenced Spencer's treatment of the numerous problems dealt with in his Sociology. Indeed one definition Spencer gives of Sociology is " the study of evolution in its most complex form."[1] He frankly admits that he was apt " to be enslaved by a plan once formed "[2] and " too much given to wandering off into the abstract."[3]

---

[1] *Study of Sociology*, p. 380.
[2] *Autobiography*, Vol. II, p. 184.   [3] *Ibid.*, p. 391.

He realized he was a " bad observer of humanity in the concrete."[1] These defects, characteristic of Spencer as man and thinker, give his Sociology a certain mechanical twist, a certain dryness that have deterred the student from its study. This is unfortunate, for there are permanently valuable elements in it which no present day sociologist dare neglect. Nuggets of gold are not generally found on the surface of the earth. They must be mined and quarried. It is so with Spencer. He needs close and careful study. Certainly the summary way in which he is dismissed by many modern sociologists and political scientists is to be deplored. To regard his *Principles of Sociology* as a recent writer does, as " an imposing but not very necessary book,"[2] is to betray a lack of appreciation of the significant impact Spencer made on the development of sociological thought. Hobhouse in England, Durkheim in France, von Wiese, Simmel and Oppenheimer in Germany, Albion Small, Sumner and Giddings in America, all outstanding sociologists, bear witness to the seminal influence exerted by Spencer's *Principles of Sociology*.

There is a widespread, but false impression, that on the basis of his metaphysical and philosophical principles, Spencer proceeded to excogitate a sociological system out of his inner consciousness. But for years Spencer had supervised the accumulation of a vast storehouse of sociological data, showing " in fitly classified groups, facts of all kinds presented by numerous races, which illustrated social evolution under all its various aspects."

---

[1] *Autobiography*, Vol. II.

[2] Crane Brinton, *Political Thought in the 19th Century*, 1933, p. 226.

" Indications of climate, contour, soil and minerals of the region inhabited by each society. . . . Some accounts of the *Flora* and *Fauna*, in so far as they affected human life, had to be given. And the characters of the surrounding tribes or nations were factors which could not be overlooked. The characters of the people, individually considered, had also to be described—their physical, moral and intellectual traits. Then, besides the political, ecclesiastical, industrial, and other institutions of society—besides the knowledge, beliefs and sentiments, the language, habits, customs and tastes of its members, there had to be noticed their clothing, food, arts of life, etc."[1] Spencer realized that if valid sociological generalizations are to be made, comparative data of this nature were absolutely essential. But Spencer did not always study the context of the passages from which his assistants had extracted the data on which he relied, and thus, at times, accepted his facts at second-hand. In their final form this store-house of facts constituted the *Descriptive Sociology*[2] and served as the basis for the *Principles.*

What did Spencer understand by Sociology? From one point of view it was the science of Superorganic Evolution; of the growth, structure, function and products of Human Societies; from another, it was the science which deals with the phenomena that result from the interactions of individuals. But Spencer's individualistic tendency

---

[1] *Autobiography*, Vol. II, pp. 172–173.
[2] 1. *English;* 2. *Ancient American Races;* 3. *Lowest Races:* 4. *African Races;* 5. *Asiatic Races;* 6. *American Races:* 7. *Hebrews and Phœnicians;* 8. *French;* 9. *Islamic Races.*

led him to write " it is much more true that Society
is created by its units, and that the nature of its
organization is determined by the nature of its units.
The two act and react ; but the original factor is the
character of the individuals, and the derived factor is
the character of the society."[1] The tendency reflected
in this passage induced him to lay greater stress on
one aspect of the " society-individual " equation
than on the other and thus involved him in various
difficulties and contradictions. Spencer, it is true,
does not set up that false antithesis—*the* individual
and human society ; society, for him, is " individuals
in interaction." But Spencer endeavours to derive
society from a pre-social state, so that Society
becomes a social contract entered into by individuals
to escape the *bellum omnium contra omnes*. Modern
sociologists do not derive Society from some previous
state ; they hold that wherever there are human
contacts, Society exists. In any case, Spencer
recognizes that Society, even if a contract, is also
a growth, a social organism. This particular contradiction, one for which he himself was responsible,
Spencer did not succeed in reconciling. But it has
to be remembered that Spencer's emphasis was laid
on societies of men, not on Human Society as such.
In this he shows a marked advance on earlier
sociologists and makes possible the presentation of
a morphology of societies, a necessary pre-requisite
to a scientific sociology.

Spencer proceeds to a brilliant analysis of what
should be the scope of a science of society,
what it should deal with, and what problems are

---

[1] *Autobiography*, Vol. II, p. 465.

most germane to it. It is of interest that this analysis is preceded by an examination into the mental and physical equipment of primitive man. Thus " setting out with social units as thus conditioned, as thus constituted physically, emotionally and intellectually, and as thus possessed of certain early-acquired notions and correlative feelings, the Science of Sociology, has to give an account of the phenomena that result from their combined actions."[1] Commencing with the development of the family, Sociology has next to describe and explain the rise and growth of political organization ; the evolution of the ecclesiastical structures and functions ; the control embodied in ceremonial observances ; and the relations between the regulative and operative parts of every society. These developments of the structures and functions, which make up the organization and life of each society, having been traced, we have then to follow out certain associated developments which aid and are aided by social evolution, the development of language, knowledge, morals, æsthetics. " Finally, we have to consider the interdependence of structures, and functions, and products, taken in their totality. Among these many groups of phenomena there is a *consensus ;* and the highest achievement in Sociology is to grasp the vast heterogeneous aggregate, as to see how the character of each group at each stage is determined partly by its antecedents and partly the past and present actions of the rest upon it."[2]

This is truly an admirable outline of sociology.

---

[1] *Principles of Sociology,* Vol. I, p. 426.
[2] *Principles of Sociology,* Vol. I, p. 431.

Spencer himself never completed this vast undertaking, and some of the most interesting sections that were to treat of progress, linguistic, moral, and æsthetic, were never written, although the germs of their formulation lie scattered in Spencer's works. As written, the *Principles* suffer from a number of defects. In the first place Spencer stressed too much what is now called cultural anthropology, which is only a division of general sociology. Secondly, Spencer was far too interested in the origin of institutions, primitive habits and the survival of ancient customs, to give much attention to the actual working of institutions and their functional character in modern society. And yet this is undoubtedly a task the sociologist must not neglect. It is remarkable, for instance, that although an enormous literature exists on the origin and functioning of the family in ancient society, its place and role in modern society are not so extensively studied. The same may be said of other institutions. Modern sociology still finds it somewhat difficult to wean itself away from anthropology. Spencer's sociology, full of remarkable insight, is after all an account of what has been well called the embryology of society. Of the adulthood of society there is little. And, finally, Spencer lacks a philosophy of history such as illuminates the pages of Vico and Comte and others. He has, it is true, a philosophy of evolution but it does not animate his sociology. On the contrary, it gives it a mechanical appearance. It is paradoxical but true that evolution in Spencer's thought is not dynamic but static. There is little in his pages of emergence of newness such as evolution in sociology implies.

Plus ça change plus c'est la même chose. This is Spencer's evolution.

These defects must not blind us to Spencer's achievements in making sociology a science, and in so brilliantly defining its scope. The problems he posits are for future sociologists to solve. His sociology remains a challenge to those who confound sociology with some petty statistical investigation. It abounds in ideas that cannot but stimulate the student to further research. It is full of pregnant observations. It rightly stresses the necessary interdependence of structures and functions in each type of society—the consensus—the nature of which we seek to discover. It aims at the discovery of fundamental correlations between the family, political and industrial institutions and society. It aims at revealing the reciprocal influences exercised by institutions on men's natures and by men's natures on them. It possesses finally a coherence and a unity that stamps the work with originality and penetration, and gives him an unique place among those who laid the foundations of modern sociology.

Sociology was to Spencer a generalizing science, concerned not with a particular society but with all societies, and seeking to discover the laws of their growth and development. He writes, " Beginning with types of men who form but a small and incoherent social aggregates, such a science has to show in what ways the individual qualities, intellectual and emotional, negative further aggregation. It has to explain how modifications of individual nature, arising under modified conditions of life, make larger aggregates possible. It has to trace, in societies of some size, the genesis of the social relations, regulative and operative, into which the members fall. It has to exhibit the stronger and more prolonged influences which, by further modifying the characters of citizens, facilitate wider and closer unions with consequent further complexities of structure. Among societies of all orders and sizes, from the smallest and rudest up to the largest and most civilized, it has to ascertain what traits there are in common determined by the common traits of human beings : what less general traits distinguishing certain groups of societies, result from traits distinguishing certain races of men ; and what peculiarities in each society are traceable to the peculiarities of its members.   In every case its object is to interpret the growth, development, structure and functions of social aggregates as brought about by the mutual actions of individuals, whose natures are partly like those of all men, partly like those of kindred races, partly distinctive."[1]

We have already seen that in the series of volumes in *Descriptive Sociology*, Spencer had accumulated an enormous amount of material for answering the problems he set himself. How was he to bring order into this mass of sociological facts ?   In the social sciences where innumerable, indefinite and remote forces have to be calculated, it is not possible as in the physical sciences to appeal to laws already ascertained or to hypotheses postulated beforehand. Instead, therefore, of beginning with deduction and confirming it by induction or experiment, Spencer began with induction, and then showed by deduction from the nature of the case that his inductive

---

[1] *Study of Sociology*, pp. 52–53.

generalizations were valid. This method, often called the Inverse Deductive or Historical Method has been very fruitful in social investigations. Whether induction or deduction comes first is not, however, very important, for in any prolonged train of thought both induction and deduction recur again and again, the order of their appearance differing with circumstances. It has been rightly pointed out that " the old logic differentiated definitely between them. Deduction was considered as an application of the general principle to a particular case, an induction as the opposite process of constructing a general rule from particular instances. As the movements run in quite opposite directions, they were thought to be mutually exclusive for any simple operation of reasoning. But as a matter of fact we always have in any act of thought both deduction and induction, only under certain conditions we have the inductive tendency predominant, in other circumstances the deductive tendency prevailing."[1]

In Spencer a skilful application of both tendencies is marked, though he did not make sufficient allowance for his *a priori* elements of thinking, those unconscious postulates and definitions, which, though not present in any process of reasoning, form the first premise in an argument. To some of these we have referred before, as von Baer's parallel between ontogenetic and phylogenetic development, the survival of the fittest, etc., which Spencer assumed as proven when drawing conclusions from them in his sociology. Others, such as Spencer's

---

[1] B. Bogoslovsky. *The Technique of Controversy*, pp. 104–105, 1928.

individualism and non-conformity, his aversion to State interference, his marked independence of thought, were more dangerous because more subjective. For all reasoning is biased by our wishes and desires. Unknown to us they colour conclusions we deem to have arrived at in a purely objective way and logically. And in this sense, of course, all reasoning begins with deduction.

Another marked characteristic of Spencer is his tendency " not to rest content with induction but to continue an inquiry until the generalization reached was reduced to a deduction."[1] He shows in his essay on Progress, that observing in many phenomena a transition from homogeneity to heterogeneity, he arrived at the generalization that this is the law of progress, and began a search for an ultimate truth from which the induction might be deduced. For Spencer was interested in showing not only that there was order in the universe but also that there were necessary relations between phenomena. In *Social Statics*, too, induction led to deduction, and abstract and concrete reasoning go on together. This tendency to complete induction by deduction follows as we shall see from Spencer's philosophical views on the nature of causation and necessity in the universe. Still another characteristic was his remarkable ability to formulate hypotheses, about which it was wittily remarked that a tragedy to Spencer was an hypothesis killed by a fact. " An hypothesis," Spencer declared, " sets

---

[1] *The Filiation of Ideas*, 1899 (reprinted in the *Life and Letters of Herbert Spencer*, by David Duncan, 1908. This essay of Spencer is fundamental to an understanding of the development of his thought.

up a process of organization in thoughts previously lying low.''[1]

His own writings illustrate very clearly the way his mind worked. Take his example of the relation between militancy and social type. He shows in the first place that certain *a priori* conditions have to be fulfilled by a society fitted for preserving itself in the presence of antagonistic societies. There must be corporate action, subservience of the operative to the regulative part and despotism. In the second place he points to many societies past and present that have been characterized by such traits although they differed in race, circumstances and degrees of development. Finally, he indicates evidence furnished by the adapted characters of men who compose militant societies. Deduction and induction, and more specifically the comparative method and the method of concomitant variations skilfully weave Spencer's facts into patterns of grand and striking design.

A few words may here be said about the comparative method which plays a large part in Spencer's Sociology. In essence this method compares, analyses and sifts the relevant from the irrelevant by varying the circumstances when examining any phenomenon. Thus in the above example Spencer drew his data from different parts of the world and from different periods of history—Russia, Dahomey, Sparta, and the lost Empire of the Incas. The characteristic common to them all was militarism. Race could not be the cause for this fundamental similarity in social organization because all these peoples were of different races. Nor could climate, habitat,

---

[1] *Ibid.*

customs, habit in which they all differed widely. Throughout his investigations Spencer stressed the view " that exhibiting sociological phenomena in such wise that comparisons of them in their co-existences and sequences as occurring among various peoples in different stages, were made easy, would extremely facilitate the discovery of sociological truths."[1]

In this new science of society Spencer was preceded by Comte, another of the greatest sociologists of all times. Sociology not only owes its name to him but also a conception of its tasks and a brilliant example of the fruitful application of the Historical and Comparative methods. Although each pursued his work independently, Comte and Spencer have much in common. Both realized the necessity of treating all social phenomena as an interrelated whole; that knowledge is experiential and relative; that scientific explanation must exclude metaphysical entities as causes; that invariable natural laws and uniformities of relation among phenomena, govern the universe. Comte developed an analogy between the individual and society, Spencer between society and the organism. Both Comte and Spencer believed that cultural changes were slow and continuous, that certain successive stages must be passed through, and that differences between peoples could be explained by the different speeds at which these stages had been traversed. Both were inclined to equate evolution with progress even though Spencer's ideal society was an anarchist individualism and Comte's a collective humanity. Even their religion

---

[1] *Autobiography*, Vol. II. pp. 264–265.

or perhaps irreligion was similar. Comte abolished religion by transforming it into the Religion of Humanity. Spencer relegated it to the Infinite Unknowable.

Their differences, arising out of different methods of approach and different philosophical preconceptions, are likewise significant. Spencer rejected Comte's notion that in the process of development knowledge goes through three stages, the theological, metaphysical and positive. He argued " that there are not three methods of philosophizing radically opposed, but one method of philosophizing which remains in essence the same. At first and to the last, the conceived causal agencies of the phenomena, have a degree of generality, corresponding to the width of the generalizations which experiences have determined ; and they change just as gradually as experiences accumulate."[1]   This is a perfectly valid point, but it does not really answer Comte's claim that at different periods of history philosophical thought has been dominated by conceptions of the above nature. Spencer also rejected the hierarchy of the sciences according to decreasing generality and increasing complexity (mathematics, astronomy, physics, chemistry, biology, sociology). " These sciences," he writes, " do not logically conform to the natural and invariable hierarchy of phenomena ; and there is no serial order whatever in which they can be placed which represents either their logical dependence or the dependence of phenomena . . . All along there has been a continuous action and reaction between the great

[1] *Reasons for Dissenting from the Philosophy of M. Comte.* Essays, Vol. II, p. 125–126.

classes of the sciences (abstract, abstract-concrete, concrete) an advance from concrete facts to abstract ideas, and then an application of such abstract facts to the analysis of new orders of concrete facts."[1] But in actual fact Spencer's own Sociology is based on such a serial order. He began with Physics or " Statics," proceeded to Biology and Psychology, and reared on these foundations a science of society. And the reason is evident, for the conclusions of these sciences form the starting-point of Sociology.

Philosophically, Comte was an empiricist. He was averse to the study of ultimate causes. A law to Comte was simply a convenient expression for showing that phenomena simply follow each other in a regular order and that a customary association exists between them. To Spencer, on the contrary, a law was a necessary and an immutable connection in a universe dominated by such laws. The uniformity of nature was more than the outcome of experience. It was a necessity of thought. " The error of empiricism," Durkheim writes, " has been to regard the causal bond as merely an intellectual construction of speculative thought and the product of a more or less methodical generalization. Now, by itself, speculation can give birth only to provisional, hypothetical and more or less plausible views, but one which must always be regarded with suspicion, for we can never be sure that some new observation in the future will not invalidate them. An axiom which the mind accepts and must accept, without control and with-

---

[1] *Reasons for Dissenting from the Philosophy of M. Comte.* Essays, Vol. II, p. 130.

out reservation, could never come from this source. Only the necessities of action, and especially of collective action, can and must express themselves in categorical formulæ . . . The imperatives of thought are probably only another side of the imperatives of action."[1]

Spencer went further than this. To him the categories of thought in some way or other mirrored the imperatives of reality. The belief in the necessity and universality of causation was a belief that every manifestation of force must be preceded and succeeded by some equivalent manifestation, and between cause and effect a natural and a necessary relation exists. Unlike Comte therefore, the discovery of final causes was essential to Spencer, and even if, in the end, all causal agencies could be subsumed under one general law, " yet the consciousness of cause remains as dominant to the last as it was at first, and can never be got rid of. The consciousness of cause can be abolished only by abolishing consciousness itself."[2] The task of Sociology should therefore be not only the discovery of co-existences and sequences, but of necessary co-existences and sequences. Society must be integrated with nature and truths of the widest generality formulated. He thus went further than Comte, to whom Sociology was the science of human action in its broadest sense, and which excluded all specialisms from its scope. To Spencer all these specialisms were necessary if Sociology were to become truly a generalizing science.

[1] E. Durkheim. *The Elementary Form of Religious Belief*, 1915, pp. 368–369.
[2] *Reasons for Dissenting from the Philosophy of M. Comte.* Essays, Vol. II, p. 127.

Unlike Comte too, he did not reject the possibility of applying to the interpretation of sociological phenomena laws applicable to another department of nature and he did not regard as chimerical the attempt to subsume all phenomena under one single law. Spencer did this in the law of evolution, the significance of which escaped Comte, who believed that species were fixed and immutable. Finally, Comte never escaped from his belief that Sociology was no more than the positive study of social physics. He ignored psychology because to him it was partly physiology (cerebral physiology) and partly sociology. Spencer, on the other hand, made a distinct step forward and devoted some attention to social biology and social psychology. And yet in the final analysis Spencer's Sociology was still a physical philosophy of society. It is true that he saw the unwisdom of divorcing society from nature, but he does not really give us any clue by which physical laws can be transformed into social laws. Comte like Spencer saw the desirability of treating social phenomena like physical phenomena, but he did not believe they were interchangeable. He rightly stressed that social facts were of a reality *sui generis* and could not be reduced to physics. He urged the application of the method of experimental investigation, which Spencer with all his zeal for physics never did. In truth, Spencer and Comte are necessary to each other and the main tendencies in modern Sociology derive from one or the other or from both. In spite of certain weaknesses and imperfections due doubtless to the pioneer nature of their enquiries, Comte and Spencer are the true founders of Sociology.

And it is for future sociologists on the basis of later science and more advanced philosophy to improve upon them.

In the thirty years since Spencer died, Sociology has made rapid strides, and its claim to scientific status, hardly accepted then, is now firmly established. The field of Sociology remains very much as he delimited it, although numerous shifts of emphasis have occurred on one or another aspect of it. Spencer's view of Sociology as a co-ordinating and generalizing science seeking to discover the general laws of the structures and functions of societies, has formed the foundation for the enquiries of later scholars such as Schäffle, Barth, Tönnies, Razenhofer, Worms, Tarde, De Greef, Novicow and Roberty.

A similar view stressing the unifying function of Sociology is expressed by Hobhouse. He writes, "General Sociology is neither a separate science complete in itself before specialism begins, nor is it a mere synthesis of the social sciences consisting in mechanical juxtaposition of their results. It is rather a vitalizing principle that runs through all social investigation, nourishing and nourished by it in turn, stimulating inquiry, correlating results, exhibiting the life of the whole in the parts and returning from the study of the parts to a fuller comprehension of the whole." In later years he marked the field of Sociology more precisely—" As its immediate objective, Sociology has in view the interpretation of social life, as, in spite of all such departmental distinctions, a unity." " Sociology is concerned with the relation of parts in a whole, and so with the concrete life that is actually enjoyed

---

[1] *Sociological Review*, Vol. I, No. 1, 1908, p. 8.

or suffered."[1]   Sociology thus becomes a synthesis of the specialisms and the interpretation of social life as a unity. This also is Durkheim's view. " Sociology " he declares, " is and can only be the corpus of the social sciences " and " this *rapprochement* (of the social sciences) under a common rubric constitutes not merely a verbal operation, but implies and indicates a radical change in the method and the organization of these sciences."[2] Again— " an adequate sociology can only have for its organ a body of sciences distinct, but animated by the sentiment of their solidarity. And it may be predicted that these sciences, once organized, will return with accumulated interest to philosophy what they have borrowed from it."[3]

A different interpretation of Sociology is put forward among others by Wiese, Simmel and Vierkandt. They wish to differentiate Sociology more precisely from the narrower social specialisms, and insist that it deals only with the forms or modes of social life, such as competition, domination, subordination, etc., common to all of them, and not with miscellaneous problems neglected by the particular social sciences. In Spencer himself traces of such an approach can be discerned, and he has a passage to this effect whose influence on Wiese is unmistakable. He writes—" We found that every aggregate of units of any order is limited in possible forms of structure by the properties of its units. Hence it was inferable, *a priori*, that, given the

---

[1] L. T. Hobhouse.   *Social Development*, 1924, p. 213.
[2] *Sociological Papers*, 1904, p. 258.
[3] *Ibid.*, p. 200.

natures of the men who are their units, and certain characters in the societies formed are pre-determined ; other characters being determined by the co-operation of surrounding conditions. The current assertion that Sociology is not possible, implies a misconception of its nature. Using the analogy supplied by a human life, we saw that just as bodily development and structure and function furnish subject-matter for biological science, though the events set forth by the biographer go beyond its range ; so, social growth, and the rise of structures and functions accompanying it, furnish subject-matter for a Science of Society, though the facts with which historians fill their pages mostly yield no material for science. Thus conceiving the scope of the science, we saw, on comparing rudimentary societies with one another and with societies in different stages of progress, that they *do* present certain common traits of structure and of function, as well as certain common traits of development. Further comparisons similarly made, opened large questions (such as that of the relation between social growth and social organization) which form parts of this same science ; questions of transcendent importance compared with those occupying the minds of politicians and writers of history."[1]

There are, however, practical difficulties involved in a purely formal interpretation. In Sociology, form and content can hardly be dissociated, and when they are, grave mistakes are made. Thus, formal sociologists too readily assume that certain types of social life are inherent in the nature of social relationships as such, whereas it is more than

---

[1] *The Study of Sociology*, p. 381.

likely that they are due to economic, biological or historical causes. Again, although appearing in different contexts, the same form may not be due to identical causes. We have but to think of subordination within the family, Church and State, to see that they may all be due to different psychological causes. In fact, few formalistic sociologists have exclusively limited themselves to form, and content, too, has been taken into consideration. It is possible that with refinement and careful application of conceptual schemes this school may produce useful results. So far work of but slight value has been produced. A position close to this is taken up by those who regard the relation between science and Sociology as analogous to the relation between arithmetic and mathematics. Among such sociologists are Giddings, Ross and Gumplowicz.

Recently a clear presentation of the main objectives of contemporary Sociology has been given by Ginsberg. These are :

1. " To determine the nature or the character of the various forms of social groupings and institutions by which they are regulated and maintained, and to trace the line of their growth or development.

2. " To determine by means of the comparative method, and as far as possible by the use of quantitative measurement, the interrelations between institutions and the degree of correlated growth. In this connection, the phenomena of diffusion and of contact are of the greatest importance.

3. " To formulate empirical generalizations or laws of such growth.

4. " To interpret these laws in the light of the more ultimate laws of life and mind."

---

[1] Morris Ginsberg. *Studies in Sociology*, 1932, pp. 16–17.

Two more present-day conceptions may be given showing how in essence Spencer's views have become incorporated into contemporary Sociology :

" Sociology seeks to discover the principles of cohesion and of order within the social structure, the ways in which it roots and grows within an environment, the moving equilibrium of changing structure and changing environment, the main trends of the incessant change, the forces which determine its direction at any time, the harmonies and conflicts, the adjustments and maladjustments within the structure as they are revealed in the light of human desires, and thus the practical application of means to ends in the creative activities of social man."[1]

Sociology " does not postulate any one-sided and simplified homo-economicus or homo-politicus. It deals with men and their relationships in all their real complexity. Homo-sociologus is a composite homo who in part is homo-economicus, in part homo-politicus, in part homo-religiosus, in part homo-æstheticus, and so on. . . . The data of each of these special sciences are insufficient to disentangle the real nature of man, his behaviour and relation-ships, and the movement of social phenomena because they are dependent on many other conditions not studied by each of these sciences. This makes necessary an intercorrelation of the factors studied by each of these sciences which leads to the inter-correlation of various forces, conditions and factors operating in man's nature, behaviour and relation-ships and through those to social phenomena generally."[2]

---

[1] R. M. MacIver. *Society : Its Structure and Changes*, p. viii, 1932.

[2] P. A. Sorokin and C. C. Zimmerman. *Principles of Rural-Urban Sociology*, 1919, p **5**.

Methods of research too have been much refined since Spencer. There are, of course, strictly speaking no specific sociological methods of investigation. Observation, classification and inference are essential as in all science. There are, however, certain techniques, the comparative method of investigation being the most widely used in Sociology. In addition there is the quantitative analysis of phenomena which is mistakenly supposed to mark the acme of scientific procedure. Much of the most important sociological knowledge is not quantitative, as evolution, diffusion of culture, etc. Then we have the typological approach which we shall discuss in some detail later ; the social survey ; the method of case study ; the ecological approach ; and finally a technique of experimentation which is as yet in its infancy.

Philosophical presuppositions necessarily influence the whole approach to Sociology. A Behaviourist or Pavlovian will try to interpret all sociological phenomena in terms of elaborate chains of conditioned reflexes. But at the moment there seems to be little possibility of reducing the categories of social science to physical categories. Social phenomena are mediated through human minds and until the relation between mind and matter as well as the nature of consciousness itself are resolved, it is wise to keep the categories distinct. It has been well said that " the choice does not lie between science and philosophy, but between good science and bad science, between better and worse philosophy."[1]

A recent tendency in Sociology has been to give

[2] R. M. MacIver. *Causation and the Social Process in " Social Problems and Social Processes,"* p. 144, Edited by E. S. Bogardus, 1933.

up the whole conception of cause and effect and replace it by that of the variable function, which implies according to Pareto—

1. " A conception of mutual dependence instead of one-sided dependence.

2. " A conception of functional relationship instead of that of cause and effect.

3. " A study of the constant elements of a social system instead of its unique, incidental and quite irregular components.

4. " A study of the uniformities and correlations in the fluctuation (in space and time) of these constant elements.

5. " Quantitative measurement of the uniformities, their fluctuations and their correlations instead of a purely qualitative description.

6. " Following this method we will obtain a series of formulas which represent a successive approximation to the extremely complex social reality and its dynamics."[1]

This conception of the variable function, although valuable, unnecessarily sets a limit to sociological discovery. With Spencer it may be argued that the search for cause and effect and of the necessary co-existences and sequences in Sociology is essential, and that the consciousness of cause can only be abolished with consciousness itself. By all means let us obtain as many correlations as we can, but correlation must not be confused with causation. Science is more than the accumulation of the similarities or identities of particulars in essence, it is a study of causes. It is a study of the essential elements in a complex situation, of those factors which seem more significant

---

[1] P. A. Sorokin. *Contemporary Sociological Theories*, 1928, p. 45.

than others in determining the phenomenon under
consideration. Finally, it may be possible to arrange
those factors in a hierarchy of significance—a task
social science must attempt.

All these problems that we have indicated somewhat
briefly show the close relationship that exists between
philosophy and sociology. The main functions of
philosophy in this connexion would be to scrutinize
its fundamental categories, interpret the ultimate
nature of reality and consider the element of value
in the universe. A social philosophy that would
deal with this last problem is necessary to a complete
sociology. For whilst sociology treats of values as
facts, social philosophy treats of facts as values.
Spencer it will be remembered followed his *Principles
of Sociology* with the *Principles of Ethics*. He wrote,
" that besides observing the interactions of the
social state, we have to observe the associated modifications of those moral codes in which moral feelings
get their intellectual expression. The kind of behaviour which each kind of regime necessitates, finds
for itself a justification which acquires an ethical
character ; and hence systems of ethics must be
dealt with in their social dependence."[1]   The story
is told that as he was sitting at his desk the drawers
of which were labelled Astrogeny, Geogeny, Biology,
Psychology, Sociology and Ethics, Spencer was
asked why Ethics was at the bottom. The reply
came quickly—Ethics was the foundation of them all.

---

[1] *Principles of Sociology*, Vol. I, p. 431.

BIBLIOGRAPHY. CHAPTER I.

BARTH, P. *Die Philosophie der Geschichte als Soziologie.* 1922.

DURKHEIM, E. *Sociologie et philosophie.* 1924.

FREYER, H. *Soziologie als Wirklichkeitswissenschaft.* 1930.

GINSBERG, M. *L. T. Hobhouse.* 1931.

GINSBERG, M. *Studies in Sociology.* 1932.

HOBHOUSE, L. T. *Social Development.* 1924.

MACIVER, R. M. *Community.* 1920.

MACIVER, R. M. *Society : Its Structure and Changes.* 1931.

PARK, R. E., and BURGESS, E. W. *Introduction to the Science of Sociology.* 1923.

REUTER, E. B. and HART, C. W. *Introduction to Sociology.* 1932.

SOROKIN, P. A. *Contemporary Sociology Theories.* 1927.

TÖNNIES, F. *Einfuhrung in die Soziologie.* 1931.

VIERKANDT, A. *Gesellschaftslehre.* 2nd ed. 1928.

Handworterbuch der Soziologie. Ed. A. Vierkandt. 1931.

VON WIESE, L. *Allgemeine Soziologie.*1 924, 1929.

WEBER, M. *Gesammelte Aufsätze zur Wissenschaftslehre.* 1922.

WEBER, M. *Gesammelte Aufsätze zur Soziologie und Sozialpolitik.* 1924.

WEBER, M. *Wirtschaft und Gesellschaft.* 2nd ed. 1925.

CHAPTER II.

Biology, Psychology, History.
(The Social Organism).

Sociology Spencer rightly regarded as a super-organic science studying all those processes and products which imply the co-ordinated actions of many individuals. It would seem therefore, that his masterly exposition of its scope, aims and methods, should be followed by an analysis of the vast accumulation of ordered facts he had at his disposal in the *Descriptive Sociology*. Instead of this, Spencer reverts to the organic level, equates biological processes with social processes, and finds the facts of sociology in the parallelisms between the animal organism and human society. Recollecting that " a society as a whole, considered apart from its living units, presents phenomena of growth, structure and function, analogous to those of growth, structure and function in an animal ; and these last are needful keys to the first,"[1] he interprets biological laws in terms of social facts, and then reasons from them as if they were social laws. And following up his initial mistake, Spencer constructs a magnificent and detailed analogical connection between the organism of society, overshadowing the element of truth in his theory, by ingenious but absurd illustrations, so that analogy, identity and reality became

---

[1] *Study of Sociology*, p. 326.

inextricably interwoven, and the nature of society, the meaning of social cohesion, for this is the real problem that agitated Spencer's mind, gets lost in their midst.

Throughout the whole of this elaborate discussion, to which a lengthy section of the *Principles*, entitled " The Inductions of Sociology," is devoted, one has a feeling that Spencer overlooked the fact that parallelisms do not establish real connections. In any case, analogical reasoning can only be productive of valuable results if the entities between which a connection is to be established are clearly understood, and their essential features known. One such entity, the animal organism, Spencer thought he understood. It is a physical system. But what is society? Is it also a physical system? On this matter Spencer is neither clear nor consistent. Here society is regarded as a physical system to be understood in terms of railways, roads and telegraph wires ; elsewhere, it is a mental system explicable only through the psychology of emotional response, language and tradition. Moreover, Spencer's assumption that he understood the nature of the animal organism should not pass unchallenged. In fact its unity, persistence and cohesion, are as yet unexplained secrets which biologists and bio-chemists are investigating. To explain, therefore, the nature of society by the nature of the organism is to explain the unknown by the unknown—a procedure that is not admissible in science. Both terms of the equation are unknown quantities. It may be said that all that Spencer wished to insist upon in his analysis was that biological truths should be taken into consideration in the interpretation of social phenomena. In this case there was no need for making that analogical superstructure an integral part of his sociological theory. Because biological laws apply to societies, plants and animals, we cannot draw the conclusion as Spencer often does, that all these groups are identical, and that the same principles of composition and activity apply to them in all cases. Because the organism is composed of cells, and society of individuals, can we say that theirs tructure and functions are identical?

But this is exactly what Spencer does affirm. As early as 1860 he had foreshadowed the development of this part of his theory in an essay, " The Social Organism." And in 1867, when the classification and tabulation of his sociological data began, they were fitted into two biological categories, structural and functional. The biological trend of Spencer's thought is clearly evident in the introduction to the first part of the *Descriptive Sociology*, where Spencer writes—" In further explanation, I may say that the classified compilations and digests of materials, to be thus brought together under the title of Descriptive Sociology, are intended to supply the student of Social Science, with data standing towards his conclusions, in a relation like that in which accounts of the structures and functions of different types of animals stand to the conclusions of the biologist. Until there had been such systematic descriptions of different kinds of organisms, as made it possible to compare the connections, forms and actions, and modes of origin of their parts, the science of life made no progress. And in like manner, before there can be reached in Sociology, generalizations having a certainty making them worthy to be called scientific, there must be definite accounts of the institutions, and actions of societies of various types and in various stages of evolution, so arranged as to furnish the means of readily ascertaining what social phenomena are habitually associated."[1]   These are valuable observations, but to the modern sociologist they appear to be vitiated somewhat by their biological setting.

Let us now turn to a consideration of Spencer's arguments.   Society must be regarded as an entity, " because though formed of discrete units a certain concreteness in the aggregate of them is implied by the general persistence of arrangements among them throughout the area occupied."[2]   What else shares this characteristic, asks Spencer ?   It is true the answer is organism.   From this, Spencer concludes " A Society is an Organism ", an inference rejected by modern sociologists.

A society, he shows, agrees with an individual organism in four conspicuous peculiarities, which are more sharply marked the higher the society or the organism :—

1. Both commence as small aggregations and insensibly augment in mass, becoming in due course thousands of times their original size.

2. Both are at first simple in structure, in fact, almost structureless, but assume in the course of their growth a continually increasing complexity of structure, which is accompanied by a progressive differentiation of functions.   Just as in the animal organism a regulative organ develops, so in Society a dominant class arises, which does not become like the rest, but assumes control over the rest ; different groups also arise following different occupations.

---

[1] *Descriptive Sociology*, Part I, 1873.
[2] *Principles of Sociology*, Vol. 1, p. **436.**

3. In their undeveloped states both manifest scarcely any mutual dependence of parts, and with the passage of time their parts gradually acquire a mutual dependence, which finally becomes so great that the life and activity of each part are made possible only by the life and activity of the rest. All these changes are mutually determined.

4. The life of both wholes becomes interdependent of and far more prolonged than the life of the component units. There is a perpetual removal and replacement of parts joined with a continued integrity of the whole.

There also are certain significant differences, but Spencer brilliantly qualifies them in such a way as to support his thesis.

These are as follows :—

1. Societies have no specific external forms ; but neither have some organisms in the vegetable and animal kingdom, argues Spencer. " If, too, it should be eventually shown, as we believe it will, that the form of every species of organism has resulted from the average play of external forces to which it has been subject during its evolution as a species; then, that the external forms of societies should depend, as they do, on surrounding conditions, will be a further point of community."[1]

Furthermore, societies regarded in their ecological setting fuse into their environment, and the traits of a pastoral society will be different from those of an agricultural or manufacturing society. Finally, by means of language, the social aggregate is rendered a living whole.

2. The units of an organism such as tissues, are

---

[1] *Social Organism.* Essays, Vol. I , p. 274.

physically continuous, but the living units of a society are dispersed persons. But here again, argues Spencer, " in the lower divisions of the animal and vegetal kingdoms, there are types of organization much more nearly allied, in this respect, to the organization of a society, than might be supposed— types in which the living units essentially composing the mass, are dispersed through an inert substance, that can scarcely be called living in the full sense of the word."[1]

" Hence the members of the body politic are not to be regarded as separated by intervals of dead space, but as diffused through a space occupied by life of a lower order."[1]

3. The living elements of individual organisms are mostly fixed in their relative positions, while units of a society are capable of moving from place to place. " But here, too, the disagreement is much less than would be supposed. For while citizens are locomotive in their private capacities, they are fixed in their public capacities. As farmers, manufacturers, or traders, men carry on their businesses, at the same spots, often throughout their whole lives."[2] " Just as in a living body, the cells that make up some important organ severally perform their functions for a time, and then disappear leaving others to supply their places; so, in each part of a society the organ remains, though the persons who compose it change."[3]

4. In the body of an animal, only a special tissue is endowed with feeling; in a society all the members

---

[1] *Social Organism.* Essays, Vol. I, p. 274.
[2] *Ibid.*, p. 275.
[3] *Ibid.*, p. 275.

are endowed with feeling. But even societies are
not without a certain differentiation, argues Spencer,
and " the classes engaged in laborious occupation
are less susceptible, intellectually and emotionally,
than the rest ; and especially less so than the classes
of highest mental culture."[1]   In conformity with
his philosophical and ethical views, Spencer makes
an admission the implication of which is to destroy
his whole argument. He writes " that while, in
individual bodies, the welfare of all other parts is
rightly subservient to the welfare of the nervous
system, whose pleasurable or painful activities make
up the good or ill of life ; in bodies-politic the same
thing does not hold, or holds to but a very slight
extent. . . . This is an everlasting reason why
the welfare of the citizens cannot rightly be sacrificed
to some supposed benefit of the State, and why, on
the other hand, the State is to be maintained solely
for the benefit of the citizens. The corporate life
must here be subservient to the lives of the parts,
instead of the lives of the parts being subservient to
the corporate life."[2]

Spencer then proceeds to follow out in detail a
structural and functional comparison between society
and an organism. He shows how societies, like
living bodies, begin as germs and grow into huge
masses. Growth proceeds by mere multiplication,
or by the compounding and recompounding of
groups, and is accompanied by increasing heterogeneity and complexity of institutions and functions,
so that the parts of society become unlike each other.
A like process occurs in individuals who become

---

[1] *Social Organism.*   Essays, Vol. I, p. 276.
[2] *Ibid.*, pp. 276–277.

increasingly differentiated and adapted to the performance of particular kinds of work and in groups
which, possessing a monopoly of skill, concentrate in
certain areas and initiate localization of labour.
A similar condition obtains in developed animal
organisms, where certain cells cluster together to
constitute, for example, the liver, which has its special
function.   Just as the formation of living organs in the
body proceeds by stages, so in the same way social
organs arise, consisting at first of a single worker, then
of a family, then of a guild and finally of a factory.
The social organism like the individual organism
can also produce offspring which abridge the stages
of development passed through by the parent and
straightway assume the developed structural characteristics of a mature society—as instanced in the
industrial evolution of Australia or the United
States.

Development of structure implies development of
function ; whereas small groups and societies show
but little subordination and organization, large
societies are closely integrated and sharply differentiated. The first main differentiation in society is
that between the regulative activities concentrated
in the hands of a chief and a warrior class, and the
operative activities pursued by an industrial class,
whose function it is to sustain the whole of society.
A parallel development is to be observed in the
living organism, which possesses a system of organs
fashioned for self-preservation and an alimentary
system for absorbing nourishment. Their evolution,
however, proceeds on different lines, for while the
material and economic environment determines the
industrial class, it does not determine the regulative

or governmental class, which arises and develops as
a result of war and struggle with surrounding
societies.

With increasing division of labour " there must
be an increasing heterogeneity in the currents of
merchandise flowing throughout that community."[1]
A distributing system represented by railways, roads
and tracks develops, that is paralleled by the vascular
system of animals.   The pulsations of the blood-flow
Spencer likens to the alternate increases and decreases
in traffic from hour to hour, day to day, week to
week.   He also shows that just as the main arterial
venous vessels are endowed with walls, which sharply
limit and define the course of blood, so the main
railways and roads are sharply marked off by lines
or fences from the surrounding country.   As the
blood-vessels become smaller, their routes become
less definite, less rigidly enclosed until we reach
the capillary vessels, which have no defined path.
Similarly, with the distributing mechanism in society
—there are small roads not fenced and less sharply
marked off from the adjacent land, and country
paths and tracks which have neither permanency or
definiteness.

Governmental institutions find their parallel in
the physical and neuro-muscular apparatus of individual organisms.   " Strange as the assertion will be
thought," writes Spencer " our Houses of Parliament
discharge in the social economy functions which are in
sundry respects, comparable to those discharged by the
cerebral masses in a vertebrate animal."[2]   The growth
of government is correlated with the growth of war,

---

[1] *Social Organism.*   Essays, Vol. I, p. 293.
[2] *Ibid.*, p. 302.

and as the area of government expands subordinate regulating centres are established. For co-ordinating the actions of the aggregate there is needed besides a governing centre, media of communication to make effective governmental commands. " By the agency of these latest internuncial structures, the social organism, though discrete, has acquired a promptness of co-ordination equal to and indeed exceeding the promptness of co-ordination in concrete organisms."[1] In fact, the telegraph wires of society may be considered as analagous to the nerve fibres of an animal. Even closer similarities apply, for both nerves and telegraph wires have to be insulated.

In both kinds of organisms the regulating system in its evolution divides into two systems to which is finally added a third partially independent. In the case of the regulating system, speed and immediate response are necessary, and that is why its main agencies are railways and telegraph wires. The sustaining system, on the other hand, has a similar apparatus but much slower in its movements, which informs it of the volume and kinds of consumption required by society. This apparatus is constituted by exchanges, markets, business agencies in the social organisms and by the sympathetic nervous system in the animal organism. Finally, a third regulating system arises. In order that an organ may continue to respond to the increased demand, there must be an extra influx of material used in its actions—it must have credit in advance of the function discharged. This purpose is achieved in the individual organism by the vaso-motor nerves

---

[1] *Principles of Sociology*, Vol. I, p. 524.

which run along the walls of the blood-vessels and which can produce contraction or expansion. The counter-part of this separate plexus of connected ganglia in the social organism is its banking and financial systems which lend out capital when increased demands are made by industrial and commercial concerns. Although this regulating system is entangled with the other regulating structures, yet it is functionally separate and of great independent power. In a developed, sustaining and distributing system of this nature money is an important element for furthering industrial growth. Money in the social organism is analogous to the blood discs of the individual organism.

This, in brief, is Spencer's contribution to the nature of society, and is a good example of his perceptive and co-ordinating powers. The analogies he regards no more than a scaffolding to help in building up a coherent body of sociological inductions. Even if the scaffolding is taken away, he writes, the inductions will stand by themselves. Actually, however, the scaffolding has to be taken away because it throws no light on the problem of social cohesion, while the inductions themselves, admitting that they can stand apart from the scaffolding, are not of great importance. That societies grow, increase in size, structure and function, may be true, but the task of Sociology is to show in detail how these truths are functionally related, how the various components of a social system interact, and to explain the products of such interaction. The view of modern sociologists is that no wide and abstract formula such as society is an organism; not even the more comprehensive formula of increasing differentiation and integration, can yield that information. Sociology must begin with limited, empirical correlations and then endeavour to subsume these under a wide and general formula.

A number of difficulties and contradictions arise in connection with the social organism when we come to other aspects of Spencer's Sociology. Higher organisms and higher societies show integration and differentiation. But what is a higher organism ? What is a higher society ? Can we use other than subjective criteria in estimating highness or lowness ? If we use Spencer's own criteria, centralized control and unified action, the military society is much more like an organism than the industrial society ; but if this is the case what becomes of the individual and the freedom and happiness which individuation assure him in an industrial state ? Spencer also saw clearly that society is discrete and consists of individuals each with a separate mind. What he does, therefore, is to throw overboard his theory of the social organism, for it is clearly incompatible with his conception of the industrial society as the highest. The notions of integration and differentiation cannot be fitted easily into the dual classification of societies. Integration applies to the military society, whereas differentiation applies to the industrial society. On occasion Spencer uses these concepts as a pair of scissors which move harmoniously together in cutting out a social pattern. At other times, he uses them separately, and with each blade cuts a different pattern.

A modern reinterpretation of Spencer's conception of society may be discussed under the following heads :—

Firstly, a society grows in size and expands in area whenever conditions permit. Growth may involve disturbances, but after a time equilibrium is attained.

Secondly, it tends to persist both as a spatial and temporal whole, each part of which is linked to the other by a relation of mutual causal interdependence, so that the character of the parts depends on the relation of each to the remainder. The whole maintains a certain balance or correlation of functions.

Thirdly, society exhibits an interdependence of parts which may range from slight to very complex cohesion. There are all kinds of societies, just as there are all kinds of organisms. Some are complex and some are simple ; some have a high degree of central control, and some a low degree ; some are patterned simply on the repetition of some unit ; others are highly differentiated, and present the bizarre complexity of the pattern in a Persian rug.

Finally, it shows a certain adaptability to its environment, and by means of persistence and varied effort carries on an unceasing process of adjustment and readjustment.

Such a functional interpretation of animal and human societies has to be amplified in case of the latter, because mind, purpose and effort toward unity may have to be postulated. Social tradition and conscious purpose are important in binding the generations to each other, and in transmitting social institutions and beliefs which the individual can modify to but a small extent. Society also becomes integrated by a thousand connecting institutions, each of which seems on the surface to run its own course, but all of which in reality are dependent on the totality of social relationships. Thus the system of transport in a society will depend on the amount of commerce, the division of labour, the financial system and so on. In the same way each individual is caught up in a network of relationships that subtly tie him to, and make him dependent on, the larger body of which he is but a unit. Even as regards the comparatively simple problem of growth human societies may frequently grow by war and conquest, which are themselves the products of very elaborate social organization. According to modern opinion these qualifications make impossible the interpretation of human society by the animal organism and completely invalidate the comparison between them. Moreover, a few specific differences exist which it is worth while to note.

In the first place, society is much more plastic than the organism in which the parts lose their independence. In societies parts may have great independence, and in some cases a certain institution may be so strong as to dominate society.

Secondly, the parts of society are themselves organisms which are very mobile compared with the analogous cells in the animal organism.

Thirdly, a society may enclose within itself a number of other societies and groupings all of which may be comparatively autonomous. The higher animal organism, on the other hand, cannot be split up into component systems, for they cannot exist apart.

Fourthly, the individual in a modern society may belong to many different groupings and may join or leave them as he wishes. The parts of an organism cannot move readily from one system to another.

Fifthly, while the organs of an animal have special functions which are not easily interchangeable, this is quite possible in society.

Finally, there is no evidence that society possesses a collective consciousness, will or mind, in any way analogous to the consciousness, will or mind of the individual organism.

Spencer saw this point and all its disastrous implications for the theory that society is an organism, and only got over the difficulty as we shall see, by postulating a militant and an industrial type of society. We must conclude, therefore, that the laws applying to society will radically differ from those applying to an organism, and that the wholes formed by individuals in their interrelations are markedly different from those formed by the union of cells.

At this point let us turn to a topic which emphasizes still more sharply the differences between society and the animal organism, and that is the marked difference between biological change and social change. Following Ginsberg's analysis, it is to be observed, that vast and important changes have taken place in history and social life, without, as far as we know, corresponding changes of much significance in the innate mental and physical equipment of *homo sapiens*. All the advances in civilization that have occurred seem to be totally unrelated to any specific racial groupings. Where mixture and intermarriage has taken place, the cultural contacts of the different races have been seemingly more significant than the biological contacts. In the transmission of culture, tradition, law, custom and technique, to another generation, or even to another people, we see the importance of the inheritance of acquired characters in social evolution ; that this is important in biological evolution has not as yet been demonstrated—certainly no mechanism for its existence has been revealed, whereas in social evolution the mechanism is evident. Moreover, while biological change is slow and non-cumulative, social change is rapid and cumulative. Witness the effects of inventions on social life. These are much more numerous and striking than what the writer conceives to be their analogues in biology, viz. mutations. The former can often be explained as a result of co-operation and imitation, but at the present time mutations cannot be explained in this way. Finally, it is to be noted that one invention may stimulate the production of others in a similar direction, or even stimulate production in later generations. The cumulative nature of social tradition, and the fact that each generation stands on the shoulders of the next, makes the problem of orthogenetic evolution, or evolution in one direction, seem comparatively simple in comparison with the problem in biology. These facts, in addition to those we have mentioned above, such as conscious purpose, language, and co-operation strengthen the conclusion that social phenomena cannot be satisfactorily explained in terms of biology, and that social facts are of a nature *sui generis*, for the elucidation of which a science of society is necessary.

Implicitly, the discussion has hitherto been the relationship between sociology and biology. Mistaken as present day sociologists believe Spencer to have been in regarding the social organism as cardinal in this relationship, he nevertheless clearly grasped the fundamental dependence of sociology on biology. " The human being," he said, " is at once the terminal problem of Biology, and the initial factor of Sociology."[1]   Hobhouse, his eminent successor in English Sociology, concurred in this view, saying that " the last word of biology is the first of sociology."   Spencer also realized the error of thinking " that the different forms of society presented by savage and civilized races, all over the globe, are but different stages in the evolution of one form : the truth being rather that social types, like types of individual organisms, do not form a series but are classifiable only in divergent and redivergent groups."[2]   Unfortunately, he did not always heed this statement in his own methodology, and was apt to erect a sequence of unilinear stages in his classification of social institutions.   He was among the first to realize the necessity of discovering what mental and physical differences exist between races, classes and other social groups, and what effects these differences have upon social structures. He saw that " the methods of inquiry which Biology uses are methods to be used by Sociology,"[3] but in the writer's opinion he had not sufficient scientific training to live up to his own injunction, and was too easily influenced by his philosophical and moral preconceptions.   He objected to the Poor Law because of its alleged dysgenic influence on the population, as a result of the suspension of Natural Selection, but never verified that this was actually the case.   His Eugenics, if it may be so called, was

---

[1] *Study of Sociology*, p. 332.
[2] *Ibid.*, p. 325.
[3] *Ibid.*, p. 324.

of a most elementary kind, and, often in the guise of a pure scientist expounding biological principles, he advocated policies which, in the writer's opinion, were the result of his preconceptions.' Nevertheless, much of the subject-matter that is now covered by Social Biology, owes its formulation to Spencer and the problems he suggested are now being investigated. The most fruitful lines of inquiry in Social Biology seem to be :—

1. " To determine the effect of individual innate differences in mental and physical characters upon the constitution of social groupings, such as classes, nations and the like, and upon the working of social institutions generally.

2. " To determine the converse operation of social institutions, by way of social selection and in other ways, upon the biological constitution of groups.

3. " To study the effects of race or group contact and mixture upon society.

4. " To ascertain and measure the intensity of the selective forces operating in man in society and the possibilities of controlling or modifying them by agencies under social control."[1]

Although Spencer attempted to refute Lester Ward's and Giddings's criticism that his sociology was based on biology to the exclusion of psychology, his refutation was not altogether convincing. It is true he had written " that psychological truths underlie sociological truths, and must therefore be sought by the sociologist,"[2] but then Spencer assumed he had at his disposal systematized truths such as he had in biology. Beyond some

---

[1] Morris Ginsberg. *Studies in Sociology*, 1932, p. 18.
[2] *Study of Sociology*, p. 377.

remarks on gregariousness and sympathy, his main emphasis was on the emotional and intellectual characters, such as fear, vanity and imitation in the primitive man. He clearly saw the need of a social psychology, and yet his *Principles of Psychology* stand unrelated in the main to his *Principles of Sociology*. He recognized the importance of correlating social institutions and mental qualities, and writes : " that for every society, and for each stage in its evolution, there is an appropriate mode of feeling and thinking ; and that no mode of feeling and thinking not adapted to the degree of evolution and its surroundings can be permanently established. Though not exactly, still approximately, the average opinion in any age and country, is a function of the social structure of that age and country."[1] This is an important problem for sociology to elucidate. According to Spencer, sympathy is the basis of all the social sentiments, which are, however, primarily egoistic. Transmitted by inheritance, and increased by use, it is able with the help of the representative powers of the mind to unite with instinct and form social sentiments. These again, because of their utility and conscious and unconscious adaptation to the conditions of life, have survived, and continue with the cumulative inheritance of acquired mental traits.

As in his biological thought, here, too, Spencer accepts perhaps too readily evidence bearing on the psychological differences between men and women, and between different races, and allows philosophical bias to intrude on his chain of reasoning. Thus, among other things, he objected to public education

---

[1] Study of Sociology, p. 386.

because " having as much as we could, suspended the civilizing discipline of an industrial life, so carried on as to achieve self-maintenance, without injury to others, we now proceed to suspend that civilizing discipline in another direction, by relieving parents from certain responsibilities, which in the order of nature fall on them."[1]

The coherence and unity of society, which Spencer had sought to interpret in terms of a social organism, can only be described in terms of psychology. For society consists of human beings in interaction, men and women endowed with impulses who need each other for realization and gratification. Struggle and conflict just as much as sympathy and mutual aid require society for their manifestations. Basically human beings need each other not only to satisfy their gentle and tender impulses, but also to exercise their assertive and aggressive tendencies. In a wider sense than they are used by Freud, love and hate are the twin roots of human society. In order to disentangle their subtle interaction and their conscious and unconscious pervasiveness an exact knowledge of the structure of the mind is needed— of the nature of instinct and emotion, of reason, desire and sentiment ; how they develop, operate and interact. That is why the sociologist is so dependent on the psychologist—they differ simply in attitude and approach. The psychologist studies mental processes for the light they throw on the operations of the mind, and the conditions of its development. The sociologist studies these same mental processes for the role they play in determining the nature and development of social phenomena. And he relates

Study of Sociology, p. 366.

them always to the material environment, the
property relationships and the other determining
factors of social life.

Just as it is unnecessary to assume a social organism
—an idea that finds different expressions in Plato,
Cicero, Hobbes, Grotius and Rousseau—so is it unnecessary to postulate a social mind or a general
will, a supersensuous entity above and distinct from
the minds of its members such as has been formulated by Hegel, Durkheim, Bosanquet, Bradley and
MacDougall. All we need for such purpose are human
beings possessed of certain psychological impulses
interacting with each other and with the traditions
they have evolved, and the material environment
amidst which they are settled. In sociology it is
necessary to avoid stressing the units against society
as Spencer does, or stressing society against the units
as Durkheim does. The emphasis should be on the
individuals in society intrinsically connected to
each other, and constituting a social whole through
their interrelations. Society, as Hobhouse rightly
pointed out, must be regarded as " a whole, constituted by the interconnection of parts which are
themselves maintained each by its interconnection
with the remainder." The unity of society must not
be exaggerated. Different aggregates exhibit different degrees of unity—compare the unity of a
football crowd, a political party, a social class,
the State. The unity of society is more subtle
and depends on many complex factors, such as
suggestion, imitation, the appeal to dominant
sentiments and the inhibition of conflicting tendencies.[1]   In developed societies the degree of unity

---

[1] See M. Ginsberg, *The Psychology of Society*, 1921.

will largely depend on the degree in which conscious
purpose is recognized by the members of particular
associations, and on the efforts of the different parts to
arrive at mutual adjustment. With increasing
consciousness, purpose, foresight and planning,
society may become more organic, and the element
of compulsion and constraint less. But this
process results throughout from the interplay
of distinct individuals who are to a large extent
self-determining. Thus it must be remembered
that the trend towards unity and cohesion which a
society manifests varies and depends on numerous
factors. These same remarks apply to those powerful associations such as states, whose unity, in so
far as there exist class divisions and sharp economic
antagonisms, is far from enduring.

Spencer's emphasis on the social organism and a
biological interpretation of society had unfortunate
effects on the development of sociology. In the first
place it diverted attention from the more fruitful
lines of inquiry that had been laid down by Comte
and Spencer himself, and led sociology to the facile
but sterile regions of Social Darwinism. Social processes were equated with biological processes and
Natural Selection was emphasized. In the second
place progress was regarded as spontaneous and automatic, and human action and effort were dismissed
as an interference with the biological laws
of nature. And finally it was easy on the basis of
the social organism to justify state sovereignty and
omnicompetence, a corporate society, a totalitarian
state and every other kind of social absolutism. In
Russia Novicow, in Austria Gumplowicz, in Germany
Lillienfeld and Schäffle, in France Worms and

Le Bon illustrate an extreme bio-sociological interpretation and a laudation of the struggle for
existence, anarchic individualism and political quietism, and state absolutism.

The relationship of sociology to biology and
psychology, having been examined, let us now turn to
a consideration of its position with respect to history.
Here again, Spencer has some pertinent remarks to
make. " What Biography is to Anthropology,
History is to Sociology," he wrote.[1] Elsewhere he said
that sociology stands related to history, much as a
vast building stands related to the heaps of stones
and bricks around it. He envisaged sociology as a
generalizing science, and criticized historians who
looked upon history as the chronicle of great men,
wars and battles, dynastic successions and the like,
and excluded from it broad social movements and
social organization.[2] History, argued Spencer, should
become descriptive sociology. " Facts should be so
grouped and arranged that they may be comprehended in their ensemble and contemplated as mutually dependent parts of one great whole. The aim
should be so to present them that men may readily
trace the consensus subsisting among them, with the
view of learning what social phenomena co-exist
with what others. . . . The highest office which the
historian can discharge, is that of so narrating the
lives of nations as to furnish materials for a Comparative Sociology ; and for the subsequent determination of the ultimate laws to which social phenomena conform."[3]

---

[1] *Study of Sociology*, p. 57.
[2] *Autobiography*, II, p. 253.
[3] *Education*, pp. 35–36.

Broadly, this view is accepted by most modern sociologists and historians. In general, the historian concentrates on events in so far as they are unique and individual and traces those special forces which influenced their origin and development, and from this angle he would investigate such events as the Reformation, the French Revolution and the rise of Christianity. The modern sociologist on the other hand, endeavours to discover those traits and relationships which were common to all special forms of social phenomena, and is not so interested in a phenomenon or relationship which is unique in time or space. His task is to find out generalizations and correlations, such as those Spencer sought to formulate " between great militant activity and the degradation of women, between a despotic form of government and elaborate ceremonial in social intercourse, between relatively peaceful social activities and the relaxation of coercive institutions."[1]

In opposition to the above view, it is claimed by Rickert and Tröeltsch that historical knowledge differs from sociological knowledge, in that it deals with unrepeatable wholes which can only be intuitively understood, and is not like sociology a generalizing discipline following the ordinary procedure of science.[2] This view makes too sharp a distinction between the knowledge of the universal and the knowledge of the particular ; and its claim that history is concerned with unique and unrepeatable occurrences is not borne out in fact. At the

---

[1] *Autobiography*, p. 265.
[2] See H. Rickert, *Die Grenzen der Naturwissenschaftlichen Begriffsbildung*, 2nd ed., 1913. For summary of Rickert's views see the article " Historical Synthesis " by Fred Morrow Fling in the *American Historical Review*, IX, Oct., 1903. See also W. Windelband, *Introduction to Philosophy*, 1921, pp. 277–299, and E. Tröeltsch, *Der Historismus und seine Probleme*, 1922.

same time, although the sociologist is concerned with generalities, he dare not neglect the study of concrete situations. History and sociology are mutually necessary to each other, the latter being interested in the discovery of general laws, the former in reconstructing the actual occurrence of events. Their difference is thus a matter of emphasis.[1]

There is finally an attitude that would deny the validity of scientific generalizations both in history and sociology, and assert that social phenomena can only be explained in terms of the great man, the genius, the natural leader, or in terms of an inscrutable and divine providence. The latter view is not within the scope of science. A similar view that history is a tale told by an idiot, full of sound and fury signifying nothing, would not however preclude scientific investigation. Indeed it should demand enquiry. The great-man theory, equally, does not preclude such investigation. Greatness itself is historically conditioned. The great man is 'not so much the arbiter of events as the product of sociological forces. The great man, writes Spencer, " must be classed with all other phenomena in the society that gave him birth, as a product of its antecedents. Along with the whole generation of which he forms a minute part—along with its institutions, language, knowledge, manners and its multitudinous arts and appliances, he is the resultant of an enormous aggregate of forces, that have been co-operating for ages."[2] This is, we consider, an all-sufficient answer.[3] Lastly, it is asserted that since

---

[1] See M. Ginsberg, *Studies in Sociology*, 1932. Chap. ii, *History and Sociology*.

[2] *Study of Sociology*, p. 34.

[3] See L. T. Hobhouse, *Social Development*, 1924, pp. 321–324, for an acute analysis.

human beings possess " free-will," sociology and history cannot be sciences, and that all life is a matter of chance. The element of chance nobody would deny, but in spite of this it is possible to discover certain generalities and regularities, as, for instance, in the rates of suicide or marriage. Again, certain events which occur do not appear to be unrelated to a preceding chain of circumstances, and we can study the events leading up to the Industrial Revolution or the Great War. It must also be borne in mind that although individual action may be willed, the products of such action are often unwilled. During a period of financial uncertainty, each individual may wish to preserve his own money by withdrawing it from the bank, and thereby unwillingly heighten the panic. Such broad tendencies and movements can in this way be studied and discovered in spite of the indeterminateness of the will. From another angle, it may be asked whether such laws, physical and social, do not limit human freedom. But freedom *is* " knowledge of necessity ". We may conclude with the following illustration : " The spectacle of a bird denouncing as an encumbrance the air by which alone it is enabled to fly would be a fitting parallel to the spectacle of those philosophers who decry that regularity of sequence through which alone has ' freedom ' any meaning."[1]

---

[1] John Fiske, *Outlines of Cosmic Philosophy*, 2 Vols., 1874. See Chap. XIII, *Sociology and Free-Will*, p. 183. See also L. T Hobhouse, *Social Development*, 1924. Chap. xiii, *Social Law and Social Science.*

BIBLIOGRAPHY. CHAPTER II.

ALEXANDER, S. *Moral Order and Progress.* 1889.

BERNHEIM, E. *Lehrbuch der Historischen Methode.* 1894.

BUCKLE, T. H. *History of Civilization.* 1857–1866.

CARR-SAUNDERS, A. M. *Eugenics.* 1926.

GINSBERG, M. *The Psychology of Society.* 1921.

GINSBERG, M. *Studies in Sociology.* 1932.

HOBHOUSE, L T. *Democracy and Reaction.* 1904.

LANGLOIS, C., et SEIGNOBOS, C. *Introduction aux Études Historiques.* 1898.

MacDOUGALL, W. *An Introduction to Social Psychology.* 1931

RITCHIE, D. G. *Darwinism and Politics.* 1889.

RITCHIE, D. G. *Principles of State Interference.* 1891.

SÉE, H. *Science et philosophie de l'histoire.* 1928.

TEGGART, F. J. *Prolegomena to History.* 1916.

TRÖELTSCH, E. *Der Historismus und seine Probleme.*

TRÖELTSCH, E. *Gesammelte Schriften.* 1922.

CHAPTER III.

TYPES OF SOCIETY.

THE essential unimportance of regarding society as an organism became apparent to Spencer in his exposition of social types and constitutions which is one of his permanent contributions to sociology. He shows a distinct advance upon Comte in confining his investigations not to the generic and rather vague term Society, but to societies, that is, to specific and definite social aggregates possessing a distinct and recognizable structure ; and in elaborating a classification of the types and forms of societies and social relationships without which a scientific sociology is impossible.

In order to generalize and discover sociological correlations, the multitudinous varieties of peoples and societies must be classified into groups. A social morphology must be attempted much in the same way as in botany and biology, and societies and institutions arranged into genera and species exhibiting essential affinities, structural and functional, analogous and homologous. To what extent any such classification may be valid, must depend, of course, on the extent to which common principles of causation can be applied to it ; but these principles as we showed in the last chapter, must be sociological and not biological principles. A morphology of biological organisms cannot be equated with a morphology of human societies. This Spencer recognizes, and admits that not only is it impossible to obtain so definite a classification of societies as of individual organisms, but also that societies exhibit so great a degree of plasticity and divergence, that an application to them of a biological scheme of classification must be used with great caution. And, indeed, although Spencer adheres to a biological terminology, he finds little use for such a classification in his grouping of societies, which he arranges according to their degrees of composition, as simply compound, doubly compound and trebly-compound, and in a less specific way according to their organization as predominantly militant or predominantly industrial. The social organism receives a passing reference, and societies are " those in which the organization for offence and defence is most largely developed, and those in which the sustaining organization is most largely developed."[1]

For the construction of a morphology the comparative method is necessary, and is applied by Spencer with great skill. We pointed out above that in essence the method is to vary the circumstances when examining any phenomenon and thereby sift what is important and relevant from what is unimportant and irrelevant. In ethnographic research it has been exceptionally fruitful, for it has given us, not a history or a developmental scheme as is wrongly assumed, but the elements for such a reconstruction in the shape of a number of photographs taken instantaneously by a number of cameras at a given time.[2] It must not be confused with the

---

[1] *Principles of Sociology*, Vol. 1, p. **538**.

[2] See L. T. Hobhouse, M. Ginsburg and G. C. Wheeler ; *The Material Culture and Social Institutions of the Simpler Peoples: An Essay in Correlation*, 1915, for an analysis of the comparative method.

evolutionary hypothesis. Much of the criticism that has been levelled against the application of the comparative method is due to the confounding of the two methods. Nor does the fact of diffusion vitiate the method, for the comparative method, too, seeks to determine the sources of cultural change. In fact, the comparative method is not incompatible with, but rather complementary to the problem of diffusion. For both require a social morphology, and both seek to trace adhesions between institutions, and discover correlations between them.

Although a social morphology need not assume evolution or development, the evolutionary hypothesis may be suggested and applied. " When we see developing in one group, as a product of known factors, a custom which has existed in another group since prehistoric times, we may fill out the prehistory of the latter on the basis of the knowledge of the former."[1] Such evolution need not be unilinear or rectilinear with a fixed and unvarying sequence of stages. In any case the problem of the temporal order of development must be studied independently by reference to chronological facts supplied by history and archæology. In biology, likewise, taxonomy and phylogeny are distinct problems " though, of course, if the taxonomic tree can be shown to coincide with the phylogenetic tree, that constitutes a striking piece of evidence in support of the theory of evolution." " In sociology the tracing of a line of evolution constitutes a problem, additional to that of morphological classification."[2]

---

[1] This statement is by Lippert, and is quoted in *The Evolution of War : A Study of Its Role in Early Societies*, by Maurice R. Davie, 1929, p. 2.

[2] Morris Ginsberg, *Studies in Sociology*, 1932, p. 13.

This problem Spencer did not pursue. In modern sociology morphology precedes the determination of evolution ; with Spencer evolution precedes and determines a social morphology. Whether applied to the physical, organic and super-organic levels, evolution was the principle that gave to these levels definiteness, coherence and form. At the same time this principle of evolution solved for Spencer the chronological problem, and the complex was necessarily later in time than the simple, the heterogeneous than the homogeneous. This in the opinion of the present writer is a methodological error, as we shall see later, and does much to detract from the value of Spencer's conclusions.

The unit in Spencer's first group, the simpler peoples, is defined as " one which forms a single working whole unsubjected to any other, and of which the parts co-operate, with or without a regulating centre, for certain public ends."[1] The classification based on the degree of political organization obtaining among them is as follows :—

Simple Societies

(Nomadic, Semi-settled, and Settled)

Headless (Leaderless)

Occasional Headship

Vague and Unstable Headship

Stable Headship

" We find reason for inferring," writes Spencer, " that the changes from the hunting life to the pastoral, and from the pastoral to the agricultural, favour increase of population, the development of political organization, of industrial organization and

---

[1] *Principles of Sociology*, Vol. I, p. 539.

of the arts ; though these causes do not of themselves produce these results."[1]

Compound societies are those in which the simple groups have their respective chiefs under a supreme chief, and where no cases of headless government appear.

Compound Societies
(Nomadic, Semi-settled and Settled)
Occasional Headship
Unstable Headship
Stable Headship

" As might be expected, stability of this compound headship, becomes more marked as the original unsettled state passes into the completely settled state : the nomadic life obviously making it difficult to keep the heads of groups subordinate to a general head "[2]

" The completely settled compound societies are mostly characterized by division into ranks, four, five or six, clearly marked off ; by established ecclesiastical arrangements ; by industrial structures that show advancing division of labour, general and local ; by buildings of some permanence clustered into places of some size ; and by approved appliances of life generally."[3]

Doubly-compound societies are all completely settled—

Doubly Compound Societies
(Semi-settled, Settled)
Occasional Headship
Unstable Headship
Stable Headship

---

[1] *Principles of Sociology,* Vol. I, p. 540.
[2] *Ibid.,* p. 541.
[3] *Ibid.,* p. 541.

These societies are characterized by more elaborate and stringent political organization, a developed ecclesiastical hierarchy, often a caste structure. " Custom has passed into positive law ; and religious observances have grown definite, rigid and complex." Towns and roads have become general ; and considerable progress in knowledge and the arts has taken place."[1]

Finally, to complete the classification a number of civilizations have to be added, all of which are trebly compound, these are Ancient Mexico, the Assyrian Empire, the Egyptian Empire, the Roman Empire, Great Britain, France, Germany, Italy and Russia.

On the basis of the above classification certain generalizations may be made, Spencer concludes, that there are societies of these different grades of composition ; that those of the same grade resemble one another in structure ; and that they arise in a similar order. " The stages of compounding and recompounding have to be passed through in succession."[2] The mutual dependence of parts which constitutes a group a working whole, must be achieved over a narrow area before it can be achieved over a wide one. War consolidates the compound society, and still more war the double-compound society. Simultaneously it becomes more complex in its regulative, distributive and industrial systems. " In this order has social evolution gone on, and only in this order does it appear to be possible."[3]

Making allowance for Spencer's evolutionary assumptions and the somewhat mechanical form of

---

[1] *Principles of Sociology*, Vol. I, p. 541.
[2] *Ibid.*, p. 543.
[3] *Ibid.*, p. 544.

his classification, it constitutes a useful one for primitive peoples. Spencer made, however, too little use of it. Hobhouse, Wheeler and Ginsberg with much more precise data and methods than Spencer had at his disposal corroborate on the whole Spencer's with results. Comparing the degree of government peoples of different economic grades, these authors found that the proportion of cases in which there is no government apart from the household, falls steadily from approximately one-half among the Lower Hunters to one-tenth in the second grade of agriculture, and to none in the higher economic grades. A similar development has been found to obtain for larger groups and the proportion of effective government rises from a quarter to nearly a third of the whole among the Hunters and in the lowest agricultural grade, to a half in the next agricultural grade, and to more than three-fourths in the highest agricultural and pastoral peoples. Here government is more than tribal in some cases, and extends over a kingdom. For the historically civilized peoples, on the other hand, such a simple scheme as Spencer's genetic classification is hardly appropriate in view of their complexity, different institutions, histories and modes of life.

His second classification, based on the constitutional traits of two opposite types of society, the predominantly military and the predominantly industrial dominates Spencer's Sociology. With all its uncertainties and blemishes it is a remarkable tribute to Spencer's analytic and synthetic powers of mind and abounds in flashes of brilliant insight. His analysis of the influence of war upon society and political organization as resulting in centralization, regimentation, and despotism is a valid and useful contribution to Sociology.

This in substance is Spencer's account. " The militant type is one in which the army is the nation mobilized while the nation is the quiescent army, and which therefore acquires a structure common to army and nation."[1] That structure involves centralized control in war and peace and a marked tendency for the military chief to become also the political head, despotism and rank. Along with this form of earthly government goes a like form of supernatural government mirroring the former in ranks, powers and militancy ; and an ecclesiastical organization which teaches that absolute subordination is the supreme virtue and " disobedience the crime for which eternal torture is threatened."[2] In this type of society industry serves solely to supply the needs of the military. Everybody and everything is subject to military discipline. An ideology develops concerning the relation between the State and the individual—" the claims of the unit are nothing and the claims of the aggregate everything."[3] Finally, the co-operation by which the militant society is maintained is a compulsory co-operation. This " social structure adapted for dealing with surrounding hostile societies is under a centralized regulating system, to which all the parts are completely subject : just as in the individual organism the outer organs are completely subject to the chief nervous centre."[4]

---

[1] *Principles of Sociology*, Vol. I, p. 545.
[2] *Ibid.*, p. 551.
[3] *Ibid.*, p. 551.
[4] *Ibid.*, p. 552.

The industrial society is the opposite type. It is peaceful, and in its early stage possesses scarcely any political organization, and such as exists is elective and democratic. The sustaining or industrial organization is well developed ; coercive rule is on the decline and free institutions and representative government arise. " Regions whence changes towards greater political liberty have come, are the leading industrial regions."[1] Such societies will have appropriate sentiments and beliefs. " Right of private judgment in religious matters gradually establishes itself along with establishment of political rights. In place of a uniform belief imperatively enforced, there come multiform beliefs voluntarily accepted ; and the ever multiplying bodies espousing these beliefs instead of being governed despotically, govern themselves after a manner more or less representative."[2] Slavery and feudalism give way to free associations, unions of workers, associations of employers, and political societies. Instead of the militant, the industrial mode of regulation ramifies now into all minor departments of social activity, and " multitudinous objects are achieved by spontaneously evolved combinations governed representatively."[3] This type of society will have its own ideology. " In place of the doctrine that the duty of obedience to the governing agent is unqualified, there arises the doctrine that the will of the citizens is supreme, and the governing agent exists merely to carry out their will."[4] Finally, the co-operation

---

[1] *Ibid.*, p. 555.
[2] *Ibid.*, p. 555.
[3] *Ibid.*, p. 556.
[4] *Ibid.*, p. 556.

by which the multiform activities of the society are
carried on is a voluntary co-operation ; like the
organism its regulating apparatus becomes diffused
and decentralized.

These two types are ideal types. Actually, a
number of factors obtrude, and obscure these essential traits, such as the racial composition of society ;
the effect of the immediately preceding mode of life
and social type ; the nature of the habitat ; the
structure and customs of the neighbouring societies ;
and finally the mixture of races, which Spencer considers the most potent factor of all, for it determines
the relative homogeneity or heterogeneity of the
units constituting the social aggregate. He is of the
opinion that where intermixture does not occur
between two different races, social regulation implies
a compulsory and despotic system.   " Social constitutions of this kind, in which races having aptitudes
for forming unlike structures co-exist, are in states
of unstable equilibrium."[1]   Where the two different
races intermarry extensively, similar effects are
produced, because the individual hybrid " inheriting
from one line of ancestry proclivities adapted to
another set of institutions, is not fitted for either.
He is a unit whose nature has not been moulded by
any social type and therefore cannot, with others
like himself evolve any social type."[2]   Mexico and
the South American republics with their constant
revolutions belong to this class. If, however, two
races differ slightly from each other, their mixture
will have beneficial effects—" medium plasticity
allows these changes of structure constituting advance

---

[1] *Principles of Sociology*, Vol. I, p. 559.
[2] *Ibid.*, p. 560.

in heterogeneity."[1]   The Hebrews and Athenians were such racial mixtures.   England, which is " peopled by different divisions of the Aryan race, and mainly by varieties of Scandinavians, again illustrates this effect produced by the mixture of units sufficiently alike to co-operate in the same social system, but sufficiently unlike to prevent that social system from becoming forthwith definite in structure.[2] Systems such as these most easily evolve into the industrial type.

That these inductions are correct is the teaching of biology according to Spencer.   Between organisms widely unlike in kind no progeny can arise. If they are less unlike, the progeny, it is true will live, but will be incapable of propagating. Only with varieties nearly allied will a permanently fertile breed result.

There is also a third type of society that the future may evolve—" As the contrast between the militant and the industrial types, is indicated by inversion of the belief that individuals exist for the benefit of the State, into the belief that the State exists for the benefit of the individuals ; so the contrast between the industrial type likely to be evolved from it, is indicated by inversion of the belief that life is for work into the belief that work is for life."[3]

In a chapter entitled " Social Metamorphoses," Spencer turns to a verification of his ideal types. Evidence from biology is again adduced—the fact that with social organisms as with individual organisms structure becomes adapted to activity,

---

[1] *Ibid.*, p. 560.
[2] *Ibid.*, p. 561.
[3] *Ibid.*, p. 653.

and as this changes in response to new conditions, so will the structure.   If these activities become more militant or industrial, the outer and inner structures will accordingly increase or diminish. That is if there are no resistances to change which the inherited social type offers, and to those resistances caused by the partial continuance of the old traditions.   History supports biology in providing evidence of changes of societies into the military from the industrial, and *vice versa*.   In Europe, a period of peace from 1815 to 1850 was accompanied by industrial development.   Since then belligerent habits have revived, and compulsory regulations come into force from which Great Britain was not exempt.   " We have military heads of the Metropolitan and Provincial police "[1] (a strikingly modern note).   Sanitary regulations have increased, Poor-Law centralization has grown up, and " in sundry towns municipal bodies have become distributors of gas and water."[2]   " While nominally extended by the giving of votes, the freedom of the individual has been in many ways actually diminished, both by restrictions which ever-multiplying officials are appointed to insist on, and by the forcible taking of money to secure for him, or others at his expense, benefits previously left to be secured by each for himself.   And undeniably this is a return towards that coercive discipline which pervades the whole social life where the militant type is predominant."[3]

Two main conclusions follow. Firstly, that social evolution forms a part of general evolution, in that

---

[1] *Principles of Sociology* Vol. I, p. **570.**
[2] *Ibid.*, p. **571.**
[3] *Ibid.*, p. **575.**

it manifests integration, change from homogeneity to heterogeneity, and increasing coherence and definiteness. Secondly, that these inductions constitute the outline of an Empirical Sociology which shows " that in social phenomena there is a general order of co-existence and sequence ; and that therefore social phenomena form the subject matter of a science, reducible in some measure at least to the deductive form."[1]

Before considering some of the more serious objections that may be raised against Spencer's scheme, and against the biological analogies interpolated therein, it will be useful to consider a scheme which in externals is not unlike that of Spencer. Émile Durkheim, who, like Spencer, possesses powers of synthesis and analysis of the highest order, on the basis of careful study of factual data formulated two main types of society, one in which division of labour is slightly developed, and the other in which it is highly developed. He then correlated a number of social phenomena with this variable and arrived at conclusions not unlike those of Spencer. Both Durkheim's interpretation and approach are different, however, and his *De la division du travail social* contains some pertinent criticisms of the Spencerian scheme.

Let us first see the classification Durkheim proposes for the simpler peoples. Following Spencer, he rightly recognizes the importance of understanding the nature of society. But while to him society is a resultant of its constituent units and the mode of their interaction, to Durkheim it is an entity *a priori* to the individual. The essence of society

---

[1] *Ibid.*, p. 585.

may best be revealed, argues Durkheim, by research
into primitive peoples who will most likely yield the
clue to a valid system of classification, and to an
understanding of the nature of the social tie. But
what shall be the unit of study? Durkheim objects
to Spencer's unit because it is too loose a definition
including within it peoples of different degrees of
culture and civilization. The unit should imply,
argues Durkheim, a complete absence of parts, " a
mass absolutely homogeneous, whose parts are not
distinguished from each other, and consequently
would not be arranged among themselves ; which
in a word would be lacking both definiteness of
form and organization."[1] This unit (the horde) is
" a social aggregate which does not now, nor ever
has, comprised any other more elementary aggregate,
and is immediately resolved into individuals "[2]
who are only " juxtaposed atomically." Since such
an undifferentiated unit does not exist, Durkheim
postulates it, in order to explain the existing
primitive unit—the clan, which must have been
formed by the combination or repetition of this
hypothetical unit. Further compounding would
result in societies of greater complexity, and the
scheme of development beginning with the unit
would be—

The unit (horde).

The Clan.

The simple polysegmentary society (mere aggregation of clans).

The polysegmentary society simply compounded.

The polysegmentary society doubly compounded.

[1] *De la division du travail social*, 6th ed., p. 149.
[2] *Ibid.*, p. 102.

All these groups or societies are mechanical, repetitive or metameric in nature, for each part is simply the repetition of another part. They are segmentary as opposed to those in which the parts are mutually related, are complementarily functional. Organic societies are products of later development, as a result of processes we shall soon consider.

This classification bears remarkable similarities to Spencer's scheme but is open to similar objections. Firstly, it is not very helpful in explaining complex civilizations, for to regard these as resultants of compounding and recompounding unduly simplifies their actual modes of growth and expansion. Secondly, it implies at any rate a scheme of uniform development to which Durkheim was opposed. Thirdly, as against Spencer's actual unit, it postulates a unit which does not exist. And finally, it lumps together peoples of different degrees of culture and material progress.

Morphological evolution meant to Durkheim a transition from the segmentary type of society to the organic type of society and a corresponding change in the social ties, just as in Spencer's scheme it involved the transition from a military to an industrial type of society. Durkheim shows how the undifferentiated horde gradually gives way to the village type of society bound together more by the principle of territorial contiguity than by that of kinship. The population, although still organized on a partially segmentary basis, has begun to be differentiated by the division of labour. Concomitant with every decrease of the segmentary type there is an increase of the organic type; so that with increasing division of labour, both geographic and functional, world-wide commerce and manufacture, immense cities, and minute specialization of every phase of social life, societies come to be composed of occupational groups which are functionally interdependent, and organically closely knit together.

The nature of society, of social cohesion and solidarity, which Spencer had attempted to elucidate by means of the social organism, Durkheim attacks from another angle, and to understand his position it is necessary to say a few words about his conception of primitive society.

According to Durkheim, the remarkable feature of primitive life is its intense solidarity, its pervading cohesiveness. Outside and above the individual there looms a collective consciousness specifically different from the individual consciousness, which gives rise to *réprésentations collectives* dominating and controlling the individual's thinking at every point. Religion, for instance, is here based not on animism or naturalism, but is a group product. The group or clan is God and the totemic principle. Social facts are " ways of thinking, feeling, acting, exterior to the individual, and endowed with a power of coercion by reason of which they impose themselves on him."[1] Primitive mentality is characterized by compulsive categories of thought deriving from society. The individual is thus completely merged in the group and bound to it by super-individual and powerful collective beliefs, and the nature of social solidarity clearly evident.

But with increasing division of labour—to be understood not merely in its economic aspect, but

---

[1] *Les régles de la méthode sociologique*, p. 8.

as specialization in every phase of life—with the transition from the metameric to the organic type of society, the group loses its hold over its units, who tend to become more autonomous, independent, and heterogeneous. But, nevertheless, social solidarity persists, the social group remains as cohesive as ever. How is this to be explained? asks Durkheim. He finds the answer in the process of the division of labour itself, which makes the units of society functionally dependent on each other, and which is associated with new social ties and a new ideology that take the place of the old ones.

Durkheim then proceeds to a brilliant analysis of the correlative changes that occur in the whole complex of institutions and beliefs with the metamorphosis of the mechanical into the organic type— an analysis that is reminiscent of Spencer's deep and penetrating generalizations. Let us briefly review the main characteristics of a society— primitive society—in which division of labour is only slightly developed, and of an organic society in which division of labour is very highly developed.

In the first, mechanical, type of society the essence of religion in the group itself gives rise to vague, magical and impersonal powers, the symbol of which is the totem. Patriotism is intense, local and tribal. Morality is uniform and rigid, and its infringement provokes collective resentment and repression. Since society dominates every department of life, criminal law preponderates over civil law, and most crimes are crimes against society. Here the function of law is not restitution but punishment. Opinion is unanimous and every person feels, thinks and acts in the same way. The absence of class and social distinctions necessarily results in a political system which is democratic, and in an economic system which is communistic. Such differentiation as exists is due to heredity only, but this does little to disturb the mechanical and regular responses of individuals. In such a society social solidarity is likewise mechanical and homogeneous, and the collective consciousness reigns supreme.

In the organic society, the forms of religion are different. At first, polytheism is dominant, and later monotheism, whose god mirrors the social type by becoming individualized and depersonalized. Local and tribal patriotism wanes and yields to internationalism and cosmopolitanism. As the control of society over all actions lessens, laws lose their emotional character and crimes their sacrilegious nature. Restitution, rather than vindictive punishment is the function of law. Contractual relationships replace those of status, and co-operation replaces compulsion. Politically, society becomes more specialized and less democratic, while in the economic system, private property and economic individualism begin to preponderate. Vertical and horizontal mobility characterizes society and individuals become heterogeneous instead of homogeneous. Behaviour becomes more individual and personal in proportion as there is a decrease in the volume of collective consciousness as compared with individual consciousness. Public opinion becomes multiform instead of unanimous, and tastes, beliefs and customs become diverse and varied. The role of heredity becomes less, especially as regards the transmission of occupation and status. Social solidarity is now organic, and rests upon the fact that every member of society, as a result of the division of labour, is no longer self-sufficient. The dependence of one individual upon another, and functional mutuality now constitute social solidarity.

It is clear that in form there are a number of striking similarities between Spencer and Durkheim in their treatment of types of societies. Spencer's " simple society " is like Durkheim's " unit or horde " ; both writers emphasize the process of compounding and re-compounding ; Spencer's military and industrial types are analogous to Durkheim's mechanical and organic types ; to Spencer the decrease of militarism was correlated with an increase in industrialism—to Durkheim the decline of the mechanical type was associated with the rise of the organic type of society ; and, finally, in many respects Spencer's industrial society with its emphasis on the contractual nature of social relationships is not unlike that of Durkheim's organic society.

But these are only surface similarities, indicating nevertheless the profound influence Spencer exercised over Durkheim. In fact, Durkheim makes some very pertinent criticisms of Spencer's typological construction, and shows that there are significant differences between them. These it is well worth giving, together with some general comments on Spencer's scheme.[1]

While Spencer was of the opinion that centralization and militarism submerged the individual, who only regained his freedom through industrialism, Durkheim suggests that the individual is most absorbed

---

[1] *De la division du travail social*, 6th ed., pp. 170–209.

in society when militarism and centralization are absent. For it is in the most primitive society, where differentiation hardly exists, that the individual is so completely a part of his group that he has no separate individuality. Indeed, Durkheim adds, centralization is necessary if individuality is to emerge. Just as in the higher organisms there is a centralization of the nervous system, so in higher societies is it necessary to have centralized government. This is a repetition of what Huxley had already written about Spencer's social organism.[1] In complex societies, not less but more government is necessary, for where contractual relations ramify throughout society, a strong and centralized government is necessary to see that contracts are observed. Not only is there an increase of contractual relations, argues Durkheim, but there is also an increase of non-contractual relations as society develops—instance the relations between husband and wife, and parents and children. To regard as Spencer does the distinction between militarism and industrialism as purely contractual, is to obscure the real nature of social solidarity. But most serious of all, Durkheim argues, is Spencer's assumption that militarism and individualism mean the same thing in different contexts of history. Is it valid he asks to compare the democracy of a primitive tribe with the democratic system that prevails to-day?

That some of these objections to Spencer's types are valid can hardly be doubted. But there are two very serious objections that Durkheim hardly realized, and which Spencer did not see at all. Spencer

---

[1] See T. H. Huxley, *Administrative Nihilism*, 1871, and Spencer's not very satisfactory reply, *Specialized Administration*, 1871.

argued that the process of history partly involves
the rise of the industrial type of society, and that
in the fullness of time the complete development of
an industrial type is assured. But in the last
generation or so two significant developments have
occurred that seem, according to some sociologists,
to refute Spencer's conclusions. In the first place,
since Spencer died there has been a growth of
economic imperialism or of what may be described as a combination of industrialism and
militarism. And in the second place, there
has been a growth of the socialized state,
wherein government and centralization take an
important part in the control of industry. The
growth of capitalism and the struggle for markets is
tending to make each state a highly-organized industrial unit that is at the same time highly militant.
War itself, it has been argued, has generally economic
motives behind it, and is waged for the control of
markets or necessary commodities such as oil or
rubber. Government tends to become more and
more involved in the activities of financial or
industrial interests, and in a totalitarian state may
completely control and manage industry. There
might at the same time be a tendency towards
Socialism, and in this case, the state would own and
control the means of production, and through this
almost every department of life. Spencer, who
vehemently attacked the participation of the State
in industry, and indeed thought that industry and
militancy were utterly opposed, lived to see their
close alliance. He saw too the growth of imperialistic exploits, and although he sharply criticized
the Boer war and similar ventures, he did not see

the implications, of the above tendencies for social development nor could he see how they affected his own theoretical constructions.

It may also be added that Spencer's verification of his types by an appeal to biology and to his interpretation of the law of evolution, is an appeal to evidence that is not conclusive, as is shown more than once in this book. What reason is there for thinking that the industrial type is more complex and more differentiated than the military type, and that therefore its development is implicit in evolution? His argument that races closely akin are more likely to form stable political constitutions on mingling, than races which are very dissimilar, may be true, but to explain this fact as Spencer does on racial grounds, seems to some modern thinkers a simplification of a very complex problem. The study of the biological effects of race mixture presents great problems owing to the difficulty of disentangling the purely genetic effects from the social and environmental. Spencer assumes that his generalizations regarding racial mixtures and racial qualities, will prove to be the final pronouncements of science.

Although Durkheim chose his data with as much care as did Spencer, and used the comparative method more cautiously, his types of society reveal some serious defects. He assumes a super-individual mind or a collective consciousness for primitive society. He assumes that in such a society, the individual is completely merged in the mass, and has no individuality whatever. The truth of a number of his correlations has still to be ascertained, for instance, was property always a communal possession in primitive times ? He finds the cause of all social development in the growth—in the volume and density of societies, which leads to increasing competition and the division of labour. For only in this way could people continue to make a living and live side by side in society. But it would be easy to point to societies which have grown slowly or not at all in volume and density, such as the French, but have nevertheless made rapid social advances, and to others, such as the Russian, whose population has grown very rapidly, and yet have remained backward. It would be truer to say that volume and density in societies are the effects rather than the causes of material advance. Moreover, Durkheim is inclined to isolate the factor of division of labour, the variable with which he correlates all the other social changes, and make it independent of other factors.

The schemes of Spencer and Durkheim are invaluable contributions to sociology. They possess a scope and a generalizing power that justify a science of society ; they show insight and penetration ; they seek to discover fundamental correlations ; and finally, they help us to understand the processes of history. Few of these typological constructions, and there have been many, rival those of Durkheim and Spencer. Comte wrote of a theocracy wherein the temporal power is subordinate to the spiritual, and of a sociocracy where these would be perfectly harmonized, and social development would be guided for the benefit of all humanity. Bagehot singled out government by authority, and government by discussion. From a study of the evolution of law, Maine constructed societies based on contract and societies based on status. Ratzenhofer spoke of the military or conquest state, and the culture state. Ross develops a scheme including these stages—clericalism, militarism, officialism, liberalism, capitalism and individualism. Tarde distinguished between a teleocracy governed by desires, and an ideocracy ruled by ideas. Ward's contribution was physiocracy, plutocracy and sociocracy. Giddings on the basis of general psychological characteristics, classifies societies into eight main types—sympathetic, congenial, approbational, despotic, authoritative, conspiral, contractual and idealistic.

A scheme that has some affinities to Durkheim's is implied in the distinction Tönnies makes between " Gemeinschaft " and " Gesellschaft." The. former dominated by the principle of kinship is equivalent to the mechanical society, whilst the latter, characterized by willed and voluntary relations, is equivalent to the organic society. The main features of " Gemeinschaft " are common will, common beliefs, religion, custom, natural solidarity, common property, sovereignty of group interests, and the subordination of the individual to society. " Gesellschaft," on the other hand, exhibits individual will, public opinion, doctrine, fashions and fads, contractual solidarity, private property, sovereignty of private interests and the exaltation of the individual above society.

A classification that has been very fruitful in comparative sociology is the one drawn up by the authors of the *Material Culture and Social Institutions of the Simpler Peoples.*[1] The criterion adopted was

---

[1] L. T. Hobhouse, M. Ginsberg and G. C. Wheeler, *The Material Culture and Social Institutions of the Simpler Societies : An Essay in Correlation*, 1915.

the degree of mastery over the environment as evidenced by tools, instruments and techniques, and the classification obtained was :

a. Lower Hunters (including Fishers and Gatherers) who live by gathering—no substantial dwellings—no spinning, no weaving, no pottery).

b. Higher Hunters—live more by fishing and hunting and possess some of these arts.

c. Agriculture 1.   *f.* Pastoral 1.

d. Agriculture 2.   *g.* Pastoral 2.

e. Agriculture 3.

The principles running through and dominating these groups are kinship, numerous ramifications of intermarriage and territorial contiguity.

For the classical and ancient civilizations Hobhouse proposed the principle of authority, and these main forms of society[1]:

a. Absolute Monarchy.   *c.* Empire.

b. Feudal Monarchy.

Finally, growing up at the same time, and becoming ever more definite are societies based on the principle of citizenship :

a. The City State.   *b.* The Country State.[2]

At this point it may be appropriate to make some brief remarks on the construction of types or the typological method. A good starting point is a passage by Durkheim, which it is worth quoting in full, for the bearing it has on Spencer's Sociology.

---

[1] L. T. Hobhouse, *Morals in Evolution*, 1923.

[2] The most useful classifications are those employing economic criteria, *e.g.* Bucher's—(1) house economy, (2) town economy, (3) national economy, (4) world economy. Hildebrands—(1) natural economy, (2) money economy, (3) credit economy. Marx's—(1) economy of antiquity, (2) asiatic economy, (3) feudal economy, (4) bourgeois economy.

Durkheim writes : " For the sociologist as for the historian, social facts vary with the social system of which they form a part ; they cannot be understood when detached from it. This is why two facts cannot be profitably compared merely because they seem to resemble each other ; it is necessary that these societies themselves resemble each other, that is to say that they be only varieties of the same species. The comparative method would be impossible if social types did not exist, and it cannot be usefully applied except within a single type. What errors have not been committed for having neglected this precept ! It is thus that facts have been unduly connected with each other, which in spite of exterior resemblances, really have neither the same sense, nor the same importance, the primitive democracy and that of to-day, the collectivism of inferior societies and actual socialistic tendencies, the monogamy which is frequent in Australian tribes, and that sanctioned by our laws.

" If we do not wish to fall into these same errors, instead of scattering our researches, over all societies possible, we must concentrate them upon one clearly determined type."[1]

Durkheim perhaps unduly limits the comparative method, but he does show how important it is not to bring different peoples together into one category. One must also be careful not to use in classification criteria implying a casual relationship when such a relationship is to be proved. Many studies that distinguish economic stages on the basis of the degree of social and political structure, thus postulating a necessary relation between them, are invalid

[1] *The Elementary Forms of Religious Life*, 1915, p. 94.

for this reason. And, finally, it is important not to postulate a sequence of stages, where the data do not warrant it.

These points must be borne in mind in any construction of types. The typological method, takes many forms and attempts to classify societies, cultures and instructions. In spite of the vast amount of typological literature on the forms of societies and institutions, it has little scientific value. Only within recent times have attempts been made to devise categories that will describe the essential nature of societies. And to do this requires not only comprehensive knowledge, but also an ability to go behind the multitudinous concrete characters and grasp the characters that are requisite, the typical traits of a society or an institution. Moreover, analysis and synthesis must be well balanced to be productive of fruitful results.

These qualities were possessed in a high degree by Max Weber. His methodological works are important contributions to the typological method, and raise a number of significant problems in connection with it. That this method constructs abstract ideal types, instead of accurately describing facts, is untrue, and Weber could rightly reply that facts alone give no point of view. What usually happens is that the investigator with his value-ideas selects from his collection of facts a proportion on which to build his point of view. The ideal type is a mental construction arrived at by concentrating upon certain features and combining them with other features, not necessarily always associated with them, so as to get a coherent whole, a pictured unity. Such an ideal type, say, of town economy, is not an average of all town economies at different ages and in different parts of the world, but a concept containing only essential features. It is not an hypothesis, although it may suggest an hypothesis. It is not a picture of the real, but it helps us to understand the real. It is not a definition, nor is it an average. It is simply a heuristic construction in order to facilitate comparison. It may have to be modified after comparing it with its actual prototype or on the other hand, reality may be judged by the extent to which it deviates from the ideal type.

We may, for example, take Max Weber's construction of the "town-economy." To determine its essential characteristics, it was necessary to classify and compare different types of towns. It was found that the main characteristic was not size, or the preponderance of agricultural or industrial occupations, but the grouping of a large number of people connected with each other in a variety of ways, from which were lacking personal acquaintanceship and mutual recognition. Its ties are therefore not community ties or neighbourhood ties, but certain associational groupings. It is therefore distinct from the village. It is also a market settlement. With these features in mind, a comparative and historical study of towns was made, tracing their development and differentiation from previous social structures, and their relationship to other aspects and phases of the social life. Finally, the main types of towns were totality of contrasted, their historical development determined, and the factors entering into their development evaluated.

Later in life, Weber was drawn away from factual studies, and emphasized aspects of sociology, that brought him near to the Formal school of sociology which we examined in the first chapter. He realized that both history and sociology are characterized by the selection of facts and of values, of phenomena which are valuable from or in their human significance. In this they are distinct from the natural sciences which concentrate upon phenomena, having something in common, with as large a number as possible of other phenomena. But if history is to yield sociological truths, the individualizing method of history must be replaced by generalizations regarding social processes. Thus, from the historical types we have built up, we can abstract one feature or form, such as domination, on the basis of which citizens obey the commands of authorities. We pass from history to sociology by doing this, because here we have a form or a type dealing with regular forms of behaviour, and giving one to suppose that in particular situations people will behave in certain ways. Here we get rules or " Regeln " of sociology.

To obtain these must be the function of sociology, and the only way to obtain them is to isolate and abstract a small number of phenomena from the whole complex in which they are embedded. A higher stage will yield laws of a still wider generality and validity which will deal only with those types of meaningful behaviour that are conscious and accessible to the understanding. From this point of view, meaningful behaviour is the essence of sociology and demarcates it from the natural sciences. Weber's work increasingly emphasizes the " understanding " of behaviour (verstehende Soziologie) and tends more and more in the direction of highly abstract categories and classification.

From the writer's point of view these tendencies are to be deplored.   Indeed, on the basis of " verstehende Soziologie " it would be difficult if not impossible to construct a morphology on the lines of Spencer or Durkheim. If we cannot understand the behaviour of a people living in a different environment and in a different cultural epoch, attempts at classification and generalization are nullified. Moreover, this conception of sociology unduly minimizes the significance of unconscious and emotional behaviour in social life. True, such behaviour is mainly the concern of the social psychologist, but his conclusions are necessary to sociology.

It is to be added that Weber's actual work is not confined within the narrow framework of his theoretical presuppositions. He studies the significance and impact upon society of Protestantism, Capitalism, Confucianism, etc., and illuminates his works with wide and penetrating generalizations concerning the development of society and institutions, that follow the lines of a sociology such as Spencer envisaged. Weber's ideal type leaves open the problem of evolutionary stages or sequences. But it is possible to pass from the ideal type to a morphology, and from a morphology to evolution. It is true that the earlier schemes of development with their stages of social evolution were unsatisfactory. But this is no argument against the necessity of solving the problem by more careful methods. The classification of societies, whether it be empirical or heuristic, is a necessary preliminary. Here Spencer and Weber meet on common ground. Weber himself showed that the ideal type can be used in the study of development, and that the laws of evolution, if care be taken not to regard them as forces or empirically valid, constitute ideal constructions of heuristic importance. A complete social morphology would facilitate the task of comparison, and the discovery of causation in social processes. In this sociological task Spencer was the pioneer whose work was carried on by men like Hobhouse, Durkheim and Weber.

BIBLIOGRAPHY. CHAPTER III.

DURKHEIM, E. *De la division du travail social.* 2nd ed. 1902.

DURKHEIM, E. *Les regles de la méthode sociologique.* 1895.

HOBHOUSE, L. T. *Morals in Evolution.* 1915.

HOBHOUSE, L. T. *Social Development.* 1924.

HOBHOUSE, L. T., WHEELER, G. C., and GINSBERG, M. *The Material Culture of the Simpler Peoples.* 1915.

MÜLLER-LYER, F. *The History of Social Development. Trans. by Elizabeth C. Lake and H. A. Lake.* 1920.

WEBER, M. *Aufsätze zur Wissenschaftslehre.* 1922.

WEBER, M. *Wirtschaft und Gesellschaft.* 2nd ed. 1925.

WEBER, M. *The Protestant Ethic and the Spirit of Capitalism. Trans. by Talcott Parsons.* 1930.

CHAPTER IV.

Woman, Family, Race.

Spencer's type of society, and especially his distinction between the militant and industrial types, must be kept in mind throughout his Sociology, if we are to understand his discussion of political and industrial institutions, and of the role of the family and the position of woman in society. These types constitute the keystone of his whole sociological and evolutionary arch. Again and again Spencer demonstrates that at any given stage of development, there is a necessary consistency between society's institutions, arising from the fact that the functioning of one institution is dependent on the functioning of the others, and that in the course of time, a certain balance or equilibrium obtains among them. This observation by Spencer is a valuable contribution to sociology, and deserves further exploration and analysis.

In this chapter we shall confine ourselves to a brief examination of Spencer's views on the family and some kindred problems, and the way in which he relates them to his evolutionary scheme and to his typological construction. Our main topics deal with the position of women and children in primitive times : the forms of the family and sexual relationships—promiscuity, group marriage, exogamy, the matriarchy, polyandry, polygamy, and monogamy ;

and the antagonism between individuation and genesis ; and we shall show to what extent recent research modifies Spencer's conclusions.

It must be remembered that Spencer's views on all these matters were greatly influenced by a number of assumptions against which the student of sociology should be on his guard. He presumed that whatever has evolved is the fittest and that the latest evolved is always the best. Survival value and ethical excellence become interchangeable terms, and to him those domestic relations, "which are the highest as ethically considered, are also the highest as considered both biologically and sociologically."[1] His second assumption was to identify evolution with progress, and therefore, Spencer has to postulate a period of promiscuity antecedent to monogamy which is the highest rung on the ladder of evolution. His third assumption was that the process of evolution is rectilinear or unilinear, so that everywhere and always, one stage of the process must necessarily be followed by the next until the whole series is completed. From this point of view, there is but one and irreversible order of development for the family—promiscuity, polyandry, polygamy and finally monogamy. In justice to Spencer, it must be said that he frequently disclaimed evolution of this kind, and that in many cases his evolution has reference not to any particular society, but rather to the broad and general tendencies of civilization or humanity.

With these assumptions in mind, Spencer finds no difficulty in portraying the treatment of women in primitive times. It was "cruel to the utmost

---

[1] *Principles of Sociology*, Vol. I, p. 600.

degree bearable "[1] and there was " no check to the tyranny which the stronger sex exercised over the weaker "[2] save in so far as their preservation for the maintenance of the race was felt necessary. " The slave class in a primitive society," Spencer states, " consists of women."[3]

The facts he adduces in support of this thesis can, however, be shown from later researches to be one-sided. A very detailed study of the Central Australians, who are very primitive, if not the most primitive tribes, showed that woman " is generally well treated, and able to influence masculine decision, regardless of all theory as to her inferiority or impurity " and that " it is precisely among the rudest people that she enjoys practical equality with her mate."[4] Westermarck from a very careful survey of the evidence came to the conclusion that although, among the lower races in general, the married woman is in the power of her husband, she enjoys a remarkable degree of independence, is treated with consideration, and exercises in some cases such a great influence over her husband, that she is regarded as his superior.[5] Finally, Hobhouse, Wheeler and Ginsberg indicate that among the most simple groups the husband can dissolve the marriage at will on the slightest grounds, but that this right is in the majority of cases also granted to the woman.[6]

This cumulative evidence modifies considerably

---

[1] *Principles of Sociology*, Vol. I, p. 713.
[2] *Ibid.*, p. 713.
[3] *Ibid.*, p. 717.
[4] B. Spencer and F. J. Gillen, *Native Tribes of Central Australia*, 1899.
[5] E. Westermarck, *Origin and Growth of Moral Ideas*, 1906.
[6] L. T. Hobhouse, G. C. Wheeler, M. Ginsberg. *Material Culture and Social Institutions of the Simpler Peoples*. 1915.

Spencer's account. Marriage by capture, which he assumed to be the most primitive and universal form of marriage, does not imply, as Spencer thought it did, that the husband had absolute rights over the woman. Nor does marriage by purchase, where women are exchangeable for cattle, imply that the woman is without personal rights. It is true that in general the social position of women is inferior to that of men, but it does not follow that their treatment was such as Spencer imagined. He does not sufficiently distinguish their treatment from their legal status, and the magical and religious notions concerning them—all of which may differ at any given time, owing to disturbing causes. And he too readily assumes that the position of woman is a gauge or a criterion of the general culture of a people, and of its social and moral progress. Even if it were such a criterion, what conclusions can be drawn from a comparison of woman in prim Victorian times, and her position in some long ago hypothetical era when wild and fierce hordes roamed the world. In fact, the course of civilization was not, as Spencer believed, to narrow the gulf between man and woman, but to widen it, when property and culture became the prerogative of man.

The earliest division of labour, Spencer argues, was between man the master, and woman the slave. " Omitting those activities for which women are during large parts of their lives incapacitated, or into which they cannot enter in considerable numbers without fatally diminishing population, we cannot define the division of labour between the sexes further, than by saying that before civilization begins, the stronger sex forces the weaker to do all the drudgery, and that along with social advance, the apportionment somewhat mitigated in character, becomes variously specialized under varying conditions."[1] This argument, as put by Spencer, has not the assent of all anthropologists. The majority, including Westermarck and Lowie are of the opinion that on the whole primitive division of labour was equitable, and that it by no means condemned woman to lifelong drudgery. Among hunting peoples, while the men were away pursuing game, women gathered berries, wild roots and shellfish. They planted seeds and gathered in the harvest in the agricultural stage, and in the pastoral stage they engaged in the dressing of skins, and the spinning and weaving of clothes. This more or less equitable apportionment of tasks, however, is not universal, for religious, magical, and especially specific economic factors operate to make certain occupations a man's prerogative, or to exclude women from the general economic life. In this case their treatment too, possibly worsened. But the view that in early times the woman was a drudge probably has its origin in the mistaken interpretations of travellers who saw the women heavily loaded and burdened during a migration or a march, while the men were seemingly unburdened and free. But it was necessary for the men to keep their hands and arms disengaged and be ready at any moment for attack. Spencer himself qualifies his argument by admitting this point[2] and by further admitting that " even among the rudest men, whose

---

[1] *Principles of Sociology*, Vol. I, p. 720.
[2] *Ibid.*, p. 718.

ordinary behaviour to their women is the worst, predominance of women is not unknown.''[1]

Spencer rightly emphasizes the importance of economic factors in determining the treatment of woman and her position. He shows that in the case of marriage, through services rendered to the wife's people, she was more likely to be valued than one that was bought or stolen. Moreover, the husband entered the wife's family for the period of his service, and was considered an unwelcome visitor, rather than as a lord and master of his family, which he only became when he was back in his own tribe. But more important in determining the status of woman were the kinds of occupations followed. Where the occupations of the men and women were similar, the women were on a greater level of equality with the men. Thus, where men and women hunt together, or where the women are proficient in catching fish, their status will be higher than usual, though still inferior to that of men. In the early phases of agriculture, it is known that woman played an important role, for gardening with the hoe was woman's distinctive employment. But later with the domestication of the ox, which was used for ploughing—an achievement that was due to man— her status became worse. Another result was that the care of herds became generally a man's occupation. Indeed, were it not because of such disturbing factors to which we have alluded above, the correlation between economic grade and the status of woman, would be much more exact than it is. Even the very unsatisfactory assessment of her status made in the *Simpler Peoples* indicated that in the

---

[1] *Principles of Sociology*, Vol. I., p. 715.

Agricultural societies as a whole, the position of woman was slightly better, and in the Pastoral a little worse, than among the Hunters.[1] Lowie, who is reluctant to admit a necessary correlation between the economic factor and the position of woman on the ground " that the preservation of an accidental complex is entirely possible " and that " the empirical association of inferior status with non-participation could evolve once, was disseminated as a unit, and has persisted from sheer conservatism," has finally to admit that " the economic factor is an efficient cause, but at its best only one of a series of determimants."[2]

Spencer's most valuable contribution to this topic is his determination of a series of correlations between the position of woman and types of social organization.   His most important conclusions are that there are positive correlations between the low position of woman and militancy, and her high position and industrialism.   Hence he states " that among peoples otherwise inferior, the position of woman is relatively good where their occupations are nearly the same as those of men, seems allied to the wider truth, that their position becomes good in proportion as warlike activities are replaced by industrial activities ; since, when the men fight while the women work, the difference of occupation is greater than when both are engaged in productive labours, however unlike such labours may be in kind."[3]

---

[1] L. T. Hobhouse, G. C. Wheeler and M. Ginsberg. *The Material Culture and Social Institutions of the Simpler Peoples*, p. 173.

[2] R. H. Lowie, *Primitive Society*, 1924. *See* his discussion on the treatment of women.

[3] *Principles of Sociology*, Vol. I, p. 722.

These correlations Spencer links to another series of correlations he had already obtained between militancy and polygyny, and industrialism and monogamy. And since, he goes on to argue, polygyny implies a low position of women, and monogamy a high position, it follows that a decrease of militancy and an increase of industrialism are general concomitants of a rise in their position.

This argument has an element of truth which only more precise and narrower correlations could determine. Spencer's own correlations are too wide, and not sufficiently specific. What, it may be asked, is there in common between the militancy of primitive times and the elaborate militarism of modern times, between the industrialism of uncivilized tribes and the industrialism of powerful capitalist empires ? Unless their specific content is determined, and the constant elements of each type ascertained, and the limits laid down within which the correlations hold, Spencer's analysis, however much thought-provoking, does not seem convincing to later enquirers. As we shall see later, his correlations between industrialism and monogamy, and militancy and polygamy, which he adduces to support his analysis must be completely rejected, for there seems to be no necessary connection between the type of family and the type of society. Spencer himself admits that the evidence he brings forward, relating both to simple and compound societies and to people differing in race, religion, culture, customs and beliefs, is of unequal value and difficult of interpretation. But nevertheless he concludes that in peaceful societies there is an elevation of women, and in

militant societies a subjection.   He feels that additional reasons are needed in support of his position,
and he shows that approximate equality in the
numbers of the sexes, a requisite to their equal
treatment, would result from diminishing militancy
and increasing industrialism.   He also shows, that
in proportion as the supply of males, available for
increasing " social ostentation " becomes larger, less
and less work would fall on women, who in this
event would have superior offspring and thus equip
society better in its struggle for existence.

It is necessary only briefly to refer to Spencer's
analysis of the status of children, for in essentials it
mirrors the status of woman.   In primitive times,
there is neither moral obligation, nor moral restraint,
and the cruel treatment of children is limited only by
the necessity of perpetuating the tribe.   Their treatment improves and especially that of male children,
when their value as future warriors, avengers in
blood-feuds, and perpetuators of a family's name
and property, are recognized.   In militant societies,
boys, and especially girls, are cruelly subjected, but
in industrial societies their treatment improves,
boys and girls approach equality, and both are
regarded as individualities.   This is a very good
example of Spencer's logical way of treating a
subject, and the lengths to which he will go, to
be logically consistent.   All things at the beginning
are indefinite and incoherent and extremely cruel.
But later, higher forms of life evolve, and love for
children grows up.

Let us now consider Spencer's analysis of domestic
institutions, the forms of the family, and the relations between the sexes.   It is to be noted that he

takes up a guarded attitude that hovers in uncertainty between some kind of original promiscuity, the compulsory capture of women, and monogamy. Early sexual relations, he regards as unregulated, indefinite and inconstant. " In the loose groups of men first formed, there is no established order of any kind ; everything is indefinite and unsettled. As the relations of men to one another are undetermined, so are the relations of men to women."[1] The evidence Spencer presents is of unequal value, with implications capable of other interpretations than his own. He speaks of formal marriage ceremonies, thus predicating a period when living together began informally ; of the absence of ideas and sentiments which today are considered appropriate to marriage; of the slight estimation put upon chastity ; and, finally, of frequent incestuous relations. But all this, Spencer warns us, must not be taken as synonymous with "absolute hetairism," or absolute promiscuity—for early man endowed with strong proprietary sentiments, was ever ready to fight for the personal possession of women. Qualified promiscuity is admitted, with its logical derivative maternal descent, for only the connections between mother and child would be obvious. Moreover, promiscuity must hinder social evolution, for does not progress imply increasing coherence and definiteness ? Again, promiscuity must be antagonistic to settled political control, and unfavourable to the welfare of offspring who would be lacking paternal care. Natural selection, therefore, would eliminate it in favour of societies with forms of family approximating more

---

[1] *Principles of Sociology*, Vol. I, p. 602.

closely to the Victorian period in which Spencer
lived.

It is evident that the primitive relations of the
sexes, as well as the earliest forms of marriage, are
shrouded in the mystery of prehistoric times. But
the assumption that sex relations were ever totally
unregulated is hardly plausible in view of the fact
that wherever there was society, there was regulation
of some sort, conscious and unconscious. Spencer
writes about " loose groups of men," where " the
wills of the stronger, unchecked by political restraints
unguided by moral sentiments, determine all behaviour."[1] He accepts a pre-social stage, a Hobbes-
ean conception of primitive times, when life was
unpleasant, mean, brutish and short, and individual
men, even if combined in mechanical hordes, did
whatever was right in their own eyes. This, however, is a purely hypothetical construction. Society
is coeval with man, and the simplest social
organization postulates a small number of families
living together on their own territory, and in continuous contact, friendly or unfriendly, with other
social groups. These families need not necessarily be
of the bilateral type, nor need only kinship ties knit
this group together. Strangers and other individuals
could be incorporated in the group, and described
in terms of kinship. In the writer's opinion
society from the beginning was wider than the
kinship group. Society therefore is not an expression
of kinship, but kinship is an expression of society.
Kinship in all its forms is but an expression of society's
cohesion. Only upon such a view, and not one that

---

[1] *Principles of Sociology*, Vol. I, p. **631**.

derives society from the isolated family, can the pre-servation of human culture, language and tradition be understood.

That even the simplest social group would leave sexual relations unregulated is hardly conceivable, for at all times sex is disruptive and antagonizing, as well as binding and unifying, and needs a certain control and regulation. The popularity of promis-cuity as the initial phase in human development, is partly due to the evolutionary school of anthro-pologists who conceived evolution as passing through a regular sequence of stages, and partly as a natural reaction to patriarchal theory that interpreted society in terms of an original combination of mono-gamous units. Morgan's scheme is the most thorough-going of all, and Spencer's resembles it very closely.

According to Morgan, there originally prevailed complete sexual licence unrestricted even by incest regulations, the stage of absolute promiscuity. This was followed by group marriages of two kinds—a group of brothers own and collateral, marrying a group of sisters own and collateral, and another kind where a group of unrelated men were actually or potentially wedded to a group of unrelated women. In turn, there succeeded syndrasmy or pair marriages, with polygamous marriages as a privilege of wealth and rank. And, finally, monogamous marriages. Such individual marriages may be subordinate to the clans of the mothers, in which case social organiza-tion would take the form of a matriarchate ; and at a later stage they may be subordinate to the gentes of the fathers, and social organization would take the form of a patriarchate. According to Morgan, the process of social history is the triumph of the bi-

lateral kinship group, of monogamy and the patriarchate, over group marriage, the matriarchate and
the unilateral kinship group.[1]

If promiscuity had ever possessed that universality ascribed to it, one would imagine that the
evidence in its favour would be much more plentiful
than it is. But Westermarck[2] does not enumerate
more than thirty-one such cases, and even as regards
these, there is no unanimity as to their interpretation.
The most primitive groups in existence to-day, such
as the African Bushmen, the Wood Veddas of
Ceylon, the Andamanese and the Pygmies of Africa,
are predominantly monogamous, and among them
promiscuity has never been recorded. We do find
some examples, it is true, that approach promiscuity,
and which involve the complete sexual access of
one group to another. But it is difficult to determine
whether this is a relic of an earlier custom, when
such groups were actually married to each other.
Again, although during certain festivals present-day
European peasants indulge in periods of sanctioned
sex licence, it would be hazardous to infer a previous
stage of general promiscuity. The classificatory
system of kinship as opposed to our own descriptive
system of kinship, does not necessarily support
Morgan's views. As such, the system is concerned
not with biological, but with social relations, with
the social position of an individual within a group,
and not with his blood relations.

It is often attempted to obtain data in favour of or
against promiscuity by pointing to the sexual relations existing among the higher animals such as

---

[1] L. H. Morgan, *Ancient Society*, 1877.
[2] E. Westermarck, *History of Human Marriage*, 1921.

apes. Both Westermarck and Briffault do this, although it is evident that such a procedure is not altogether justifiable. It has been pointed out before (*see* chap. II.) that in the writer's opinion the application of biological categories to sociological phenomena is inadmissible, all the more so when we treat of such complex social forms as promiscuity or monogamy. Whatever determines the sexual relations and forms among animals belongs to categories that cannot be related to the human being and human society, where every phase of behaviour is conditioned by tradition and culture.

The psychological argument against promiscuity based on the emotion of jealousy in man may have more weight. Naïve observers of savage tribes were ready to believe that jealousy was unknown among them when such customs as wife-lending came to their notice. It is obvious, however, that this custom may be rooted in something more powerful than this emotion, such as a magical injunction. Moreover, even where wife-lending is practised, marital infidelity is strongly resented. This problem is admittedly very complex. It is difficult for us to enter into the psychology of primitive man, and it is certainly unwise to judge him by standards that apply to us.

The evidence as regards a closely related problem, that of group marriage, is much more satisfactory, and a certain number of authentic cases have been ascertained in Central Australia and in North Eastern Siberia. It implies that a group of men have sexual rights with certain other women besides their individual wives, and that the women have similar rights with reference to other men besides their

husbands. This custom is, however, strictly circum-
scribed, and the true husbands and wives are distinguished in terms both of status and terminology
from the other mates. It does not seem to be
universal or primal, and instead of being an indication of promiscuity may possibly be derived
from individual marriage by an extension of sexual
rights beyond the limits of the family.

What seem to be universal in one form or another
are restrictions forbidding marriage within a certain
group—exogamy. Spencer's ingenious theory (one
among hundreds of others) need not detain us long.
Early man was ever at war, argues Spencer. Victory
would be followed by pillage and the carrying off
of women as prizes. Woman-stealing becomes,
therefore, an incident of successful war ; and the
possession of one taken in war becomes a badge of
social distinction ; all warriors worthy of the name
would endeavour to steal wives in order to show
their fitness and justify their warrior-ship. Form
of marriage in which sham capture of the bride
occurs, Spencer suggests, are indicative of a
period when marriage by capture was universal.
Endogamy on the other hand would characterize
peaceful and primitive tribes, and only as societies
became less hostile would it prevail and become the
concomitant of the higher forms of the family.

This explanation is thought to be untenable by
many modern sociologists. It assumes universal
hostility and war among early peoples which Spencer
himself contradicts when he ascribes endogamy to
conditions of peace. Marriage by capture has according to the latest evidence adduced by Malinowski

Westermarck, Goldenweiser and others, has never been general; it occurs rather as an exception to a regular marriage system; and is incompatible with matrilocal marriage. Sham capture marriage may not be a relic of real capture, but an expression of maidenly modesty, a magical ceremony intended to ward off evil spirits, or a test of the bridegroom's fitness to marry. Finally, this theory throws no light at all on the prohibition of incest, which is practically universal.

It must be admitted, however, that more recent theories are not much more satisfactory.[1] An interesting approach to the problem has been developed by Hobhouse, who, by postulating an impulse that would keep distinct the parental and sexual sentiments, shows that the main functions of exogamy would be to check in-and-in-breeding, and to act as a cohesive force binding people together.[2] This last function was also emphasized by Tylor, who wrote: " Exogamy is an institution which resists the tendency of uncultured populations to disintegrate, cementing them into nations capable of living together in peace and holding together in war, until they reach the period of higher military and political organization."[3]

Spencer does not commit himself to the supposition of a universal matriarchy. What he implies is rather a system of mother-right which followed upon and was bound up with a period of promiscuity. He shows that under promiscuity the connection

---

[1] E. Westermarck, *Recent Theories of Exogamy. Sociological Review*, Jan., 1934.

[2] L. T. Hobhouse, *Morals in Evolution*, 1923.

[3] E. B. Tylor, *The Matriarchal Family System. The Nineteenth Century*, XL., p. 93.

between mother and child would be more obvious, and there would arise a habit of thinking of maternal rather than of paternal kinship. He shows further that male parentage is habitually known, though disregarded where the system of kinship is in the female line, and he criticizes Sir Henry Maine for assuming that descent has always and everywhere been in the male line and for his patriarchal theory of society. Not only is descent in the female line common all over the world, and not only is it observed among little organized or " pre-infantine " groups, but it occurs in nations which have evolved complex structures. In such communities not only blood descent but also succession to rank, property and titles, would go through the mother.

Beyond these remarks, Spencer says little about what has been mistakenly called a matriarchate. Although it is true that the lower we go in the scale of civilization the more prevalent is the type of social organization in which the mother is socially more important than the father, and that many civilizations show traces indicating their transition from such a stage, it is not easy to interpret these facts. There is great doubt that such a stage has ever been universal or been passed through by all societies. Where descent is through the mother, property and ceremonial rites will go through her brother or her husband. Even in such societies many disabilities attach to women. The headship of the clan is inherited through the mother, but not by the mother, and passes from her brother to her son, and from her son to her daughter's son. In many cases the woman, instead of being subjected to her own husband, is subjected by her family. In view of these facts, a matriarchate or the rule of women is highly problematical, and the term mother-right is much more appropriate if we wish to point to a social organization where rights go through the mother and are dependent on the mother.

There has recently been a brilliant attempt to reconstruct society as dominated by " Mothers."[1] Here the centre of the family would be the mother with all her children and daughter's children. Her husband and daughters' husbands would be excluded from it. Descent would naturally be in the female line because paternity was uncertain and even unknown, and sexual associations were matrilocal. In such a society, the influence of the mother would be supreme, since from her there would radiate all those industries, activites and sentiments that were vital to the life of an early society. Moreover, war and private property had not yet developed, and thus there was no occasion for the dominance of man. Domination only came to him with their develop- ment and with the beginning of a settled agricultural life. Then the foundations of social life were trans- formed, social power passed over to the man, who now became the head of the family, and who now brought into it his wife. Whatever the truth of this theory, Briffault's main thesis that the part played by woman in very primitive times was greater than at a later period, is possibly, but not demonstrably, correct. It is evident, at any rate, that the psycho- logical basis both of the family and the social group would be different under such conditions, and that although the family would not be knit so firmly together, social cohesion would be greater and

---

[1] Robert Briffault. *The Mothers*, 3 Vols. 1927.

property would be communally owned.   That the
growth of private property had revolutionary significance for social life is becoming much more
recognized by anthropologists.   Goldenweiser writes
that the " androcentric trend of property and property prerogatives has played an important part in
history.   Everywhere and always, it has reflected
as well as enhanced that systematic disenfranchise-
ment of woman, which constitutes one of the least
pleasing aspects of human civilization."[1]

Following the elimination of promiscuity as an
unsuccessful adaptation to social life, Spencer proceeds to argue, experiments in indefinite polyandry
and indefinite polygamy would arise.   Polyandry
was of three forms—where a group of brothers
married one woman, a group of unrelated men
married one woman, and finally where a combination
of polyandry and polygyny was practised.   All these
forms are due to poverty or to female infanticide.
Spencer's suppositions that these forms are universal,
that they appeared in the order given, and that they
all arose in response to the same conditions, have not
been substantiated.   Among the groups that practice
polyandry the Tibetans are agriculturists, the
Eskimos are hunters and the Todas are pastoral.
That poverty is an essential condition of its appearance has also been disputed.

Polyandry is succeeded by polygamy, a topic
which Spencer discusses in a most illuminating
manner.   He shows that although it is widespread
and persistent, it is limited by a number of factors,
the most important of which are the economic

---

[1] A. Goldenweiser. *Early Civilization*, p. 260, 1923.

conditions of a people and the number of women available. So that in general, the majority will possess but one wife, and only the rich and powerful few, will have a number of wives. " While probably a majority of primitive tribes permit polygamy, biological and in some measure social conditions, prevent the majority within any one group from availing themselves of their theoretical prerogative."[1] Causes favouring polygamy would be warfare and the capture of women, the economic benefits to be derived from having a number of wives working for one husband, and often the desire of a single wife to have companions or concubines to share with her the burden of her labours. Finally, there is an important psychological reason—" Since in every society the doings of the powerful and the wealthy furnish the standards of right and wrong, so that even the very words ' noble ' and ' servile,' originally expressive of social status, have come to be expressive of good and bad in conduct, it results that plurality of wives acquires in places where it prevails, an ethical sanction."[2] The ordinary individual would aspire to imitate the rich. Polygamy, in general, will therefore characterize societies that are differentiated in wealth and status.

These conclusions are borne out by the investigators of the " *Simpler Peoples*," who found that the practice of polygamy extends almost continuously from the lowest Hunters upwards. Spencer rightly shows the importance of distinguishing its practice and its permission, for even where permitted, it may be impracticable, owing to a number

---

[1] *Principles of Sociology*, Vol. I, p. **656**.
[2] *Ibid.*, p. **657**.

of reasons. It may, perhaps, also be mentioned that polygamy would tend to be limited by matrilocal marriages, for here permission to take a second wife would depend on the wife's parents.

Finally, Spencer turns to a discussion of monogamy, which he regards as the ultimate and final form evolution has brought into flower. It grew slowly, but even among barbaric groups, where sexual behaviour was unregulated, the union of individual men with individual women must have occurred. Monogamy is humanity's natural form, and other forms were probably due to disruptive influences brought about by increasing aggregation. He writes : "It may be that during certain transitional stages between the first extremely scattered, or little gregarious stage, there have arisen various conditions favouring various forms of union, so causing temporary deviations from the primitive tendency."[1] "Be this as it may, however," he continues, "it is clear that monogamy has long been growing innate in the civilized man."[2] Evidently, Spencer is being carried away by his ethical preconceptions, in spite of the fact that he himself points out certain natural conditions, such as the equality in the sex ratio and the growth of private property, upon which monogamy is dependent. In any case, there is no evidence for regarding it as innately determined.

In an analysis of the general social characteristics of monogamy and polygamy, Spencer shows his generalizing powers at their best. Why, he asks, is polygamy superior to promiscuity and

---

[1] *Principles of Sociology*, Vol. I, *p.* 673.
[2] *Ibid.*, p. 673.

polyandry? Because, he answers, it results in a higher birth-rate, and therefore yields greater man-power in war. It determines descent according to the male, and thereby conduces to political stability. It stimulates ancestor worship. It consolidates society. It decreases infant mortality, and makes the blessings of matrimony available to those, who under a more unfortunate system, may have been compelled to remain spinsters. But polygamy has also grave defects which ioutweigh its advantages. It prevents the development of those higher emotions which are fostered by the association of the sexes under monogamy. It dulls domestic affection, and creates discord within the family. It elevates one wife, but reduces the rest to a servile condition. It blunts the moral feelings. Sooner or later it is bound to decay, and is characteristic only of a period of barbarism. It reflects that society of which it is a product, and is itself permeated with barbaric features.

Just as polygamy is superior to the more primitive forms of marriage, so is monogamy superior to all the rest. It is the final and ultimate form. It conduces to a higher birthrate because fewer are excluded from having wives. It assures political stability because it eliminates dynastic intrigues characteristic of polygamous societies. It promotes ancestor worship and " whatever favours stability in the dynasties of early rulers, tends to establish permanent dynasties of deities, with the resulting sacred sanctions for codes of conduct."[1] It creates " a permanent deep sense of æsthetic interest "[2] in

[1] *Principles of Sociology*, Vol. I, p. 671.
[2] *Ibid.*, p. 672.

those sentiments of love, passion and romance characteristic of an era of monogamy. It develops to the highest degree marital and filial affections. It tends to prolong the lives of individuals. It lacks the jealousies and disruptions inevitable within the polygamous family. And, finally, it exhibits intimacy and cohesion, qualities which are valuable to any society in its struggle for existence.

In spite of the fact that Spencer considers monogamy as the highest ethical form, he retains his sociological approach when he shows that different forms of the family have grown up under special conditions and that under other conditions correlative forms of the family would develop. Thus under pastoral conditions, a group would naturally evolve male descent, strong cohesion, co-operation both industrial and defensive, and subordination to the patriarch. The government of society would reflect the government of the family, and distinctive ideas, sentiments, customs and social arrangements typical of the patriarchal type of society would develop. At every stage of society the forms of family and the forms of government act and react upon each other. Here, Spencer opens up a vast series of problems which have been explored by the Le Play school on the one hand, and are being explored by psychologists on the other. It is realized that a close and intimate relationship exists between the social structure and the family, and that it is necessary to disentangle the psychological forces acting on both. It is evident that the distribution and effectiveness of both power and initiative will markedly differ in the modern monogamous family from that of a patriarchal family, in which authority will be concentrated in one person, and that the corresponding changes on the social structure and especially upon government will be different.

Spencer attempts to discover correlations between his social types and the forms of marriage. In the first place, he asks whether societies of different degrees of social composition habitually present different forms of domestic arrangement. The answer is : No, although " one kind of connection between the type of the family, and the degree of social composition, may, however, be alleged. Formation of compound groups, implying greater co-ordination, and the strengthening of restraints, implies more settled arrangements, public and private. Growth of custom into law, which goes along with an extending governmental organization holding larger masses together, affects the domestic relations along with the political relations ; and thus renders the family arrangements, be they polyandric, polygynic or monogamic, more definite."[1] In the second place, he asks if the domestic arrangements are associated with militancy and industrialism. The answer, he says, is clear and precise. An advance from the primitive warlike society to the highest industrial society has gone along with an advance from prevalent polygamy to exclusive monogamy. Spencer goes beyond the correlation to the causal factor and finds it in declining militancy and increasing industrialism. This, he says, is the only factor common to all the peoples who are otherwise divided by race, language, culture, customs and tradition.

---

[1] *Principles of Sociology*, Vol. I, pp. 674–675.

Even if the correlation were exact between a decline of militancy and a decline of polygamy, it would not follow that one is the cause of the other. The correlation itself as we said before is open to objections. There may be a necessary connection between his types of society and between polygamy and monogamy, but Spencer does not show what the nature of that connection is.

What of the future of the family? Since of all the numerous genera and species of families those which are found in advanced societies are the most coherent, definite and complex, it follows that evolution can only be in the same direction. The monogamic form must therefore become more perfect. Spencer might have been content to leave this task to evolution, but he cannot forget his philosophical preconceptions. State interference has proceeded too far, and if the imminent dangers of family disintegration are to be averted the ethics of the family must be kept distinct from the ethics of the State.

And what of the future of women? " It must be concluded that no considerable alteration in the careers of women in general can be, or should be, so produced ; and further, that any extensive change in the education of women, made with the view of fitting them for business and professions, would be mischievous. If women comprehended all that is contained in the domestic sphere, they would ask no other."[1] This shows a different outlook from that of the Spencer who had, earlier in life, advocated the emancipation of women.

---

[1] *Principles of Sociology*, Vol. I, p. 757. For his earlier views, see *Social Statics*, pp. 71–77.

To sum up. Spencer postulated the following stages of the evolution of domestic institutions : a stage of qualified promiscuity and indefinite sexual relations—a stage wherein there were connections more or less enduring between one woman and several men, polyandry, and between one man and several women, polygamy—and the ultimate stage of monogamy.

The modern sociologist rejects Spencer's evolutionary plan and his ethical valuations, and insists that society has always regulated and controlled the sexual relationships of its members ; that in response to diverse conditions different forms of the family have developed ; that no form of the family is inevitable or primary; and, finally, that whether monogamy is destined to be the ultimate form of marriage, only the future can answer.

Spencer himself recognized the importance of different economic and social conditions in moulding different family forms, but his enthusiastic advocacy of evolutionary stages gave rise to inconsistencies. He rightly points to the necessity of investigating the psychological forces underlying domestic institutions and their relations to the totality of social life. He discovered correlations between type of family and type of society, and pointed out a line of research that could be fruitfully followed up. His results, however much in need of qualification, are always illuminating and suggestive. It is unfortunate that Spencer limits himself only to the primitive society and only to its biological functions. He has, it is true, some remarks on the threatened break-up of the contemporary family, but it is evident that the structure and functions of the family in modern society, as a sociological problem, did not interest him. This is, however, a criticism that may be levelled against most sociologists. Only now is it being studied as a living and not as a dead institution, and it is undoubted that with the available technique of psycho-analysis, sociologists will be enabled to solve many of its problems.

It now remains to say something about Spencer's philosophical and biological rather than sociological framework of thought, into which he fits the family and the relations of the sexes. This is the antagonism between individuation and genesis, between the individual and the species.

" Grouping under the word Individuation," he writes, " all processes by which individual life is completed and maintained ; and so enlarging the meaning of the word Genesis as to include all processes aiding the formation and perfecting of new individuals ; we see that the two are fundamentally opposed. Assuming other things to remain the same —assuming that environing conditions as to climate, food, enemies, etc., continue constant ; then inevitably, every higher degree of individual evolution is followed by a lower degree of race multiplication, and *vice versa*. Progress in bulk, complexity, or activity involves retrogress in fertility ; and progress in fertility involves retrogress in bulk, complexity or activity."[1]

Since the function of the family is the maintenance of the human race, Spencer finds no difficulty in showing that the highest form of the family is the one which best reconciles the needs of the species

---

[1] *Principles of Biology*, Vol II, pp. 429–430.

with the needs of its individuals. Nature achieves this conciliation by reducing mortality between birth and reproductive age to a minimum, and by subordinating to the least possible extent the lives of the adults to the rearing of children. But among savages, on the other hand, this conciliation is slight. There is great juvenile mortality, infanticide and early death. There is early reproduction and maturity and exhaustion. " The marital and parental relations are sources of pleasure neither so high nor so prolonged as in the civilized races." And then after children have been reared, the remaining life of either sex is brief : often being ended by violence ; often by deliberate desertion ; and otherwise by rapid decay unchecked by filial care."[1]

Here we have another good example of Spencer's aptitude in fitting social facts into biological categories. Its importance for the present writer lies in the fact that Spencer has now " both a relative and an absolute standard by which to estimate domestic institutions in each stage of social progress."[2] Not only induction, but also deduction, therefore, support the conclusion " that the domestic relations which are the highest as ethically considered are also the highest as considered both biologically and sociologically."[3]

But if the species is to survive, the love and care which evolution has brought to flower within the highest form of family must not be extended to life at large. Here struggle and conflict are essential. In the family it is a law of nature that the least

---

[1] *Principles of Sociology*, Vol. I, p. 600.
[2] *Ibid.*, p. 600.
[3] *Ibid.*, p. 600.

worthy shall receive most aid, and if parents did not conform to it, the species would disappear in a generation.[1] But in the species, for the mature another law applies—the law that the race is to the swift, and victory to the strong. " Clearly, with society as with a species, survival depends on the conformity to both of these antagonist principles. Import into the family the law of society, and let children from infancy upwards have life-sustaining supplies proportioned to their life-sustaining labours, and the society disappears forthwith by death of all its young. Import into the society the law of the family, and let the life-sustaining supplies be great in proportion as the life-sustaining labours are small, and society decays from increase of its least worthy members. It fails to hold its own in the struggle with other societies which allow play to the natural law that prosperity shall vary as efficiency."[2]

This formula, that the ethics of the family and the ethics of society must be kept distinct, we shall examine later. It involved Spencer in numerous difficulties. His solution was that ultimately the antagonism between individuation and genesis, between society and society, shall cease. Everything will merge into universal harmony and return to the stillness of universal death. Evolution, which had seen the rise and growth of woman, family and species, rings down the final curtain upon them, and the play of life is ended.

---

[1] *Principles of Sociology*, Vol I, p. 708.
[2] *Ibid.*, p. 709.

BIBLIOGRAPHY. CHAPTER IV.

ATKINSON, J. J., and LANG, A. *Social Origins and Primal Law.* 1903.

AVEBURY, LORD. *The Origin of Civilization.* 1902.

BRIFFAULT, R. *The Mothers.* 3 vols. 1927.

CRAWLEY, A. E. *The Mystic Rose.* 2 vols. 1902.

FLUGEL, J. C. *Psycho-Analytic Study of the Family.* 1922.

FRAZER, SIR J. G. *Totemism and Exogamy.* 4 vols. 1910.

FREUD, S. *Totem and Taboo.* 1919.

GOLDENWEISER, A. *Early Civilization.* 1923.

HOBHOUSE, L. T. *Morals in Evolution.* 1912.

KROEBER, A. L. *Anthropology.* 1923.

LOWIE, R. H. *Primitive Society.* 1921.

McLENNAN, J. F. *Studies in Ancient History.* 1886.

MALINOWSKI, B. *Sex and Repression in Savage Society.* 1927.

MALINOWSKI, B. *Sexual Life of Savages.* 1929.

MÜLLER-LYER, F. *The Family.* 1930.

RIVERS, W. H. *Social Organization.* 1924.

WESTERMARCK, E. *History of Human Marriage.* 3 vols. 1921.

CHAPTER V.

SOCIETY, STATE, GOVERNMENT.

THE distinction between Society and State, never made explicit by Spencer, would seem to lie, according to him, in the fact that Society is a growth and the State an artefact, one a social organism, and the other a social contract. This distinction, as thus drawn, is not essential. The State was not constituted by a contract, nor can it be traced to a definite beginning ; it is also a growth, emerging within Society with the development of ordered government. What does seem essential is the reserve of force, of compulsion attaching to the State, in its main function of regulating and defining the rights and duties of its members. Spencer came very close to this conception, in discussing two kinds of organization, " one arising directly from the pursuit of individual ends, and indirectly conducing to social welfare, develops unconsciously and is non-coercive. The other, arising directly from the pursuit of social ends, and indirectly conducing to individual welfare, develops consciously and is coercive."[1] But in this distinction, he saw the difference between the industrial and military types of Society, and left undetermined the relationship between State and Society, sometimes regarding them as synonymous, and sometimes differentiating them in a manner that obscured the clarity of his thought. It is

[1] *Principles of Sociology*, Vol. II, p. 263.

necessary for the sociologist to know precisely the meanings of the terms he uses.

Society is the whole complex of indeterminate relationships of human beings in contact. It cannot be derived from a pre-social state because it is coeval with man. Society is an amorphous structure giving rise to further societies, but not exhausted by them. It is thus distinct from *a* society, a specific group having its own history, and possessing a recognizable structure wherein its members have defined or definable relations to each other. Such a society will contain institutions that will regulate the relationships of the individuals to each other or to any section of Society by means of prescribed and established usages. The family, for instance, whatever be its form, will control and regulate the sexual needs of the members and their desire for children. In such a society there will also be associations established for the fulfilment of certain functions and purposes. Such associations may range from insignificant local clubs to powerful and omnicompetent states, which will possess a monopoly of force and authority, and tower above all other associations. Like Society, an association—which is in essence a sub-society—may generate institutions and endow them with special apparatus. This is especially true of the State, which although a sub-species of Society, may dominate Society, or better still, the community. By this term is meant the entire population of a territory which is bound together by a common way of life, a common rule regulating the ordinary intercourse of life. Community is the society organized in its own territory, possessing distinct physical and social limits.

It has been customary to talk of the origin of the State. It would be truer to say that at particular historical times, and as resultants of many factors, States have arisen out of communities or societies. But if their histories are different their basis is similar. States have developed and persisted because communities require organization. They become communities organized for certain purposes, for aggression and defence, for the maintenance of the fabric of law and order, and for the preservation of the common rule. And since a community organized is better equipped in the struggle for existence than a community unorganized, the paraphernalia of State becomes widespread and characteristic of the higher civilizations.

But the State must not be identified with Society or community, for it comprises but a fraction of the common life. Moreover, it may be superimposed on a community by conquest and be alien to it. But even where it has grown up organically, its main sphere of action lies in fashioning conformity to externals only. It can forbid people to speak in criticism of it, but it cannot forbid people thinking. It can compel obedience, but obedience will be given only to the extent that the State has satisfied the needs and desires of its members. If it has not done so, sooner or later people will revolt. The State may be overthrown, but Society, as such, will not therefore cease to exist.

We have spoken of the State being overthrown. The State is best understood in terms of government—of those who are responsible for the organization of the community. Where this organization expresses the general and widespread needs of the community, the government will be representative. But where a certain section or class is dominant within the State, the government will represent that class. The modern State is a grouping of powerful interests conflicting with each other and struggling for supremacy, utilizing the government as an agency, by which and through which temporary adjustments are achieved.

A sociological interpretation of this nature makes impossible the confusion between State and Society— a misconception that has left its impress in the errors of Rousseau, Hegel, Bosanquet, and other exponents of the metaphysical theory of the State. Such a confusion leads sooner or later to the suppression and absorption of the individual in a general will ; it makes the State, to use Hegel's own expression, a self-conscious ethical entity, a self-knowing and actualizing personality, that can do no wrong ; it regards the State as an end in itself, overriding the rights of its citizens, and transcending the morality of the individual ; and freedom in Hegel's view lies in slavishly obeying the State.

This conception of an absolute, sovereign and omnicompetent State is not accepted by the modern sociologist, who argues that minor associations have a real or general will no less real or general than that of the State. He denies the identity of that particular form of political organization which we call the State, with the subtle and intricate totality of human relationships. He asserts that the State arises out of Society, and that we can only tell how far it embodies a common will when we scrutinize its system of rights, the formation of public opinion, its administration of law, its government and its institutions.

This brief introduction is necessary in order that we may follow Spencer's account of political institutions. His analysis it is to be observed retains a remarkable naturalistic approach which calmly and dispassionately dissects each institution as it comes under review. It clearly lays bare the intimate relationships between economic and political systems, between the State and government, and constitutes an excellent antidote to the metaphysical theories we mentioned above.

Spencer's main thesis is that the origin and growth of state organizations are to be found in war, which is waged mainly for economic reasons. This view possesses, as we shall see, a large element of truth ; but it is necessary first to discuss Spencer's emphasis on war, struggle and conflict, all of which loom so large in his sociology.

Spencer like Hobbes before him regarded war as the universal condition of primeval man. This is an exaggeration. It is evident that although primitive people are not entirely peaceful, they are much more so than peoples in an advanced stage of development. For only with an advanced social structure and technique is it possible to obtain the organization needed for the waging of war. The importance of the economic factor in war can hardly be minimized. Spencer rightly shows that the necessity for " incorporation of materials of growth " frequently led to the breaking out of hostilities and the waging of fierce and bloody warfare.

" We must recognize the truth," Spencer proceeds to argue, " that the struggles for existence between societies have been instrumental to their evolution.

Neither the consolidation and re-consolidation of small groups into large ones, nor the organization of such compound and doubly-compound groups, nor the concomitant development of those aids to a higher life which civilization has brought, would have been possible without inter-tribal and international conflicts. Social co-operation is initiated by joint defence and offence ; and from the co-operation thus initiated all kinds of co-operations have arisen. Inconceivable as have been the horrors caused by this universal antagonism, which, beginning with the chronic hostilities of small hordes tens of thousands of years ago, has ended in the occasional vast battles of immense nations, we must nevertheless admit that without it the world would still have been inhabited only by men of feeble types sheltering in caves and living on wild food."[1]

Here Spencer claims too much. It is undoubted that war has played a very important part in the integration of Society, but to claim that all the qualities of civilization are due to it is an exaggeration. Indeed, it involves a number of difficulties to whose consideration we shall soon come. The view that extensive territorial units have been the product of war and conquest has been adopted by many sociologists, including Bagehot, Gumplowicz, Ratzenhofer, Oppenheimer, Lester Ward, Albion Small and Steinmetz.[2] It is, however, necessary to

---

[1] *Principles of Sociology*, Vol. II, p. 241.

[2] Rudolf Steinmetz in his *Sociologie des Krieges* expresses views very similar to Spenser, although he rejects Spencer's law of the transition for the militant to the industrial peaceful type.

remember that elements of peace and co-operation have also entered into the composition and structure of large states. Kropotkin stressed this point in his *Mutual Aid*, and Novicow insisted that the State arose, not as a result of war, but to protect property. Both schools of thought are united in thinking that economic factors have been the root of war when it became general, and that its significance for the creation of states cannot be overlooked.

Spencer thought that the struggle between groups was a phase of natural selection, and to use Tennyson's words a manifestation of "nature red in tooth and claw." But the question immediately arises whether there be any guarantee that the conflict of groups exercises a selective influence upon individuals—for that in essence is the problem of natural selection. The defeated or conquered group is only in rare cases exterminated, generally it is incorporated within the victorious people. But assuming there is group selection, it may be asked selection for what? If it be selection for military prowess, the problem remains how qualities necessary for civilization and the maintenance of huge and settled peaceful societies ever arose. This difficulty Spencer easily explains by reverting to his industrial type of society.

He continues : " But now observe that the inter-social struggle which has been indispensable in evolving societies will not necessarily play in the future a part like that which it has played in the past. Recognizing our indebtedness to war for forming great communities and developing their structures, we may yet infer that the acquired powers, available for other activities, will lose their original activities. While conceding that without these bloody strifes, civilized societies could not have arisen and that an adapted form of human nature, fierce as well as intelligent, was a needful concomitant, we may at the same time hold that, such societies having been produced, the brutality of nature in their units which was necessitated by the process, ceasing to be necessary with the cessation of the process, will disappear. While the benefits achieved during the predatory period remain a permanent inheritance, the evils entailed by it will decrease and slowly die out."[1]

This view involves according to some sociologists certain difficulties. They ask why should the benefits of struggle and war persist and the evils disappear ? How can the origin of ethical qualities be explained when their possession meant one's elimination in the struggle for existence ? Huxley as we shall see later was non-plussed for an explanation, while Spencer keeps distinct the ethics of the State and the ethics of the family and advocates one standard of morality for those within the group, and another for those outside it. Yet Spencer looked ardently forward to the cessation of war, and to an era of universal peace. But it is legitimate to ask whether this would not involve, instead of two standards, an extension of the same standard of morality for those included in the group and those outside it.

From war and the origin of the State let us now turn to Spencer's illuminating and masterly analysis of the nature and conditions of social cohesion. Unlike most political theorists, Spencer does not

---

[1] *Principles of Sociology*, Vol. II, p. 242.

explain the nature of the State by the magic formula that man is a social or political animal. He points to a number of relevant factors—such as the habitat, which may be fitted to support large aggregates, or which may impede co-operation by lacking facilities for intercourse. Natural barriers may be present or absent, and thus make difficult or easy the keeping together of individuals under a coercion which is at first necessary. " From Roman times downwards, the formation of roads has made large social aggregates possible."[1] Other factors are the physical, mental and moral qualities of the people (Spencer assumed innate instincts that would hinder the formation of social aggregates) and especially the degree to which the units are similar or dissimilar. The type of family must not be ignored, for the greatest social cohesion will mark those groups that possess a common family tradition, a common male ancestor, joint ancestor-worship, and similar ideas, sentiments and feelings. Force by itself is an unsure foundation, for a State based on it may easily collapse. Spencer utters the warning that " our own Indian Empire, too, held together by force in a state of artificial equilibrium, threatens some day to illustrate by its fall, the in-cohesion arising from lack of congruity in components."[2] But the most important factor in social cohesion is the fear of enemies and war—" joint exposure to uniform external actions, and joint re-actions against them have from the beginning been the leading causes of union among members of societies."[3] With the increase in size of the social aggregate, greater cohesion becomes necessary, which

[1] *Principles of Sociology*, Vol. II, p. 270.
[2] *Ibid.*, p. 278.
[3] *Ibid.*, p. 278.

results " from an adapted human nature and a resulting development of social organization.''[1]   At
first advancing organization is accompanied by
decreasing vertical and horizontal mobility.   But
at a later stage " the restraints which the social
aggregate exercises over its units, decreases as the
industrial type begins greatly to qualify the militant
type ; partly because the societies characterized by
industrialism are amply populous, and have superfluous members to fill the places of those who leave
them, and partly because in the absence of the
oppressions accompanying a militant regime, a
sufficient cohesion results from pecuniary interests,
family bonds and love of country.''[2]

Spencer next discusses the growing differentiation
that goes on concomitantly with integration.   The
distinctions between men and women become greater,
a slave class develops, and society becomes divided
into classes.   All these changes result from changes
in the economic structure of society and from war.
" From the beginning,'' Spencer writes, " the militant
class, being by force of arms the dominant class,
becomes the class which owns the source of food—
the land.   During the hunting and pastoral stages,
the warriors of the group hold the land collectively.
On passing into the settled state their tenures
become partly collective and partly individual in
sundry ways, and eventually almost wholly individual.   But throughout long stages of social evolution landowning and militancy continue to be
associated.''[3]   Primogeniture and the universal fact

---

[1] *Principles of Sociology*, Vol II, p. 278.
[2] *Ibid.*, p. 284.
[3] *Ibid.*, 308.

that to him that hath shall be given tend to increase social and economic inequality.

The ruling class based on a monopoly of economic power soon attaches to itself an air of superiority. Its better food, clothing, and shelter tend to establish physical differences to the further advantage of the ruling class, and to the disadvantage of the ruled. These acquired differences Spencer believed to be transmissible by inheritance. And finally, " there are the respective mental traits produced by daily exercise of power. The ideas and sentiments, and modes of behaviour, perpetually repeated, generate on the one side an inherited fitness for obedience ; with the result that in the course of time, there arises on both sides the belief that the established relations of classes are the natural ones."[1]

The industrial type of society Spencer assumed would sweep away all class distinctions, because in it wealth would not be connected with rank, and all would be equal before the law. But although rank does not play the significant role it did in military society, and although every one is equal before the law, it may be asked how far has industrial society really abolished class distinctions. The military, nobility and landed gentry simply gave way to other groups, who possessing or controlling the wealth of Society, were to all intents the ruling class.

This closes Spencer's analysis of the State, and he turns to an examination of government. Governments, even if based on power are of themselves not powerful. " but are the instrumentalities of power.

[1] *Principles of Sociology*, Vol. II, p. 302.

This power existed before government arose ; governments were themselves produced by it ; and it ever continues to be that which disguised more or less completely works through them."[1] That power is public opinion, " the accumulated and organized sentiment of the past." In political life as in religion, we cannot escape the dead hand. " The ruler, in part the organ of the wills of those around, is in a still greater degree the organ of the wills of those who have passed away ; and his own will, much restrained by the first, is still more restrained by the last."[2] In a class society, the expression of public opinion takes on a more complicated form, and Spencer rightly points out that " under such conditions the political head either derives his power exclusively from the feeling of the dominant class, or else, setting the diverse feeling, originated in the upper and lower classes, one against the other, is enabled to make his individual will the chief factor."[3] In such a society the government is the expression of a dominant class.

The differentiation of government next occupies Spencer's attention, although his penchant for fitting everything into a mechanical framework, and for tracing its genesis, colours his conclusions. Out of the general mass, to use Spencer's biological metaphor, there will be differentiated a nucleus and a nucleolus. Similarly, from out of the general populace, there will emerge a group of leading men and a chief, among whom in turn further differentiations will take place.

---

[1] *Principles of Sociology*, Vol. II, p. 318.
[2] *Ibid.*, p. 323.
[3] *Ibid.*, p. 325.

The first component of the triune political structure is the political headship, which is acquired by one whose fitness for this position is acknowledged as resulting from greater age, superior strength or will-power, wider knowledge, quicker insight or the possession of wealth.   And Spencer turns to a valuable examination of the factors that will tend to make the headship permanent, and their correlation to various social conditions.   War and religion are the most important factors.   The first will establish the ruler's prestige, and the second will reinforce it by crediting him with supernatural power and the control of ghosts.   Mother-right is less favourable than father-right to the establishment of permanent political authority, for the latter conduces more to family cohesion, subordination, and ancestor-worship whereby natural authority receives the sanction of supernatural authority.   In a society which worships gods, the earthly ruler partakes of god's divine nature—the divine right of kings.   To obtain the god's assistance therefore, sacrifices must be made to the king.   Rebellion is wicked and hopeless, for it is an offence both against earthly and divine rule.

Just as certain conditions determine whether the warrior chief becomes an absolute monarch, so other conditions determine whether the group of leading men, the nucleus, or the second component of the triune political structure, become a small oligarchy widely separated from the people. Originally this group is a representative body of numerous tribes in association.   But if each of the tribes, united by militant co-operation, is despotically ruled, is based on patriarchal authority, or on the government of men of supposed divine descent, a powerful oligarchy arises that admits no popular intervention in its affairs.   But if patriarchal authority is weak, and peace instead of militancy characterizes the society, the compound authority is no longer an assembly of despots but governs by right of appointment.   Militancy ever tends to direct power in the hands of a few; industrialism to power in many.

From this foundational framework Spencer derives every other political institution.   How do consultative bodies arise?   Out of the union of the first and second components.   Its germ is the council of war, formed of leading warriors who deliberate in the presence of their fellows.   When Society becomes settled and organized, the power of the assembled people is limited to accepting or rejecting the proposals made, and the members of the consultative body, summoned by the ruler, give their opinions only when invited to do so.   Where the king is strong and absolute, those who might have formed a consultative body become appointed advisers only; where he is powerless the consultative body retains power and may become an oligarchy.

Representative bodies form the third element in the triune political structure, and arise from the mass of the people, when with the decline of militancy their subjection disappears.   The progress of industrialism dissolves the old relations of status and substitutes the new relations of contract.   This industrial mass is animated by new sentiments and feelings, and it is in these that the origin of free forms of government is to be sought, and not in the king's jealousy of the aristocracy, nor in the alliance of the plebeians and the aristocracy against royal exactions. It may perhaps be thought that Spencer did not find such a psychological explanation quite satisfactory, for he adds that the people's power derives ultimately from the fact that they are the taxpayers who feed the State's exchequer. In time their elected representatives, especially as the industrial portion of the community gains power, become a distinct body separate from the original consultative body.

Cabinets and ministries, too, derive from the ancient past. At first they are included in the primitive consultative body, but later they become differentiated into specialized parts. Their functions also, originally vague and irregular, afterwards acquire definiteness. With the decline of monarchical power their functions come to be the execution of the public will.

Other organs of the executive are local governments and judiciaries. Local government may be traced back to the necessity of respecting the substantial autonomy of vanquished societies. With increasing integration, however, local rulers lose their authority, and become subordinate to the central executive, discharging whatever duties they are allowed to retain by permission of the king's agents. Where central despotism prevails, local despotism prevails; where state freedom is a fact, local freedom is a fact; and a change either way in the major government is followed by a kindred change in the other.

The judiciary is closely related to the executive system, " according as the social activities develop one or other elements of the primitive triune body, there results one or other form of agency for the administration of law. If continued militancy makes the ruling man all-powerful, he becomes absolute judicially as in other ways : the people lose all share in giving decisions and the judgments of the chief men who surround him are overridden by his. If conditions favour the growth of the chief men into an oligarchy, the body they form becomes the agent for judging and punishing offences, as for other purposes : its acts being little or not at all qualified by the opinion of the mass. While if the surrounding circumstances and modes of life are such as to prevent supremacy of one man, or of the leading men, its primitive judicial power is preserved by the aggregate of freemen, or is regained by it where it re-acquires predominance. And where the powers of these three elements are mingled in the political organization, they are also mingled in the judicial organization."[1]

Under militarism the judicial organization is officered by the sacerdotal class or military class, or both ; under industrialism it falls into the hands of the class which controls property, and therefore power. Under both types of society the judicial organization develops *pari passu* with central government and differentiates from the ecclesiastical courts and from courts-martial, into civil courts and criminal courts.

This, in brief, is Spencer's survey of political institutions and like all his surveys it is masterly. As we pointed out above, it is weakened by its extreme evolutionism, which in Spencer's

---

[1] *Principles of Sociology*, Vol. II, p. 511.

hands meant the search for origins. In general, his method of approach is static, and there is lacking an appreciation of the dynamic factors of social change, which while preserving political institutions in their ancient forms, transform their underlying forces. Thus the forces economic and psychological behind democracy in the modern world have little relevance to those making a primitive group democratic. Their composition is totally different. Spencer sometimes forgets that although the form may be the same, the content is different. He is at his best in his correlations between political institutions and types of Society. But his zest for correlations often makes him neglect causation and the necessity for studying not only social structure, but also social process.

Let us now turn to Spencer's searching analysis of the nature of law in early and in modern Society. Law, whether written or unwritten, formulates the rule of the dead over the living. "To the injunctions of the undistinguished dead, which, qualified by the public opinion of the living in cases not prescribed for, constitute the code of conduct before any political organization has arisen, there comes to be added the injunctions of the distinguished dead, when there have arisen chiefs, who, in some measure feared and obeyed during life, after death give origin to ghosts still more feared and obeyed."[1] The commands of the king become fused with the commands of the god, and thus in primitive society rules of conduct have a religious sanction. Only with the development of Society and the growth of

---

[1] *Principles of Sociology*, Vol. II, p. 535.

different forms of activity and intercourse does there come into existence a body of laws of known human origin. Human and divine law differentiate, and law has now a civil and not a religious sanction. " According to the nature of Society, one or other sanction predominates ; and the sentiment appropriate to it obscures the sentiments appropriate to the others without, however, obliterating them. Thus, in a theocratic society the crime of murder is punished primarily as a sin against the god ; but not without there being some consciousness of its criminality as a disobedience to the human ruler who enforces the divine command, as well as an injury to a family, and by implication to the community."[1]   But in other cases, the loss entailed on the family of the victim is the injury recognized. and murder is not distinguished from manslaughter. In ancient Rome, for instance, the feeling enlisted on behalf of the public order was that which mainly enforced the punishment.   And in our Society, the strongest feeling of reprobation is excited, not because there has been a breach of peace, but because a life has been taken away, with which is joined the feeling of the threat to social safety which such acts imply.

This is largely true, but it does not by any means exhaust the problem of moral obligation.   The nature of the sanction against murder is much more complex, and even in the primitive conception all the components are not mentioned.   In civilized communities of to-day the notion of retribution is very prominent in this conception which is still suffused with emotional and mystical content.

---

[1] *Principles of Sociology*, Vol. II, p. 531.

Spencer then says : " At the same time, there goes on a parallel change of theory. Along with a rule predominantly theocratic, there is current a tacit or avowed doctrine, that the acts prescribed or forbidden are made right or wrong solely by divine command, and though this doctrine survives through subsequent stages (as it does still in our own religious world), yet belief in it becomes nominal rather than real. Where there has been established an absolute human authority, embodied in a single individual, or as occasionally in a few, there comes the theory that law has no other source than the will of the authority : acts are conceived as proper or improper according as they do or do not conform to its dictates. With progress towards a popular form of government, this theory becomes modified to some extent; though the obligation to do this and refrain from that, which is held to arise from State enactment, its force is the public desire. Still it is observable that along with a tacit implication that the *consensus* of individual interests affords the warrant for law, there goes the overt assertion that this warrant is derived from the formulated will of the majority : no question being raised whether this formulated will is or is not congruous with the consensus of individual interests. In this current theory there obviously survives the old idea that there is no other sanction for law than the command of embodied authority ; though the authority is now a widely different one."[1]

This is a very important observation, but more relevant to the problem of political obligation than

---

[1] *Principles of Sociology*, Vol. II, pp. 532–533.

of moral obligation and the nature of law. It is evident that law is more than the consensus of individual interests—it also involves sympathy with the individual, a desire for equal treatment and fair play. It is often said that its basis is State authority, the command of the sovereign will; and, in opposition, it is maintained that there are other associations in the State with wills of their own to whom an individual will more readily give his allegiance than to the State. Both these views are wrong, for it is not in will, whether personal, associational, or State, that the basis of political obligation is to be sought, but in the character of what is willed. If this is supposed to express the common good, allegiance is readily given, but otherwise there is always the possibility of strife and revolution.

But the consensus of individual interests can only be achieved in the industrial state, and Spencer really solves the problem of political obligation by relegating it to this type of society. He writes: " So long as the social type is one organized on the principle of compulsory co-operation, law having to maintain this compulsory co-operation, must be primarily concerned in regulating status, maintaining inequality, enforcing authority ; and can but secondarily consider the individual interests of those forming the mass. But in proportion as the principle of voluntary co-operation more and more characterizes the social type, fulfilment of contracts and implied assertion of equality in men's rights become the fundamental requirements, and the consensus of individual interests the chief source of law ; such authority as law otherwise derived continues to have, being recognized as secondary, and insisted upon only because maintenance of law for its own sake, indirectly furthers the general welfare."[1]

Spencer solves many problems by his social types, but he also sets many problems. We will examine the most important of these by turning to another analysis of Spencer's conception of the State and of the industrial and military types of Society.

We said before that the State is the community organized for certain purposes. Spencer realized that Society whether based on voluntary co-operation (the keystone of the industrial type) or on involuntary co-operation (the keystone of the military type) involves organization and definite and stable political institutions. But though at each stage better immediate results may be achieved by completing organization, they must be at the expense of better ultimate results. In the first place, it means restrictions on the actions of the units composing the aggregate, for to some extent they must be subordinated to the communal interests. In the second place, it implies a deduction from each individual's wealth for the upkeep of the central organization. Maintenance of the State is costly, and the cost may be greater than the evils escaped—in fact, anarchy with all its miseries may be preferable. And, finally, an established organization is an obstacle to reorganization, and the rigidity may be so great that a change is impossible. And here Spencer gives an analogy which implies that which may have shocked him—revolution. He writes: "The stones composing a house cannot be otherwise used until the

---

[1] *Principles of Sociology*, Vol. II, pp. 536–537.

house has been pulled down. If the stones are united
by mortar, there must be extra trouble in destroying
their present combination, before they can be re-
combined. And if the mortar has had centuries in
which to consolidate, the breaking up of the masses
formed, is a matter of such difficulty, that building
with new materials becomes more economical than
rebuilding with the old."[1] The problem of rigidity
versus flexibility occupied much of Spencer's attention. Instead of succession by inheritance, which is
the principle of rigidity, there may be succession by
efficiency, which is the principle of social plasticity
and social transformation. But social mobility, and
succession such as allows the relatively young to
exercise authority, can only appear in their complete
form in the industrial type of Society. Once again
we come to his conception of an industrial Society,
a conception that dominates and unifies the architecture of his Sociology.

In a previous chapter we examined these types of
Society more from the point of view of method, as
a typological construction. Here we propose to deal
in greater detail with their characteristics, and the
generalizations Spencer develops.

The main features of the militant society-products
and survivals of a struggle for existence will be : a
capacity for corporate action ; a maximum fighting
power sustained and supported by the working part ;
effective combination of combatants and non-com-
batants ; the subordination of life, actions and
possessions of the individual to Society ; a despotic
controlling agency commanding centres and sub-

---

[1] *Principles of Sociology*, Vol. II, p. 253-254.

centres throughout the whole of Society. Otherwise
described, such a society will be regimented on a
military basis. It will be both negatively and positively regulative, and will tell each individual not
only what he should not do, but also what he shall
do. Such a society will be rigid, because the cohesion,
subordination, combination, and regulation to which
the individuals are subjected, must decrease their
freedom to change their social positions, their occupations and their localities. It will prohibit and
repress other associations that may compete with
the State. And, finally, such a society will attempt
to be self-sustaining, and will pursue an economic
policy of nationalism, directed towards its own
self-aggrandizement and against foreigners.

The intimate relationship between the type of
Society and its units will manifest itself in the latter—
" Making success in war the highest glory, they are
led to identify goodness with bravery and strength.
Revenge becomes a sacred duty with them ; and
acting at home on the law of retaliation, which they
act on abroad, are ready to sacrifice others to self :
their sympathies continually deadening during war,
cannot be active during peace. They must have
a patriotism which regards triumph of their society
as the supreme end of action ; they must possess the
loyalty whence flows obedience to authority ; and
that they may be obedient, they must have abundant
faith. With faith in authority and consequent readi-
ness to be directed, naturally goes relatively little
power of initiation. The habit of seeing everything
officially controlled, fosters the belief that official
control is everywhere needful ; while a course of
life which makes personal causation familiar and

negatives experience of impersonal causation, produces an inability to conceive of any social processes as carried on under self-regulating arrangements."[1]

Wherever militancy increases its impress, it is quickly seen in its influence upon institutions. In military Germany, for instance, all industrial activities are regulated by the State, the railways are State controlled, and numerous restrictions interfering with business and commerce have been promulgated. The extension of British imperialism, adds Spencer, is producing similar tendencies at home.

Existing societies are a blend of industrialism and militarism, and nowhere does the industrial society exist in a pure form. It must not be thought that it is " the diligence of its members which constitutes the society an industrial one in the sense here intended but the form of co-operation under which their labours, small or great in amount, are carried on."[2] Its essence is voluntary co-operation.

In the industrial society corporate action is longer required. Where corporate action remains, its purpose is to guard individual actions against all interferences not necessarily entailed by mutual limitation. A controlling despotic agency is not needed, but one that will express the average will—a representative agency. Its function will be to see that each citizen gains neither more nor less of benefit than his activities earn. Public action involving an artificial distribution of benefits is excluded. A regime of contract prevails, which negatives interferences between efforts and results by arbitrary apportionment.

---

[1] *Principles of Sociology*, Vol. II, pp. 599–560. *See* the clever analysis which Durkheim, following him, adopted.

[2] *Ibid.*, p. 604.

Regulation is negative only. It says thou shalt not, and not thou shalt. Numerous and diverse voluntary associations spring up. Society is plastic because it is based on the principle of efficiency. It is internationalistic and promotes world-peace because it does not pursue economic policies directed against other nations. It seeks the brotherhood of man, the federation of the world.

What will be the character of this Society? "Certain uncultured peoples whose lives are passed in peaceful occupations, prove to be distinguished by independence, resistance to coercion, honesty, truthfulness, forgivingness, kindness. On contrasting the characters of our ancestors during more warlike periods with our own characters, we see that, with an increasing ratio of industrialism to militarism, have come a growing independence, a less marked loyalty, a smaller faith in governments, and a more qualified patriotism ; and while, by enterprising action, by diminished faith in authority, by resistance to irresponsible power, there has been shown a strengthening assertion of individuality, there has accompanied it a growing respect for the individualities of others, as is implied by the diminution of aggressions upon them, and the multiplication of efforts for their welfare."[1]

History indicates a tendency towards industrialism. Nations have grown up administering huge territories, and eliminating war within those areas. Wars become less frequent and do not involve the whole population. Whilst in the past the workers existed for the fighters, now the fighters exist for the

---

[1] *Principles of Sociology*, Vol. II, pp. **639–640**.

workers. The system of status has everywhere displaced the system of contract, and this decrease of compulsory co-operation has diminished the restraints over individual actions. There is greater mobility, both occupational and territorial. Men are not now obliged to profess certain political opinions, nor are they prohibited from expressing their political views. They are not regulated in dress or mode of living. They are free to join societies of all kinds, social, religious and political. The chief function of the ruling power is to administer justice, for the fear of aggression is less. In every way the decrease of militancy and the increase of industrialism have meant a change from a social order in which the individuals exist for the benefit of the State, to a social order in which the State exists for the benefit of the individuals.

But these benefits must be regarded less as the immediate results of industrialism than the remote results of non-militancy. " It is not so much that a social life passed in peaceful occupation is positively moralizing, as that a social life passed in war is positively demoralizing."[1] Democracy, therefore, is not the best of all political systems, but the least bad. Forms of government, however, are not really important. What is important are the units and their moral endowment. The State must wither away and leave social activities to free and independent individuals. State functions should be reduced to a minimum, and private enterprise increased to a maximum. An indispensable condition for the attainment of the highest social order is the abolition of war.

---

[1] *Principles of Sociology*, Vol. II, p. 640.

A few words may here be said about the concepts, status and contract which figure so largely in Spencer's Sociology in the form of industrialism and militarism. Spencer's contemporary, Sir Henry Maine, who coined the formula, regarded it as the law of progress. He writes : " The word Status may be usefully employed to construct a formula expressing the law of progress thus indicated, which, whatever be its value, seems to me to be sufficiently ascertained. All the forms of Status taken notice of in the Law of Persons were derived from, and to some extent are still coloured by, the prowess and privileges anciently residing in the family. If then we employ Status agreeably with usage of the best writers to signify those personal conditions only, and avoid applying the term to such conditions as are the immediate or the remote result of agreement, we may say that the movement of progressive societies has been a movement from Status to Contract."[1] In other words, men's social positions are first determined by their membership of a group, and afterwards by contracts to which they pledge themselves.

But this progress, regarded as universal both by Maine and Spencer, is not to-day so obvious as it was in an era of unrestricted competition and free contract. Moreover, the formula implies one continuous, universal and permanent line of evolution. But social evolution is not of this nature ; it follows many divergent and often conflicting lines. In fact, this formula is only of limited applicability. It applies in general to property, but not to

---

[1] Sir Henry Maine, *Primitive Society and Ancient Law*, Ed. 1930, p. 181.

personal relationships, " Status may yield to contract," says a famous lawyer, "but cannot itself be reduced to contract."[1]

It is evident that in his Sociology Spencer had modified his views from those in " Man Versus the State," where his attitude to the State and its political institutions was much more uncompromising and hostile. He now realized that political institutions and the State had served useful purposes in the past. He admitted that the State, even if it cannot command thou shalt, can still say thou shalt not. But Spencer did not indicate wherein the distinction actually lies. He objected to State interference, but can one draw a distinction between self-regarding activities in which the State cannot interfere and other regarding activities in which it can ? In actual practice, this cannot be done, and to delimit the State's activities *a priori* is to impose a limit on a rapidly changing world. At any particular time, a proposed extension or delimination of the State's activities should be judged on its merits. Spencer, however, was very positive—the State should not take on public education, attempt colonization, erect lighthouses, work a postal system, or set up a mint. Sanitation, poor relief, public health, were not its province, for otherwise it would interfere with the wise and inexorable decree of nature that only the fittest shall survive.

That the functions of the State shall be negative only, follows logically from Spencer's views as to the nature of progress. For if progress is automatic,

---

[1] Sir Frederick Pollock, in his introduction to Maine's book. *See* note on p. 156.

self-propelling, limitless, and in accordance with what people deem desirable, interference by the State is superfluous—indeed, positively harmful. Spencer was not unmindful of the material progress of a capitalistic era of free competition, and his social philosophy mirrors clearly and unmistakably the impact it made on him. His social philosophy is in essence a refinement of the economics of the Manchester school.

The tendency to-day is to stress more and more the positive aspects of State functions, and to urge a broad and comprehensive system of social legislation that will make possible the realization of the best potentialities in man. The emphasis is on social purpose, not on unconscious mechanism. Unrestricted competition and the economic struggle for existence seem to be leading mankind not to the paradise that might be hoped for, but to the wilderness of disillusionment and despair.

Spencer abhorred the State—because he abhorred compulsion. He saw that in the last analysis the State is a repository of force, and wherever force intrudes, freedom, the true freedom of self-disciplined individuals, disappears. He dreamt of a dim and distant Utopia, where men would be free, noble and happy, and where voluntary and willing labour would carry out the world's activities. He sometimes forgot that this was a dream, and that, as things are, a regulating centre with force at its disposal is necessary. Spencer may be right in thinking that the State as we know it may wither away, but on the other hand it is an illusion that force can be altogether eliminated. Spencer's universe is static wherein all relations are fixed and determined. Here friction is impossible. But in a universe whose only permanent attribute is change, friction is unavoidable. And where there is friction there is need for adjustment and regulation. Social life is far too complicated and dynamic to do without a regulating centre that may compel such adjustment as may be deemed necessary in the interests of the whole community.

We mentioned before that Spencer never made clear the distinction between State and Society, He hovers between the conceptions social organism and social contract. He hints at a period when " wild in woods the noble savage ran," free and unchecked. Society involved their mechanical aggregation and a consequent sacrifice of their freedom. Why, he asks, " is not man adapted to the social state ? " " Simply because," he answers, " he yet partially retains the characteristics appropriate to an antecedent state. The respects in which he is not fitted to Society are the respects in which he is fitted for his original predatory life. His primitive circumstances required that he should sacrifice the welfare of other beings to his own : his present circumstances require that he shall not do so ; and in so far as his old attribute clings to him he is unfit for the social state. All sins of men against one another, from the cannibalism of the Fijian to the crimes and venalities we see around us ; the felonies which fill our prisons, the trickeries of trade, the quarrellings of class with class and nation with nation, have their causes comprehended under this generalization."[1]

If Society be a contract, it follows that rights are

---

[1] *Social Statics*, p. 30.

inherent in the individual, and are absolute and inalienable. But if Society be an organism rights are relative and derivable from the general welfare. Spencer never made up his mind how to regard them; here they are absolute, there they are relative. Land, he argues, should belong to Society since it is necessary for the general welfare; private property on the other hand must not be interfered with. The function of the State is to protect its citizens. But if so, it has been argued, why not from internal as well as from external aggression, from the rapacity of some employers and the greed of some landlords? If the State is a " joint-stock " protection company for mutual assistance, its duties are to ensure the equal rights of citizens. It must ensure those conditions that give fulfilment to those equal rights. But this Spencer did not appreciate owing to his philosophical preconceptions regarding State and Society. He was preoccupied with his ideal industrial Society with that peculiar blend of anarchism which Huxley called anarchism with the policeman.

We must not, however, overlook the permanently valuable features in Spencer's sociological analysis of political institutions. He rightly stressed the importance of war in the formation of States. He pointed to the economic roots of wars. He realized that the State exists not only for external aggression, but also for internal aggression wherever the government represents a dominant class within the State. He emphasized the intimate connection between political institutions and economic institutions. It is significant, even if he did not see all its implications, that he discussed property

among his political institutions. He was careful
to point out that the external forms such as
monarchy, democracy, oligarchy mean little for
the understanding of their real nature. It is necessary to know by whom and by what group of
interests the form is being manipulated.   His
discussion of law is penetrating. He erred in stressing co-existences too much and in paying little
attention to the dynamic factors of change, to the
political processes themselves. But here he was
misled by his generalizations concerning the militant
and industrial types of Society. He is apt to confuse
these ideal types with real States and explain the
real by the ideal, and sometimes the ideal by the
real. He used the keys of contract and status to
unlock too many doors.

BIBLIOGRAPHY. CHAPTER V.

BAGEHOT, W. *Physics and Politics.* 1872.

BARNES, H. E. *Sociology and Political Theory.* 1923.

HOBHOUSE, L. T. *Democracy and Reaction.* 1904.

HOBHOUSE, L. T. *Liberalism.* 1911.

HOBHOUSE, L. T. *The Metaphysical Theory of the State.* 1918.

JELLINEK, G. *Allgemeine Staatslehre.* 1905.

KRABBE, H. *The Modern Idea of the State.* 1922.

LASKI, H. J. *Authority in the Modern State.* 1919.

LASKI, H. J. *Grammar of Politics.* 1925.

MacIVER, R. M. *The Modern State.* 1926.

OPPENHEIMER, F. *The State : Its History and Development.*
1925.

VINOGRADOFF, P. *Historical Jurisprudence.* 1920.

WALLAS, GRAHAM. *The Great Society.* 1919.

CHAPTER VI.

Property and Economic Institutions.

In order to live property is essential. Its acquisition is a dominating force in the life of individuals and societies, and leaves an impress on every phase of their activities. That is why the history of the family, Church and State, is so often the history of property. The main task confronting every society is the satisfaction of its physical needs, and to its successful achievement a society will subordinate everything else. In our highly complicated industrial communities the immediacy and urgency of this task are disguised by the mechanical character of commodity production, and by the universal use of money as a medium of exchange. We must go to a primitive society to see the pervasiveness of this problem and to sense its intimate connection with food supplies, and the animate and inanimate environment. To a primitive society its dependence on nature, on the weather, on the earth, on plants and animals is evident. It will surround this dependence with mystical and magical influences, and endeavour to propitiate them, or compel them to act on its behalf. It will suffuse its economic activities, and notions of property and property rights, with mana, magic and animism.

At every stage of civilization the significance of property for self-realization and aggrandizement is evident. Wars will be waged to obtain property and states will become organized to control it. It is evident that it is not so much the acquisition of property itself, as its acquisition in order to satisfy other needs that makes it so fundamentally important. For property is basic if power is to be wielded and if the need for social esteem is to be satisfied. It cannot be interpreted in terms of an instinct, although all the other instincts are dependent on it for fulfilment. It is more easily understood in terms of a sentiment which, clustering around objects in our possession, will evoke the most powerful instincts in their defence, should their use be hindered, or their enjoyment frustrated. Spencer saw this clearly in his few and scattered remarks on the psychological basis of property. Although he used the expressions " Instinct of Acquisition " and " Acquisitive Instinct " he realized that " joined with the impulse to acquire property, there is what we call a *sense* of the value of property."[1] He goes on to say, " The acquisitive propensity is a character, the degrees of which and the relations of which to the social state have to be especially noted. The desire for property grows along with the possibility of gratifying it ; and this, extremely small among the lowest men, increases as social development goes on. With the advance from tribal property to family property and individual property, the notion of private right of possession gains definiteness, and the love of acquisition strengthens. Each step

---

[1] *Social Statics*, p. 19.

towards an orderly social state makes larger accumu-
lations possible, and the pleasures achievable by
them more sure ; while the resulting encouragement
to accumulate leads to increase of capital and
further progress.   This action and reaction of the
sentiment and the social state should be in every
case observed."[1]

These are very important observations for the
understanding of the way in which the acquisitive
sentiment becomes organized and manifests itself.
It is evident that its culture patterns would be
different in an "acquisitive society" from those
in a communistic society. The accumulation of
property is unknown to primitive societies, and
the production of things for future use instead
of for immediate enjoyment, plays an insignificant role.   We must know the whole economic
structure and property relationships in a community
in order to interpret the content and importance of
the acquisitive sentiment.   For this same reason, and
because of the complexity of social life, great caution
must be used in applying the results of property
and territorial distribution in animal or insect
societies, based on instinct, to sociology.   It does not
help much to explain communism or private property by pointing to alleged cases in the animal
world, or to the "fact that even intelligent animals
display a sense of proprietorship, negatives the belief
propounded by some, that individual property was
not recognized by primitive man."[2]

Even if it be difficult to fit into the framework of
primitive society our categories of communism and

---

[1] *The Comparative Psychology of Man.* Essays, Vol. I, p. 367
[2] *Principles of Sociology*, Vol. II, p. 539.

private property, one feature stands out in all investigations of primitive economics. And that, in Hobhouse's opinion, is the predominance of the corporate claims of the group over the individuals in all questions affecting the livelihood of the group. It is true that individual property in personal belongings is recognized, and that one of the claims to ownership is as Spencer pointed out, the act of taking possession. But such possessions, to adopt Hobhouse's terms, are for use not power. Possessions of the latter kind are of vital importance to the group, and the land and the main food supply, hunting and fishing, are of paramount interest to it. They will therefore generally be owned communally, or regulated for the benefit of the group. Moreover, in such primitive societies private property for power can have but small scope, and in fact, we find that the distribution of wealth is equitable within the family, clan and tribe.

Possibly, because Spencer approached this question with the formula of the original indefiniteness of the rights to individual possession, and their growing definiteness with social progress, he did not commit himself to an evolutionary sequence of stages of ownership beginning with communism, which have been advanced by Kohler, Bucher, Laveleye, Lafargue and Lewinski. He realized that the application of the means of production will vary according to the economic structure of that particular society, and that this, in turn, will profoundly modify all other institutions. We have already shown how strongly Spencer emphasizes the economic factor in his discussion of the family and political institutions. In fact, in many places he adopts an economic interpretation of history, and argues against Comte, that it is not ideas that shape the activities of men, but the activities of men that shape their ideas.

Let us first consider the question of property in land among primitive peoples. Spencer rightly shows that " while subsistence on wild food continues, the wandering horde, inhabitants of a given area must continue to make joint use of the area, both because no claims can be shown by any member to any portion, and because the making out of small divisions, if sharing were agreed upon, would be impracticable."[1] This view is conclusively confirmed by the data in the *Simpler Peoples* which demonstrate that among hunting tribes the land is usually owned in common, by the clan, sib, or local group. In other words, the individuals composing these groups have mutual rights in the enjoyment and use of the land, and these rights they hold in common as against other groups. Usually such common ownership is correlated with communal regulation of the distribution of the products. It must be added, however, that there are also a few cases where hunting lands are privately owned.[2] In some cases, too, " tribal socialism was qualified only as regards certain improvements on the land ; if a Thompson River Indian or Maidu, had constructed a deer fence or fishing station, he was entitled to the exclusive use of what his individual efforts had produced and the right descended to his heirs."[3]

Among pastoral peoples similar results pertaining

---

[1] *Principles of Sociology*, Vol. II, p. 451.

[2] L. T. Hobhouse, G. C. Wheeler and M. Ginsberg, *The Material Culture and Social Institutions of the Simpler Peoples.* 1915.

[3] R. H. Lowie, *Primitive Society*, 1920, p. 211.

to the collective ownership of land hold good.
" Where pastoral life has arisen " writes Spencer
" ability to drive herds hither and thither within
the occupied region is necessary. In the absence of
cultivation, cattle and their owners, could not
survive were each owner restricted to one spot
there is nothing feasible but united possession of a
wide tract."[1]

The communal principle still predominates in the
early agricultural stage, but private land ownership
becomes more extensive " when there comes a
transition to the agricultural stage, either directly
from the hunting stage or indirectly through the
pastoral stage."[2] for here begin to germinate the
seeds of profound transformations. Land acquires
a value and is privately appropriated.   To this
tendency there are a number of checks available—
the strength of custom and the survival of communal
habits and sentiments ; the difficulties in the way of
establishing an exclusive claim, when other individuals and peoples are still pastoral and unsettled ;
the inability to set up effectual divisions and
boundaries ; and the fact that a particular spot soon
becomes exhausted and " whatever private claim
had arisen lapses, and the surface, again becoming
wild reverts to the community."[3] Whatever precise
meaning attaches to such forms of ownership as
the Russian Mir, the Javanese Dessa, the German
Mark, it cannot be denied that they indicate the
surviving supremacy of the communal principle.

The question of the common ownership of land is
closely bound with the question of what were the

---

[1] *Principles of Sociology*, Vol. II, p. 541.
[2] *Ibid.*, p. 541.   [3] *Ibid.*, p. 542.

early stages of economic evolution.   De Laveleye, the Belgian economist, supposed that the first stage was a hunting and fishing stage when the only possessions man had, were his crude hunting implements.   This hypothetical stage was succeeded by a pastoral nomadic stage where land was common to all, and this, in turn, by an agricultural stage, where man tilled the soil and owned all things in common.   Finally, it is supposed that individual property arose, based very frequently on war and conquest.   There is probably an element of truth in the last statement although the sequence of stages is no longer regarded as invariable or universal. Spencer saw this clearly.   It is evident that in certain parts of the world pastoral nomadism could never have developed—e.g., the South Sea Islands, and that in America, agriculture grew up together with hunting, and the intermediate pastoral stage was missed. " While spreading over the earth mankind have found environments of various characters, and in each case the social life fallen into, partly determined by the social life previously led, has been partly determined by the influences of the new environment," [1] writes Spencer.   Wissler declares that " this belief (the sequence of three stages) is no longer tenable, but hunting is still regarded as the primitive form from which a tribe may pass directly to the domestication of animals or of agriculture." [2]

Spencer's enquiries led him to conclude that certain definite phases had been passed through by every people, and he enumerates many of these stages.[3]

---

[1] *Principles of Sociology*, Vol. III, p. 325.

[2] Clark Wissler, *An Introduction to Social Anthropology*, 1929, p. 66.

[3] See *Principles of Sociology*, Vol. III. Chap. XIII, *Industrial Institutions*.

The first stage was absolute communism in husbands, wives, food and houses. The distribution of cattle, game and flocks takes place among some peoples of the hunting and agricultural stages according to certain customary rules, but is not general. As regards ordinary vegetable foods this occurs rarely, and even where there may be both production and distribution on communistic principles as among several Australian tribes, the consumption of food will be exempt from these regulations. Primitive housing and dwellings exhibit great diversity in this matter. Among the hunters and gatherers, excepting the Central Australians, there is usually a common dwelling for the clan group, the family having private occupation of houseroom within it. Among the Andamanese, Central Eskimos, and Veddas, family ownership of separate huts and caves exists along with this common dwelling. When we come to the agricultural peoples, we meet with a marked preference for the separate family dwelling, although the tribal meeting house will be under common ownership. Where we do find a clan, or a sib, living in a common house, the family will occupy a separate set of rooms.[1] From this mass of evidence it is difficult to draw conclusions favouring a universal stage in consumption of products. We may, perhaps, discern a growing tendency towards " separateness," and it would be interesting to have a comparative psychological study of the notion of " privacy."

The second stage, maintains Spencer, was partial or modified communism, in which the right of private

---

[1] *See* E. Beaglehole, *Property*, 1931, for a complete discussion of this subject.

property would be recognized, but in which there would also be property in common and communal regulation of industry. A third stage would be partial communism under patriarchal rule, the father of the household directing the activities of its members, holding on their behalf all the property, and trading with their approval. A further stage shows partial differentiation of occupations within the household, and of individual ownership beyond that of personal belongings, which in some of the Hindu tribes readily passes into complete ownership by division into shares. Finally, with the development of money, both as a cause and as a consequence, there is an "emergence from the system of undivided earnings and common property into a system of divided earnings and private property."[1]

If, as yet, modern thinkers have been unable to draw up a satisfactory sequence of necessary stages in economic evolution, we may say that just as the communal principle predominated in primitive property relationships, the principle of private property is dominant at the present. The historical process by which the latter displaced the former is one of which there is full evidence both as regards its operation and its effects. This process is especially clear in the case of the means of production. In one way it was a natural and inevitable growth out of the communal land-ownership or family-ownership systems, which yielded in different ways and degrees to qualified forms of private ownership, mostly temporary, and subject to supreme ownership by the public. This

---

[1] *Principles of Sociology*, Vol. III, p. 439.

is the significance of the periodical redistribution of the land. The second and more important way was through war, conquest and consequent class differentiation. Spencer puts the position clearly : " Force in one form or another is the sole cause adequate to make the members of a society yield up their joint claim to the area they inhabit. Such force may be that of an external or that of an internal aggressor."[1] Land instead of belonging to the community now belongs to the chief, not only nominally but in practice. This comes out very clearly in the evidence of the *Simpler Peoples*, which shows that communal land, whether tribal, village or gentile, diminishes in the two higher grades at the expense of the chiefs and nobles who profit by the possession of land.[2] The communal cases are a fraction of the total number of cases analysed.

	Communal.
Lower Hunters	0·69
Higher Hunters	0·80
Agricultural I	0·64
Agricultural II	0·54
Agricultural III	0·29

With the increasing class structure of Society, we find the kings and the nobles possessing an exclusive monopoly of the land and all the means of production, and the rest of the population, slaves, serfs semi-free and peasant cultivators, all dependent on them for their means of livelihood.

Concurrent with the growth of private property in things inanimate, there is an extension of

---

[1] *Principles of Sociology*, Vol. II, p. 546.
[2] L. T. Hobhouse, G. C. Wheeler and M. Ginsberg, *The Material Culture and Social Institutions of the Simpler Peoples*. 1915, p. 251.

property in things animate—slaves. Spencer thinks that slavery is in general a consequence of war, and that both its growth and disappearance can be explained by economic factors. In the absence of industrial activity slaves are useless ; where it is present slavery expands. Moreover, " the same advance in social and industrial organization which tends to the formation of a servile class below the ordinary free man " declares Hobhouse, " works, though less surely and rapidly, to the elevation of a small class above him."[1] This is clear in the following table, which gives the proportion of communities in each economic grade in which there exists a class of nobles, and one of serfs and slaves[2] :—

	Serfs and Slaves.	Nobility.
Lower Hunters	0·02	0·00
Higher Hunters	0·32	0·11
Agricultural I	0·33	0·03
Pastoral I	0·37	0·20
Agricultural II	0·46	0·15
Pastoral II	0 71	0·24
Agricultural III	0·78	0·23

The mitigation and gradual disappearance of slavery were again due to economic factors—the supply began to run short, and it was felt advisable to take care of slaves. Spencer, like Westermarck later on, is sceptical of the view that Christianity was the great civilizer. He points to the expansion of industry and the different modes

[1] L. T. Hobhouse, *Morals in Evolution*, p. 276.
[2] L. T. Hobhouse, G. C. Wheeler M. Ginsberg, *Material Culture and Social Institutions of the Simpler Peoples*. 1915 p. 236. *See* also H. J. Nieboer, *Slavery as an Industrial System*. 1910.

of production, and writes " when slave labour and free labour came into competition, slave labour, other things being equal, decreases as being less economical.   The relative lack of energy, the entire lack of interest, the unintelligent performance of work, and the greater cost of supervision, make the slave an unprofitable productive agent."[1]

Feudalism, Spencer realizes, is a complex institution, with roots deeply buried in the past.   Under Roman rule, the function of the serfs was to " supply money for the armies, to supply corn for the armies, and to be under a rigorous rule like that of the armies."[2]   Medieval serfdom Spencer regards as an advance upon slavery, but in essence he thinks it is a degradation of free men consequent upon an epoch of compulsory co-operation proper to a military regime.   He thus dispenses with an economic analysis.   It is often the case with Spencer that he deems to have explained an institution by putting forward the military and industrial types of society in explanation.

The growth of Capitalism, the massing of private property in few hands, and the changes in the technique of production transformed the feudal era into an era of free labour and contract.   Spencer is under no illusions as to the meaning of free in this connexion, and he writes thus of the English peasants after expropriation and enclosures had stolen the land from them : " though nominally free, the labourer was coerced not only by restraints on his locomotion, and by the obligation to accept specified sums for his labour, but by the limitation

---

[1] *Principles of Sociology*, Vol. III, p. 470.
[2] *Ibid.*, p. 492.

of his liberty to labour ; for he could not choose his occupation."[1]   And, in spite of his enthusiasm for industrialism, he admits that " the industrial freedom achieved by the masses of men in the various ways above described, still remains incomplete in most countries and remained incomplete even among ourselves within the memories of living persons."[2]

We saw in the previous chapter the fundamental rôle that the notion of free contract plays in Spencer's thought.   Contract, he shows, only arises when the work and the payment for it are voluntarily exchanged, and when definite measures of value exist. " In the course of social progress, free labour and contract developed together, each making the other possible. . . . Neither can advance without the other, and neither can advance without various advances.   There is not only mutual dependence, but also a mutual dependence of influences."[3]   This is perfectly true, but his analysis does not go to the root of the problem.   It gives the form, but not the content of the industrial system.   Free contract is only valuable when the partners to it are of equal strength.   The worker is free to sell his labour and the employer is free to buy it, but it is now admitted that does not put them on the same level as regards bargaining power, or the pressure they can exert in the economic system.

It is this fact which gives Trade Unionism its peculiar significance in a capitalist Society, a significance that Spencer completely overlooked, although

---

[1] *Principles of Sociology*, Vol. III, p. 492.
[2] *Ibid.*, p. 499.
[3] *Ibid.*, p. 503.

he was probably acquainted with the Webbs' authoritative work on the subject. He writes : " If the unionist complains that the non-unionist hurts him by under-bidding him, and taking away his work, not only may the non-unionist reply that he is hurt if he is prevented from working at the rate he offers, but the employer may complain that he, too, is hurt, by being obliged to pay more to the one than he would to the other. So that the trade unionist's proceeding inflicts two hurts that one may be prevented."[1] He does, however, admit that Trade Unions seem natural to a transitory phase of social evolution, that they do perform some useful functions and that in some cases they may restrain greed and rapacity on the part of employers.

Spencer felt that everything was not all right in a world which was moving steadily and surely forward to his ideal industrial type of society. He writes : " It seems that in the course of social progress parts more or less large, of each society, are sacrificed for the benefit of Society as a whole. In the earlier stages the sacrifice takes the form of mortality in the wars perpetually carried on during the struggle for existence between tribes and nations ; and in later stages, sacrifice takes the form of mortality entailed by the commercial struggle, and the keen competition entailed by it. In either case men are used up for the benefit of posterity ; and so long as they go on multiplying in excess of the means of subsistence, there appears to be no remedy."[2]

---

[1] *Principles of Sociology*, Vol. III,, p. 539.
[2] *Ibid.*, p. 516.

Just as Spencer's views of the significance of Trade Unionism differs from those of modern Sociologists, so the meaning he attached to Socialism differed from present-day conceptions.   This is the result of his predilection for two types of Society. Instead of seeing that, sociologically considered, Socialism is an inevitable product of Industrialism, the growing socialization of the means of production, and the massing of vast armies of labourers in industrial areas, Spencer relates Socialism to his military type of Society, and argues that because, on superficial analysis, Socialism has some resemblances to Militarism it must be a species of Militarism as it involves regulation. Those who think that Socialism is only another type of Industrialism must, he considers, be completely mistaken, He writes :—

" The industrial type of Society, properly so-called, must also be distinguished from a type very likely to be confounded with it—the type, namely, in which the component individuals, while exclusively occupied in production and distribution, are under a regulation such as that advocated by socialists and communists. For this, too, involves in another form the principle of compulsory co-operation. Directly or indirectly individuals are to be prevented from severally or independently occupying themselves as they please ; are to be prevented from competing with one another in supplying goods for money ; are to be prevented from hiring themselves out on such terms as they think fit. There can be no artificial system for regulating labour which does not interfere with the natural system. To such extent as men are debarred from making whatever engagements they like, they are to that extent working under dictation. No matter in what way the controlling agency is constituted, it stands towards those controlled in the same relation as does the controlling agency of a militant Society. And how truly the regime which those who declaim against competition would establish is thus characterized, we see both in the fact that communistic forms of organization existed in early forms of societies, which were predominantly warlike, and in the fact that at the present time communistic projects chiefly originate among, and are most favoured by, the more warlike societies."[1]

Spencer was very close to Socialism in its modern sense when advocating the national ownership of the land. Militancy and the system of status are necessarily associated, he argues, with a graduated ownership of the land and with a graduated ownership of persons. Industrial progress on the other hand, with its establishment of measures of quantity and value, stimulates the complete individualization of ownership. " With the decline of militancy and the concomitant disappearance of vassalage, the obligations of the tenure diminish, and finally almost lapse out of recognition ; while simultaneously, abolition of serfdom destroys or obscures the other claims which qualified private land ownership."[2] Since neither serf nor peasant owns the land, in this important respect there is little difference between them. He then goes on to argue that land should not be privately owned, because it contravenes the right of every individual to equal freedom and equal access to the land. " As the

---

[1] *Principles of Sociology* Vol. III, pp. 604–605.
[2] *Ibid.*, p. 556.

individual, primitively owner of himself, partially or wholly loses ownership of himself, during the militant regime, but gradually resumes it as the industrial regime develops ; so possibly the communal proprietorship of land, partially or wholly merged in the ownership of dominant men during evolution of the militant type, will be resumed as the industrial type becomes fully evolved."[1]   But if land should belong to the community, some modern sociologists ask why should not the other means of production ? Technically, there is very little difference between land and capital.   Spencer argues that Socialism will not only imply regulation, but also racial deterioration, because a premium will be put on inefficiency.   Moreover, it is psychologically absurd, because it goes against human nature. " The forms of social organization are determined by men's natures, and only as their natures change can the forms become better."[2] Spencer forgets his own statement that there is a reciprocal relationship between social organization and human nature, and that human nature, whatever it is, is capable of changing.

Socialism, in Spencer's view, meant interference, and, considering the delicacy of the economic mechanism which had slowly and painfully grown up, interference was dangerous. Economic society may be described " as an involved plexus having centres everywhere and sending threads everywhere, so bringing into relation all activities that any considerable change in one, sends reverberating changes among all the rest.   From those far past days, when flint-

[1] *Principles of Sociology*, Vol. II, p. 556.
[2] *Principles of Sociology*, Vol. III, p. 579.

scrapers were used to shape clubs, the co-operation of
appliances, then commenced, has been increasing ;
until now the tools as well as the men form an aggregate of mutually dependent parts. Progress, here as
everywhere, has been from incoherent homogeneity to
coherent heterogeneity."[1]   And a socialist is no more
than a schemer attempting to alter the complexity of
Society which he does not understand. "A fly seated
on the surface of the body has about as good a conception of its internal structure as one of these
schemers has of the social organization in which he
is embedded."[2]

Spencer then proceeds to a short discussion of the
main economic processes—production, distribution,
consumption and exchange.   Production has everywhere replaced simple acquisition, and has become
more complex as men's desires and wants have
become more varied and imperious.   The first kind
of production is that subserving primary needs, but
long before these are satisfied come the desires
which beget war, the desire for admiration, leading
in the first place to the making of weapons, and in
the second place to the making of decorations.
Militarism and Industrialism result in different productive activities.   War will check the increase of
population and diminish the labour forces of a
country, and will divert capital into unproductive
channels ; it will make industry despicable and
labour degrading.   But "peace conducing to the
pressure of population and consequent difficulty in
satisfying wants, prompts continuous application,
prompts economy, prompts better methods.   Stress

---

[1] *Principles of Sociology*, p. 403.
[2] *Ibid.*, p. 403.

of needs leads men severally to adopt occupations for which they are best adapted, and by which they can make the most ; and it becomes possible for the number of special occupations to increase, as the increase of population affords men for each business. Once more the greater specialization of industries not only develops skill in each and consequently better products, but each kind of better product serves more or less to facilitate production in general."[1] This view was reproduced in a somewhat different form by Durkheim, and was examined in a previous chapter.

The evolution of production thus involves greater specialization of functions and the division of labour. The first kind of division of labour is based on psycho-physical difference as, for instance, that between the sexes ; the second kind is territorial division of labour based on difference in the environment ; further differentiation occurs when brain and manual workers become distinct, and still further when these divide and subdivide. In time it becomes possible for men to devote themselves exclusively to making aids to production, a process which Spencer calls " auxiliary production." Such production comes to play an ever growing part in economic life. We have only to think of how the farmer is dependent on the plough, harrow, rake fork, mowing machine, reaper, binder, elevator, and threshing machine to see this. But a still more striking development occurs. The making of appliances to facilitate production is followed by the making of appliances for the making of appliances, as in the steam hammer.

Distribution necessarily accompanies the division

---

[1] *Principles of Sociology*, Vol. III, p. 362.

of labour, for men can only devote themselves to different occupations when there can be transference from one to another of their various products. But distribution takes place not only with commodities but also with skill, and agencies arise to bring producers and consumers into relation. Hence there arise wholesalers, retailers, travellers, buyers, etc. Finally, " development of the animate appliances for distribution, has been accompanied by development of the inanimate appliances, the means for conveying people, goods and intelligence. These two have all along acted and reacted : increased distribution having resulted from better channels, having caused further increase of distribution."[1]

Exchange is a concomitant of distribution, but in the absence of measures of quantity and value the idea of equivalence remains vague. Barter yields to trading when food, cattle, tea or tobacco are used as currency, and with its further evolution the process of distribution becomes enormously extended and facilitated. Values can now be definitely estimated, and prices arise. A still further development takes place when bills of sale and cheques come into use.

All these processes Spencer reminds us are so interwoven and so intimately influence each other that integration of the structures of the economic system cannot but result. In this connexion, Spencer regarded as examples of the co-operation of appliances, the integration of machines. They are symbolic, he says, of " the wider and less manifest integrations . . . displayed throughout the whole industrial organization."[2]

---

[1] *Principles of Sociology*, Vol. III, p. 377.
[2] *Ibid.*, p. 399.

Spencer devotes a separate section to the professions, but they may well be considered here, since they arise as a result of the division of labour and the specialization of functions.   His account endeavours to trace every profession back to a remote origin, and assumes a genetic relationship where he cannot find one.   The danger of such a procedure he well realized, and in dealing with the Trade Union, he writes :   " Not that there was a lineal descent of trade unions from craft guilds. Evidence of this is lacking and evidence to the contrary abundant. Though very generally each later social institution may be affiliated upon some earlier one, yet it occasionally happens that social institutions of a kind like some which previously existed, arise *de novo* under similar conditions ;   and the trade union furnishes one illustration.   Akin in nature though not by descent, the trade union is simply a gild of wage-earners."[1]   This is a simplification of the real situation where the background, attitudes, methods and functions would be different.   Spencer even refers to the differentiation that has made the doctor and surgeon distinct professions, and traces them back to the primitive distinction in which one cure of diseases was to be made by reference to demons causing it, and the other by reference to injuries caused by human beings, beasts and inanimate bodies.

With his formula of differentiation and integration, Spencer discusses the origin and development of dancer and musician, orator and poet, actor and dramatist, biographer, historian and man of letters ; man of science and philosopher, judge and lawyer,

---

[1] *Principles of Sociology*, Vol. III, p. 527.

teacher, architect, sculptor and painter.   His analysis is interspersed with many valuable suggestions and illustrations.   This is how he treats of the dancer and musician :—

" In the actions of lively children, who on seeing in the distance some indulgent relative, run up to him, joining one another in screams of delight and breaking their run with leaps, there are shown the roots from which simultaneously arise those audible and visible manifestations of joy which culminate in singing and dancing. . . . Nor does it need any stretch of the imagination to perceive that these natural displays of joy, at first made spontaneously before one who approaches in triumph as a benefactor and glorifier of his people, come in course of time to be observances used on all public occasions as demonstrations of allegiance ; while simultaneously the irregular jumpings and gesticulations with unrhythmical shouts and cries, at first arising without concert, gradually by repetition become regularized into the measured movements we know as dances, and into the organized utterances constituting songs."[1]

With reference to Spencer's attempt to trace a genetic relationship in every case it may be said that certain needs are constant in civilization, and that the forms arising to subserve them are similarly constant. Do not the medicine-man and the doctor perform similar functions ?   Here Spencer shows a close affinity to the formalistic school of sociology—

" Still glides the stream and shall for ever glide
The form remains, the function never dies."

Spencer's analysis is the first systematic effort

---

[1] *Principles of Sociology*, Vol. III, pp. 200–201.

to deal with the sociology of the professions—a subject that in the present day has once again begun to attract attention.[1] Spencer is careful to relate his examination to the social background, and he shows how the professions were acted upon and reacted with government, religion and property. His lines of inquiry will doubtless be followed up.

The future, as Spencer saw it at the close of his Sociology, filled him with deep foreboding and gloom. He began to see tendencies both in philosophy and practical life that seemed at variance with the ideals upon which his whole Sociology rested. In physics, the second law of thermodynamics implied not increasing but diminishing heterogeneity—an ultimate and dead-level uniformity. In politics he saw the blurring of his distinct and separate types of Society. He noticed signs of militarism, imperialism and " political burglaries." He felt the movement towards increasing regulation and government control. " Is the movement," he asked himself, " towards the ownership of each man by others, or towards ownership of each man by himself and towards the corresponding emotions and thoughts ? "[2] The answer was not in doubt. Socialism was spreading, and with it bureaucracy and militarism. Undoubtedly the tendency was towards the subjection of the individual by the Great Leviathan—Hobbes's phrase for the State.

Modern sociologists have asked some questions with regard to this, such as : Was not Spencer con-

---

[1] *See* A. M. Carr-Saunders and P. A. Wilson, *The Professions*, 1933.

[2] *Principles of Sociology*, Vol. III, p. 583.

founding form and content, substance and shadow ? Is there a fundamental or essential similarity between military and industrial regimentation ?   Is not this modern world so delicately integrated, and is not every human being so dependent for health, safety and livelihood upon economic processes, that regulation is absolutely necessary ?   They also say that it is important to know the purpose of the regulation. In war it is for the destruction of life and property, in the economic system for the provision of such conditions as make human beings more or less free and equal.

Spencer understood the economic system in its static character, but he did not deal with those dynamic elements of change that were giving birth to a different world.   He himself lived at a time when profound changes were taking place in the economic structure of society, and the balance between social classes was altering.   The forms were more or less the same, but the forces sustaining and animating them were different.   The very same Industrial Revolution which had brought about Spencer's industrial type of Society, with its message of peace, abundance and prosperity, was inevitably leading to a frenzied search for colonies, markets, competition and imperialism.   The militaristic type of Society was not, therefore, the antithesis of the industrial type but its consequence.   Spencer could not fit his static types to the rapidly-changing contemporary events.   He saw around him " political burglaries " and imperialistic exploits.   His types were not as he thought, distinct and opposed : both were phases of a social order that possessed within itself the seeds of its own transformation.

BIBLIOGRAPHY. CHAPTER VI.

HOBHOUSE, L. T., WHEELER, G. C., and GINSBERG, M. *Material Culture of the Simpler Peoples.* 1915.

HOBSON, J. A. *The Evolution of Modern Capitalism.* New and revised ed. 1926.

MARSHALL, A. *Principles of Economics.* 1890.

MARX, K. *Das Kapital.* 3 vols. Vol. I., 1886.

MOON, P. T. *Imperialism and World Politics.* 1926.

MÜLLER-LYER, F. *The History of Social Development.* 1920.

PIGOU, J. *The Economics of Welfare.* 1920.

TAWNEY, R. H. *Acquisitive Society.* 1921.

TAWNEY, R. H. *Equality.* 1931.

WEBB, S. and B. *The Decay of Capitalist Civilization.* 1923.

WEBB, S. *History of Trade Unionism.* 1920.

WEBER, M. *General Economic History.* Trans. 1923.

WITHERS, HARTLEY. *The Case for Capitalism.* 1920.

WOOLF, L. S. *Imperialism and Civilization.* 1928.

CHAPTER VII.

Ghosts, Ancestors, Gods.

In a memorable sentence, Spencer declared that
"while the fear of the living becomes the root of
political control, the fear of the dead becomes the
root of religious control."[1]   In accordance with this
statement it would seem that a psychological analysis
of fear and other emotional components of religion
is indicated. Spencer's account of the origin and
development of religion does not include this analysis.
With the assumption that there exists a universal
attitude of fear towards the dead, Spencer proceeds to
the discussion of every phase of religious life, belief,
worship, ritual, sacrifice, fitting one into the other
with marvellous skill and ingenuity.   In the opinion
of the present writer Hartland was right when he said
of Spencer's Euhemerism that it is "a child (one
among many) of his passion for explaining everything
quite clearly, for stopping up all gaps and stubbing
up all difficulties in his synthesis, rather than an
all-sufficient account of the beginning of religion."[2]

The value of Spencer's sentence quoted above is in
showing the intimate connexion that exists between
political and religious control, and how religious
organizations and beliefs are acted upon and interact

[1] *Principles of Sociology*, Vol. I, p. 426.
[2] *Legend of Perseus*, Vol. I, p. 203, quoted in *Encyc. of Religion and Ethics*.   Article: Ancestor-Worship.

with the general structure of society. His discussion of religion and his analysis of ecclesiastical institutions supplement each other.

Whatever the role of fear in the religious attitude, modern sociologists believe that it is only one component among many others such as love and awe, frustration and frenzy, trust and dependence, joy and anxiety, incompleteness and hope. These emotional elements do not become of themselves religious until they are organized and canalized into sentiments centring round a vague apprehension of something in reality as supernatural, extraordinary and mysterious, something on which we can project our secret wishes and desires, that can compensate us for life's shortcomings and console us when death approaches. On this emotional foundation ceremony, ritual, dogma and prayer arise. Emotion, and action in response to emotion, come to be supplemented by a belief in a supernatural realm widely different from the real workaday world and possibly in spiritual agents animating it. But beliefs of this nature are not essential, and that, in the present writer's opinion, is why Spencer's and Tylor's minimum definition of religion as a belief in spiritual beings is not satisfactory. Animism as such is not religious, although it contains within it the potentialities of religion. For animism peoples a universe with spiritual beings to whom worship and veneration may be paid, it provides objects round which religious sentiments may cluster. Finally, all these elements would need to be reinforced by an account of the institutions that arise to serve religious beliefs, such as churches and congregations, an aspect of religion which, since Durkheim's researches, cannot be ignored.

Spencer concentrates his attention mainly on two matters, which he regards as essential to religion— the ghost theory or the theory of the double, and the doctrine of ancestor-worship. These he treats very fully and subsumes under them every religious phenomenon. Let us outline his main arguments.

Primitive man, if we attempt to make explicit the working of his mind, was dominated by the notion of the duality of nature. For wherever the savage turned he saw things appearing and disappearing— changing skies, lightning, rainbows, sun, moon and stars, mirages, waterspouts and winds. He observed that plants and animals were changing and trans- forming, and that things were visible at one moment and invisible at another. This duality is confirmed by shadows, echoes and reflections, and with this notion the primitive man introduces order into the chaos of his sense impressions. " One may say that as the protoplasm forming an unfertilized germ, re- mains inert until the matter of a sperm-cell is joined with it, but begins to organize when this addition is made, so a loose mass of observations continues unsystematized in the absence of an hypothesis, but under the stimulus of an hypothesis undergoes changes bringing about a coherent systematic doctrine."[1]

This " unconscious hypothesis " receives support from dreams, and masks the primary distinction, of which primitive man is aware, between the animate and inanimate, between the living and the not-living. Dreams are actual occurrences for does not the dreamer do things, visit places and talk to persons ? How otherwise explain dreams than that there is

---

[1] *Principles of Sociology*, Vol. I, p. 121.

another self, a double, which goes away during sleep and comes back on waking? How otherwise explain somnambulism, swoon, apoplexy, catalepsy and unconsciousness? Moreover, this belief in another self harmonizes with the duality of nature's phenomena, their appearance and disappearance, visibility and invisibility. Things have their doubles, too. Spencer, in addition to the above exposition, also stresses the fact that " dream experiences necessarily precede the conception of a mental self ; and are the experiences out of which the conception of a mental self eventually grows."[1]

An extension of this belief to death and resurrection is natural. The primitive man observes various degrees of insensibility—it may last a few minutes or days—it may last so long that the body becomes cold. In this case the double refuses to come back, and attempts must be made by gifts of food or by punishment to compel its return. If it does not return now it will return later. " Such resurrection shown by the universal fear of the dead to be vaguely imagined even by the lowest races, becomes clearly imagined in proportion as the idea of a wandering duplicate is made definite by the dream theory."[2] Until the wandering soul returns to the body care must be taken not to injure or hurt the body, and " beginning with the small mound necessarily resulting from the displacement of earth by the buried body, we come at length to such structures as Egyptian pyramids."[3] The body may be embalmed or hidden away, and

---

[1] *Principles of Sociology*, Vol. I, p. 441.
[2] *Ibid.*, p. 414.
[3] *Ibid.*, p. 162.

funeral rites, such as mutilation, cutting off hair, etc., will arise in order to propitiate the presently reviving dead.

At first the second self is equally visible and material as the self—it suffers hunger, thirst, fatigue and pain, and destruction. Later it becomes invisible, ethereal and indestructible. The world and everything in it become peopled with ghosts, demons, spirits and souls. Firstly, there are the souls of deceased parents and relatives, vivid and distinct as compared with the souls of ancestors. Secondly, there are the wandering doubles of persons, asleep or insensible. Thirdly, the souls of waking persons who have temporarily left them. Fourthly, there are the souls of beasts, plants and inert objects, and finally, there are souls of friends and souls of enemies.

The souls are supposed to live a life not unlike that of the living. They eat and drink and fight as before, but now there are no limits to their gratification. They will need their weapons and clothing, etc., which are therefore buried with the dead person. They will crave for companionship—hence immolations and human sacrifices. Their social, economic and political institutions, their conduct, sentiments and ethics will closely mirror those of the living. Between the souls of the living there will be communion—" the living pray for the dead ; and the canonized dead are asked to intercede on behalf of the living."[1]

Their abode may be close at hand or in the forest, and food will be left for them. If migration had occurred, they will be said to dwell far away, down

---

[1] *Principles of Sociology*, Vol. I, p. **192.**

a river or across a sea, and canoes and horses will be left with the dead. " Where the places for the departed, or for superior classes of beings, are mountain tops, there is a transition to an abode in the heavens, which at first near and definite, passes into the remote and indefinite."[1]

The dead are more numerous than the living and offer " the potentiality of countless supernatural agencies capable of indefinite variation."[2] Any strange or extraordinary event can now be explained with this machinery of causation—epilepsy, convulsive actions, delirium, insanity, sneezing, yawning, disease and death. These are the actions of malicious ghosts which must be expelled, and thus will arise the arts of exorcism and sorcery, and the professions of medicine-man and magician. Friendly and beneficent spirits on the other hand must be propitiated, prayed to and worshipped.

This completes Spencer's account of the Ghost-Theory of which he was the prime author, and which was later developed by Tylor and others. Let us turn now to his account of ancestor-worship, which, according to him, is a logical derivative of the almost universal belief in a reviving other-self of the dead man. By ancestor-worship he means worship of the dead, be they of the same blood or not ; and he argues, that every religion has its roots in ancestor-worship.

The following evolutionary stages were indicated by Spencer, each successive stage declining in generality :

1. The almost universal belief in a double.
2. The belief in his existence after death.

---

[1] *Principles of Sociology*, Vol. I, p. 214.   [2] *Ibid.*, p. 217.

3. Ghost propitiation at the funeral and subsequently.

4. Persistent ancestor-worship.

5. Ancestor-worship of the more distinguished ancestors.

6. Their exclusive worship if the ancestors were leaders of a conquering race.

The lowest cultures lack ancestor-worship which only becomes possible at higher stages of economic development, when people have given up their nomadic life. At a still later stage ancestors are transformed into deities, and funeral rites and worship of the dead into religious worship. Thus, " in their normal forms and in their abnormal forms all gods arise by apotheosis."[1]

" We may infer *a priori*," writes Spencer, " that in conformity with the law of Evolution there will develop many unlike conceptions out of conceptions originally alike."[2] Idolatry and fetishism are thus divergent developments of ancestor-worship, as are also plant- and animal-worship. Nicknames too can be easily explained, for after countless years had passed, the nickname and the thing of which it is a name would be confused, and it would be assumed that the founder of the family was a plant or an animal.

Deification of nature has a similar root. " Partly by confounding the parentage of the race with a conspicuous object marking the natal region of the race, partly by literal interpretation of birth-names, and partly by literal interpretation of names given in eulogy, there have been produced beliefs in descent

[1] *Principles of Sociology*, Vol. III, p. 19.
[2] *Principles of Sociology*, Vol. I, p. 299.

from Mountains, from the Sea, from the Dawn, from animals which have become constellations, and from persons once on earth who now appear as Moon and Sun."[1]

Finally, powerful ancestors with strange and weird powers, medicine-men, inventors, and warriors will become deities. " And so the universality of anthropomorphism has the sufficient cause that the divine man as conceived, had everywhere for antecedent a powerful man as perceived."[2] " Instead of it being true that ideas of deity, such as are entertained by cultivated people, are innate, it is contrariwise true that they arise only at a comparatively advanced stage as results of accumulated knowledge, greater intellectual grasp and higher sentiment."[3]

In *Ecclesiastical Institutions*, Spencer has a passage correlating the attributes of the deity with the industrial and military types of Society. " Ascribed characters of deities are continually adapted and readapted to the needs of the social state. During the militant phase of activity the chief god is conceived as holding insubordination the greatest crime (as it is then legally considered the greatest offence), as implacable in anger, as merciless in punishment ; and any alleged attributes of milder kinds occupy but small space in the social consciousness. But where militancy declines and the harsh despotic form of government appropriate to it is gradually qualified by the form appropriate to industrialism, the foreground of the religious consciousness is increasingly filled with those ascribed

---

[1] *Principles of Sociology*, Vol. I, p. 384.
[2] *Ibid.*, p. 409.
[3] *Ibid.*, p. 411.

traits of the divine nature which are congruous with the ethics of peace : divine love, divine forgiveness, divine mercy are now the characteristics enlarged upon.''[1]

This closes Spencer's contributions to the sociology of religion. He stresses the close relationship between religious development and between social, scientific and moral development. It is evident that the more closely knit and greater political systems became, the more noticeable was the effect on polytheism, which gradually gave way to some sort of monistic conception. Emotionally and intellectually too there seems to be a trend to unity and harmony of the many separate and divergent strands of religion and their confluence into one broad stream.

Spencer's account does not, however, cover the whole ground. We propose, therefore, to deal with the following topics in the order indicated—animism animatism, magic, ancestor-worship, and the problem of Supreme Beings.

Spencer's scheme is mechanical and uniform, and is in accordance with his philosophical scheme— to use his own word, synthetic. He constructs an orderly evolutionary sequence with a number of fixed and definite stages, and the criterion adopted for this arrangement is that of increasing complexity. This may be regretted because Spencer begins with the warning that evolution must not be regarded as an intrinsic tendency to become something higher and that retrogression has been as frequent as progression.

His treatment of animism is not as penetrating as

---

[1] *Principles of Sociology*, Vol. III, p. 163.

that of Tylor's. Tylor derived his notion of the soul as something different from the body, from the primitive man's consideration of two sets of biological phenomena, firstly, from sleep, ecstasy, illness and death ; and, secondly, from dreams and visions, in which the dreamer not only does and sees things, but things from near and far come to him. Thus he traces all spirits ultimately from dreams. Spencer, however, derives the human spirit, soul, or ghost from the dream, and then peoples all the rest of nature with ghosts, a procedure which is a much more intellectualist construction than Tylor's, but which does not fit in as well with the evidence we now possess of animistic notions entertained by primitive peoples. Where Tylor went astray was in his attempt to derive all religions from animism alone, an attempt that was no more successful than Spencer's. He writes, " It seems as though the conception of a human soul when once attained to by man, served as a type of model on which he framed not only his ideas of other souls of lower grade but also his ideas of spiritual being in general, from the tiniest elf that sports in the long grass up to the Heavenly Creator, Ruler of the World, the Great Spirit."[1]

Recent research has shown that animism is by no means as universal as was originally thought, and that it is not equally well developed among all races. Its maximum development is among the Melanesians, Indonesians, West Coast Africans and some of the peoples of South America, and some North American Indians. But even here, not

---

[1] E. B. Tylor, *Primitive Culture*, Third ed., 1891.   Vol. II, p. 110.

everything is supposed to have a soul ; in general, inanimate objects were excluded from this category, except objects of fantastic and curious shape. It is also evident that certain nature-spirits such as of the earth, the sun and fire, need no animistic explanation, for they could easily derive from personification or mythologizing. It also seems probable, that not every explanation in terms of spirit is necessarily related to the experiences of sleep and dreams. Primitive man may infuse into natural phenomena his own personality as wishing things and wanting things, and in this way interpret causality in terms of beings like himself.

Both Spencer's and Tylor's duality has by later authorities been modified since it was discovered that some men and animals may have attributed to them a number of souls, each of which is connected with a certain faculty, although most commonly only two souls are postulated, one belonging to the body and connected with the life, and the other a shadow soul, a phantom which may owe its origin to memories of the dead, and with which may be connected a belief in future life. There may also be souls of the head and souls of the heart, a right-hand soul which goes to the " One Country " and a left-hand soul which becomes a daemon. There may be four souls, or seven souls, the number often corresponding to the mystic number of the tribe.

These considerations have suggested to Lévy-Bruhl the view that a belief in the multiplicity of souls or spiritual entities, is earlier than belief in a double.[1] The latter belief has only, however, a

---

[1] L. Lévy-Bruhl, *Les Fonctions Mentales des Sociétés Inférieures*, 1910.

limited distribution. Wundt, in "Mythus und Religion," suggested that the generalized notion of a free and separable soul must have been preceded by body-souls which, though connected with the body or with different parts of it, are completely distinct from the soul or psyche which is regarded as the breath- or shadow-soul. This soul may be the source of daimons and superhuman powers.[1]

These are the main developments that have taken place in the theory of animism since Spencer's time. They modify his position as they have modified that of Tylor. If it is still taken as the most common form of primitive belief, its claims are not as extensive now as they were. At most it is but one of the elements that will enter into the religious cult. This is theology rather than religion. It is now thought that wherever such an explanation in terms of spirit, quasi-material or sub-human, is present, there is the possibility of it assimilating to itself other elements, and interpreting them in its own terms. It affords, as Spencer pointed out, a machinery of causation of which primitive mentality may make use on those rare occasions when it theorizes.

Animism itself, when closely examined, indicates a stage of thought and feeling which possibly preceded it, and with which it has become closely fused. For the primitive mind does not clearly draw distinctions between mind and matter. Plants, animals and inanimate objects are much on the same level as human beings. The primitive mind treats them as alive, and feels a mystic bond with them. Animatism (an expression coined by R. R. Marett)[2] as

---

[1] W. Wundt, *Mythus und Religion*, 3 Vols., 1905, pp. 6–9.
[2] R. R. Marett, *The Threshold of Religion*, 1914, p. 14.

we may call this attitude, was hinted at by Tylor when he wrote of the animation of all nature as supplementing the belief that innumerable spirits people the world. Animism, as Hobhouse has well said, is " animation made more concrete and definite."[1] By a sort of empathy, things take on human feelings such as effort and strain, relief and quiescence. They are treated spontaneously as human-beings are treated, since wish-fulfilment predominates in man's attitude to things. Nature becomes endowed with vague, elusive and undifferentiated powers. Here we come upon a very important principle for the understanding of primitive cults.

Of course, not all things are endowed with this " livingness," for the distinction between the living and not-living is always observed, is essential to the very continuance of life. Only curious and weird objects will be credited with inherent power, with a form of communicable energy (again making explicit what of necessity is vaguely felt and ill-understood) that can hurt or do good to an unusual degree. Here we have the germs of the concept " mana," which inhering in things makes them sacred, and objects of religious attention and behaviour. The Melanesian wizard has mana which makes him mysterious and supernormal. This power, which has its root in animatism needs no indwelling spirit to explain its nature and effects. Similar conceptions are widespread—we find it in the Sioux " wakan," the Iroquois " orenda," the Algonkin " manitu," and the Australian " arunquiltha." It may fuse with animistic explanations when the latter are present. Souls may be derived from mana,

[1] L. T. Hobhouse, *Morals in Evolution*, 1923, p. 374.

but need not be ; on the other hand, things which are not souls may have mana. It is all-pervasive, but is neither animistic nor magical, it may be conceived impersonally or be personified. Spirits when they have mana become mysterious and fearsome, and evoke something akin to the religious emotion, which the ordinary spirit cannot do. Extraordinary individuals may wield mana, but as a condition they must abstain from the ordinary " noa." It is originally accessible to everybody, and gives such help as they need for them to come to terms with the mysteries that beset life from within and from without. It finds response in emotional action, and in a ritual that is found satisfying. Mana will tend to become institutionalized and ceremonialized for the benefit of society, and at a later stage it may become equated with the divine right of a ruling class. In mana we come upon an extensive region, completely unknown to Spencer, which cannot be included in animistic theory, and the exploration of which is essential for the understanding of the growth of religion. For it contributes the awe and wonder so integral in the religious consciousness ; it gives a name to the mysterious, supernormal and supernatural, all of which are contributory elements in religion.

In the primitive world Natural objects may therefore be regarded as alive or inhabited by spirits, and may also be regarded as being united by certain occult connections which are assumed to exist as a matter of fact. These connections which constitute the raw materials of magic do not, as Spencer thought, involve spirits who, therefore, mistakenly subsumed all magical practices under animism. As

Freud suggests, the moving principle in magic is man's desired objects. This principle postulates the omnipotence of thought, and mistakes imaginary connections for real ones. Thus to make explicit its suppositions, it will distort the principle of identity by believing that if a man's hair or nail-parings are destroyed, the man himself will wither away. To attack a man, attack his shadow, or operate on his food, would be magical maxims. This we may call contagious magic. Another form, homeopathic magic, rests on a similar principle. In order to hurt your enemy, make an image of him and stick pins into it ; to make rain, squirt water ; to get sunshine, kindle a fire. The idea involved is that these processes are the same, and the causing of one will cause the others. A third form of magic postulates powers and influences existing in, and separate from, things. To make fruitful a barren tree (presumably male) place upon it a woman's petticoat ; to get rid of a toothache strike a nail into a tree. This kind of magic easily fuses with animism, and the magical influence will turn into a spirit, or perhaps a spirit will become attenuated into an influence.

The nature of magic and its relationship to religion on the one hand, and to science on the other, have been the cause of much discussion and many theories. Let us discuss in brief some of them.

Frazer argues that magic is prior to religion and that it is the parent of science, because the uniformity of nature and the belief that the same results will follow under identical conditions, which is the basis of magic, must have been known before any religious cults arose. Magic is everywhere the same, but religions are different the world over. Magic differs from religion in not making use of conscious personal agents ; but it is similar to science in assuming the uniformity of nature. Actually it is false science and gradually gives way to true science.

This position is intellectualistic to an extreme degree, and credits primitive man with a logic that he probably did not possess. Only by realizing this can one accept Frazer's view that to think of impersonal, regularly recurrent forces is a less complicated process than to think of irregular non-recurrent personal forces. It is also not true that magic is uniform and that religion is not. Again, magic, like religion and unlike science, involves an act of faith ; it often reverts to religion and prayer when it fails. "Both magic and religion," writes Goldenweiser, "have in common the acceptance of the supernatural level and their association with the religious thrill—the magical situation may be contrasted with the religious one, by the element of constraint involved, the will or power of the magician dominating the situation, whereas in the religious setting, the will of the devotee is at best but a will to believe, whereas the will of the god or other divine personage becomes the dominant determinant factor bringing in its wake worship, supplication, prayer and the like."[1] Durkhiem's distinction between magic and religion is sociologically important as indicating one of the factors that led to the decline of magic and the victory of religion. He shows that throughout

---

[1] A. Goldenweiser, *Early Civilization*, 1922, p. 347.

the ages religion was supported and upheld by a bond closely connecting the Church and its congregation. Magic, on the other hand, never possessed such a bond, the relationship between the sorcerer and his clients being of a totally different nature. To Levy-Bruhl magic is a phase of prelogical non-casual thought characteristic of primitive man, and his deep sense of mysterious and dreadful powers.

The most acceptable view according to modern thinkers is to regard both magic and religion as separate compartments of super-naturalism, without claiming priority for one or the other. Functionally they cannot be dissociated, for both are methods for obtaining power, or good luck, or control over things in ways which are not dependent on natural causes. Historically they diverge, and religion came to be " a propitiation or conciliation of powers superior to man, which are believed to direct and control the course of nature and of human life."[1] Magic was driven out of sight, possibly because it had to show its immediate effectiveness, which religion did not always do. According to Freud magic is succeeded by religion in which man surrenders part of his power to supernatural beings, and is in turn succeeded by science which teaches him how to achieve power through limitation.

Spencer's derivation of all religious cults from ancestor-worship cannot be sustained in the light of recent research. There is not a single religious cult in the world which consists of ancestor-worship alone. Moreover, it has a distinctly limited distri-

---

[1] Sir J. Frazer, *Golden Bough*, Vol. I, 1922, p. 221.

bution—among the Bantu, Negroes, Melanesians, parts of Asia, among the Peruvians and Pueblo Indians, in China and Japan—and is by no means universal, as was originally assumed. Instead of ancestor-worship being the root of religion, it is a comparatively late product, reaching its highest development in comparatively recent times.

There are also numerous nature deities worshipped which cannot be explained as being originally ancestral. There are further cases where the cult of the warrior has developed to a very high degree, and yet the devotion shown to him is much less than that shown to the regular gods, and these are not necessarily ghosts of the dead. The ritual in both cases differs, that attending hero-worship being different from the ritual surrounding worship of a god, an indication that the two cannot be equated. Excluding nature gods, the evidence to-day is considered not to support Spencer's view that, in the last analysis, every god is the ghost of a particular human being.

A number of pertinent objections were also raised by Andrew Lang. What reason is there, Lang asks, for ghosts to be prior in evolution to gods, and why must the gods be of animistic origin ? Could they not be conceived as anthropomorphic or theriomorphic ? Wundt believed that animals were worshipped as ancestors before any human being or gods became the recipients of a religious cult. According to Lang, all savage religions have a notion of God the Maker, God the Master, who is regarded as a being who existed before death came into the world, and who created all men. He is regarded as the custodian of morality and is worshipped in a way that no ghost is. Why should not these high gods have arisen independently, why must they grow out of the less worthy ones ?

These arguments receive their clearest expression in the work of Father Schmidt, who puts forward the view that the most primitive religion consists in the worship of a Supreme Being, a High God, who is omnipotent, eternal, omniscient, the preserver and the founder of all law. It is only in later times, he argues, that his true nature becomes overlaid with superstitions and other cults that arrogate to themselves all worship. This extreme position is not accepted by the majority of anthropologists. It is clear that, from the scanty, contradictory data that exist, it is impossible to reconstruct monotheism as the most archaic of all beliefs. Certainly nowhere does the Supreme Being possess the attributes he is alleged to have, neither is he appealed to for protection, nor is he propitiated. In most cases he turns out to be a vague ancestor, the personification of striking natural features like the sky, or a generalized conception of mana. The high god seems to be the expression and the product of one of the oldest traits of mankind, the art of story telling, of myth making, whereby supernatural things are explained, and the world peopled with spirits and powers, heroes, monsters, and creators. To such a creator, the life of the tribe may be attributed, the making of the sky and nature. In time such a mythical being may take on a religious character, but generally he is beyond knowledge. He is a good and great spirit that will do no harm. It is the evil spirits or perhaps the spirits of the departed that must be propitiated.

Reviewing the evidence, Hobhouse came to these conclusions—

" 1. The conception of a creator has arisen apart from civilized influences among some people even of a very low culture.

" 2. High gods, as a supreme sun or sky god, or a culture hero such as Baiame, are more common and are also found in low grades.

" 3. A supreme god is very rarely the object of a cult, but ' high gods ' are frequently the originators of custom and concerned in its maintenance, are sometimes gods of the dead, and are occasionally addressed in prayer.   To this extent we must qualify the generalization that magic and some form of animism, animatism, or the cult of the dead form the working creed of the simpler peoples."[1]

The element in Spencer's theory of ancestor-worship that receives the support of modern enquirers is that one source of religion, of the worship of gods who are more than spirits, who have some personality and a cult, and who exercise certain superhuman functions, may be a distinguished ancestor or a real hero raised high in honour above the ordinary dead.

But ancestor-worship as such is not religion, because it is the cult of dead ancestors and not of deities. It is an expression of the love, fear and awe which the living feel for the dead, and which develops into tendance to the dead. Even this is only the beginning of ancestor-worship. From the earliest times man, prompted by emotion, showed acts of affection and homage to the dead, by gifts of food and raiment. First came the act and then the reasoning about it. For the cult to grow certain conditions were requisite such as increasing

[1] L. T. Hobhouse, *Morals in Evolution*, 1923 p. 396.

family and political stability. The patriarchal family with its strong property sentiment, and with the desire of the survivors to maintain friendly relations with the departed, was fertile soil for the development of this cult. Moreover, to Society such a cult would be highly advantageous, promoting political stability by strengthening the bonds of tradition. Ancestor-worship was always being threatened by religion. Polytheistic nature-worship and animism made serious inroads upon it, militated against its growth and made it the limited cult that it is.

These elements that we have passed in review, pave the way for the more specific great religions that swept the world. " At the beginning of the development of religion there stand certain remarkable things which form as it were its vestibule . . . such things as the idea of purity and impurity, beliefs concerning the dead and their tendance, concerning the soul and the cult of the soul ; magic, folk tales, myths, the worship of natural objects . . . the curious ideas concerning ' power ' . . . fetishism and totemism, cult of beasts and plants, daimonism and polydaimonism ; in all of which there is no more than a certain haunting element of the numinous. Before all these vestibules, came a yet ' earlier stage,' in which all these existed only as the purely natural products of primitive imagination, belonging to the times of primeval simplicity in which they had not yet even that much flavour of the numinous."[1]

To a god or gods, the writer believes, these elements become attached. One way to the divine is through the hero, another through the nature spirit. Where

[1] R. Otto, *The Idea of the Holy*, 1926, p. 146.

his place of worship stands, where his shrine is, there he is the local god. When his people expand and grow in territory, the god becomes more power-ful, and merges in himself smaller gods. He personifies and directs the great natural forces, and governs and controls their functions. He fights with other gods, and if his people is victorious so is he. If his people become conquerors of many lands, he subjugates their gods. He becomes supreme in heaven when the monarch becomes supreme on earth.

Spencer in later years became more reconciled to religious institutions and the important part they had played in social life. He came to see how they can be used to maintain and strengthen social bonds, and how they conserve beliefs, sentiments and usages favourable to social stability. " As furnishing a principle of cohesion by main-taining a common propitiation of the deceased ruler's spirit, and by implication checking the tendencies to internal warfare, priesthoods have promoted social growth and development. They have simultaneously done this in sundry ways : by fostering the spirit of conservatism which maintains continuity in social arrangements ; by forming a supplementary regulative system which co-operates with the political one ; by insisting on obedience, primarily to gods and secondarily to kings ; by countenancing the coercion under which has been cultivated the power of application ; and by strengthening the habit of self-restraint. . . . To the last as at first, subordination, religious and civil, is uniformly insisted on, " fear God, honour the king " ; and providing subordination is manifested with sufficient emphasis moral shortcomings may be

forgiven."[1]   Ecclesiasticism   he regarded above all
others as the principle of social continuity.   It
furthers social growth and development by main-
taining a common propitiation of a deceased ruler's
spirit.   It fosters the spirit of conservatism by
favouring the old social order.   It maintains a
respect for private property.   It obediently
co-operates with the political system and insists
upon obedience not only to god, but also to the
king.

For all these reasons Spencer believes religion and
religious institutions should survive and represent
(in which way we are not told) our relations to the
Unseen, to the Unknown, and to one another.
" Those who think," he writes, " that science
is dissipating religious beliefs and sentiments, seem
unaware that whatever of mystery is taken from the
old interpretation is added to the new."[2]   Science
only leaves us in the presence of the avowedly
inexplicable.   " One truth must grow ever clearer—
the truth that here is an Inscrutable Existence
everywhere manifested, to which the man of science
can neither find, nor conceive either beginning or
end.   Amid the mysteries which become the more
mysterious the more they are thought about, there
will remain one absolute certainty, that he is ever
in presence of an Infinite and Eternal Energy from
which all things proceed."[3]

---

[1] *Principles of Sociology.*   Vol. III, Ecclesiastical Institutions,
p, 149.

[2] *Ibid.*, Vol. III, pp. 171–172.

[3] *Ibid.*, p. 175.

BIBLIOGRAPHY.   CHAPTER VII.

BERGSON, H.   *Les Deux Sources de la Morale et de la Réligion.*
1932.

BERTHOLET, A., and LEHMANN, E.   *Lehrbuch des Religions-
geschischte.*   2 vols.   1925.

DURKHEIM, E.   *The Elementary Forms of Religious Life.*   1915.

FRAZER, SIR JAMES.   *The Fear of the Dead.*   1933.

FRAZER, SIR JAMES.   *The Golden Bough.*   12 vols.

FREUD, S.   *The Future of an Illusion.*   1925.

GOLDENWEISER, A.   *Early Civilization.*   1923.

HOBHOUSE, L. T.   *Morals in Evolution.*   1915.

HOPKINS, E. WASHBURN.   *The Origins and Evolution of Religion.*
1924.

JEVONS, B.   *An Introduction to the History of Religion.*   2nd ed.
1902.

MALINOWSKI, B.   *Science, Religion and Reality:* Magic Science
and Religion, Ed. by N. J. T. H. NEEDHAM.   1925.

OTTO, R.   *The Idea of the Holy.*   1926.

PREUSS, K.   *Glauben und Mystik.*   1926.

SCHMIDT, W.   *The Origin and Growth of Religion.*   1931.

TAWNEY, R. H.   *Religion and the Rise of Capitalism.*   1926.

WESTERMARCK, E.   *Origin and Development of Moral Ideas.*
1926.

CHAPTER VIII.

FACTORS OF SOCIAL CHANGE.

A SOCIETY, no less than an individual human being, an animal organism, or an inorganic product, exhibits in the course of time certain changes. We have but to glance at the history of any particular society to find that nothing has remained fixed and static, and that the only permanence belongs to change itself. Time devours its children and plays havoc with ancient and venerable usages and institutions, which disintegrate or change their forms. Taking a long stretch of time, we find different economic systems, new political institutions, a different class composition, changes in language, religion, science and art, a different numerical distribution of the inhabitants, and possibly a change in the quality of the people. Some of these changes we can measure as the growth of population or the increase in the number of institutions. Others we can infer by comparing the external features of an institution at an early and at a late stage of its development. We may compare one element of change with another—the culture of a society with man's biological equipment, see whether they change together, and at what speeds.[1] Other elements, such as fashion, art or inventions, may possess distinctive cycles of change whose duration we may determine. Changes

---

[1] W. F. Ogburn, *Social Changes*, 1923.

may proceed slowly or rapidly, with the " inevitability of gradualness " and evolution or with the inevitability of catastrophe and revolution.   In their aggregate we call all these changes social change.

Social change is manifestly complex for the reason that a change in one department of life will bring about changes in other departments of life, and all at different and varying rates.   Thus a change in the technique of production will have effects not only in the industrial sphere, but also in politics and in the balance of political power, in the relations of the classes, in the family, in art and in literature. " Such a simple occurrence," Spencer writes, " as the discovery of gold brings multitudinous results— an inrush of people, growths of towns, new social arrangements, gambling hells, demoralization, besides much wider effects—new businesses, new lines of traffic, and the changes presently caused throughout the world in the relative values of gold and goods."[1]   Moreover, one change will produce other changes and these still others, in cumulative fashion, so that it can be compared to a stone thrown into the water, producing ever-widening ripples.   This comparison, of course, simplifies the complexity of reality, for whereas in the water we see the starting point and the connecting ripples we do not always see them in social change ;   nor do we always know which came first.   Cause and effect are inextricably interwoven, and the effect of one cause in the series of changes becomes itself a cause.

This is what Spencer meant by his Law of the Multiplication of Effects and by his term " fructifying causation."   He shows that in Society one cause

---

[1] " Party Government " in *Facts and Comments*, p. 97.

produces a number of unlike effects, " every active force produces more than one change—every cause produces more than one effect."[1]   And again, "This multiplication of effects which is displayed in every event of to-day, has been going on from the beginning ; and is true of the grandest phenomena of the universe as of the most insignificant.   From the law that every active force produces more than one change, it is an inevitable corollary that during the past, there has been an ever-growing complication of things."[2]   The mechanical implications of this picture must be qualified by some sort of organismic or dialectical conception, wherein cause and effect are reciprocal and circular, act and re-act on each other, and wherein the effect is not merely the same as the cause, but also different.   In a final analysis it must be remembered that all changes, adjustment, balance and equilibrium in Society are mediated through human beings who are both causes and effects in the intricate connectedness of social life.

For the sake of convenience it is necessary to isolate, if possible, the factors, agents and conditions of social change, and to classify them into groups. Evidently social change must be sought in the interacting individuals composing Society and in the environment in which they are placed.   In other words, it is necessary to know the physical environment, the biological laws to which man with all other organisms is subject, his psychological structure and functions, and finally the way he interrelates and interacts with the other individuals in Society, and the way societies interact with each other.   Sociology aims at discovering the relations between these

---

[1] *Progress*, Essays, Vol. I, p. 37.
[2] *Ibid.*, p. 38.

different factors of social change and possibly arranging them in their relative importance. Sociology further attempts to unravel and disentangle all these fundamental conditions of social change and persistence, and relates to the more ultimate laws of life and mind all such empirical generalizations at which it arrives. In this chapter we shall deal with Spencer's conception of the environmental, biological, psychological and sociological conditions ; for they form a framework of reference in which we can place all the factors of social change.

Spencer points out that social change of whatever kind, excluding of course the intervention of a deity, is ascribable to the characters of the individuals of an aggregate, the intrinsic factors—and to the conditions under which they exist—the extrinsic factors. These he calls the primary factors of social phenomena. There are also derived factors resulting from the interaction of societies and the environment which he calls the secondary factors. We shall now consider each group in turn.

The intrinsic factors relate to the physical, emotional and intellectual traits of primitive man. " Considered as a unit the individual man has physical traits, such as degrees of strength, activity, endurance which effect the growth and structure of Society. He is in every case distinguished by emotional traits which aid or hinder or modify the activities of the society and its developments. Always too, his degree of intelligence and the tendencies of thought peculiar to him, become co-operative causes of social quiescence or social change."[1]

Spencer then discusses the physical structure of

---

[1] *Principles of Sociology*, Vol. I, p. 9.

primitive man as compared with modern man. Physically primitive man is inferior in size to modern man, for there is a connection between barbarism and inferiority of size. His lower limbs are relatively smaller, his alimentary system larger, since it must be adapted to an irregular and inferior supply of food. He is less muscular and he is less able to persist in muscular action for a long time ; but he is more hardy, more indifferent to pain, and matures somewhat earlier.

The data Spencer offers in support of his statements chosen from the limited sources of his time are very miscellaneous, but his preconception in favour of evolution seems to have coloured his conclusions. He himself pointed out that as regards size, some primitive peoples are over six feet in height. The question of stature, assuming that conditions are normal, appears to be therefore connected with race.[1] The Australian aborigines, the survivors of a very primitive race, are on the average about 62 inches in height. But Polynesians are 69·33 inches ; Negroes of the Congo, 69 ; Iroquois Indians, 68·28 ; Esquimaux, 65·10 ; Malays, 62·34 ; and Lapps, 59·2 inches. Different races have different statures, which is not due only to their habitats. To modern students it does not seem possible to conclude " that since in the conflicts between races, superiority of size gives advantages, there has been a survival of the larger . . .

---

[1] In this connection it is important to note the investigations of Sir Arthur Keith who suggests that racial characters are, to a large extent, determined by the activity of the hormones. An inherited glandular structure would provide the mechanism for the fixation of racial types. (see " The Differentiation of Mankind into Racial Types," Report of the British Association 1919.)

implying that the primitive man was somewhat less than is the average civilized man."[1]   The same argument applies to the size of limbs and the alimentary canal.   Differences there may be, but not such as to mark the primitive from the modern man, but rather one racial group from another.

As regards muscular strength, the problem is much more complicated, but making allowance for weight, height, food, etc., much evidence has accumulated since Spencer wrote, and it is doubtful if his conclusions can still be substantiated.   Hardiness—the capacity to endure hardship is very much dependent on training and manner of life.   There are women living in the countryside to whom child bearing is as easy as to primitive woman.   Spencer's observation that primitive man readily recovers from wounds which would be fatal to Europeans, is nowadays doubted ;   that he has greater ability to bear injurious actions or painful sensations is not borne out by recent investigations, although different enquirers express differing views.

Physiological maturity like height is dependent on so many factors, that it is difficult to conceive that early maturity is an innate characteristic of primitive man.   But from the data he had at his command, Spencer concluded that, climate and other conditions being equal, the inferior races must reach puberty sooner than the superior races.   He also believed this trait was associated with cerebral development and argued that the growth and structure, being completed in a shorter period, imply less plasticity of nature, and thus the rigidity of

---

[1] *Principles of Sociology*, Vol. I, p. 42.

adult life sooner makes modification difficult, and increases the obstacle to progress.

In dealing with the intellectual traits of primitive man, Spencer confirms the testimonies as to the acute senses and quick perception of the uncivilized man, " for in virtue of a general antagonism between the activities of simple faculties and the activities of complex faculties, this dominance of the lower intellectual life hinders the higher intellectual life."[1] Experimental investigation has, the writer thinks, exploded this belief, although a number of eminent anthropologists still support the Spencerian view. Rivers, Woodworth and others tested a number of American Indians, Negritoes from the Philippine Islands, Malayan Filipinos, Ainus from Japan, Africans, Eskimos and Patagonians, for vision, hearing, smell, touch and pain, and found no differences. Even in the higher mental processes, such as in the Form Board Test the average differences were slight and overlapping.[2]

Little is known of racial differences in emotion and temperament. These are so interwoven with the traditions and habits of a community that it is extremely difficult to unravel their innate basis. It is difficult with regard to individuals in the same community, and much more difficult with different peoples in different environments. But to Spencer no obstacles were insurmountable and in a section Primitive Man—Emotional, his main characteristics are summed up thus, " as he existed when social

---

[1] *Principles of Sociology*, Vol. I, p. 77.
[2] See T. P. Garth, *Race Psychology*, 1932, and R. S. Woodworth, *Racial Differences in Mental Traits*, Science, Feb. 4, 1910, pp. 171–86.

aggregation commenced." These are impulsiveness leading to explosive, chaotic and incalculable behaviour which make combined action very difficult ; improvidence and a light-hearted careless absorption in the present ; a lack of the sentiments of cohesion ; and a love of approbation from which arises subordination to tribal opinion, and some consequent regulation of conduct. Primitive man is also deficient in sympathy as is evidenced by his treatment of women and by his cruelty, by his early maturity, and by his addiction to fixity of habit which makes him averse from innovation and change.

" Being less evolved," Spencer writes, " we must expect to find him deficient in those complex emotions which respond to multitudinous and remote probabilities and contingencies. His consciousness differs from that of the civilized man by consisting more of sensations and the simple representative feelings directly associated with them, and less of the involved representative feelings."[1] Given a more complex environment, emotions would become more complex in the process of adaptation (so argues Spencer) and each succeeding generation would inherit this capacity. He further asserts that these traits constitute the original nature of man—" On the hypothesis of evolution, the civilized man, passing through phases representing phases passed through the race, will early in life betray this impulsiveness which the early race had."[2]

The most original part of Spencer's exposition is that dealing with the intellectual traits of primitive man and his primitive ideas. His traits of mentality,

---

[1] *Principles of Sociology*, Vol. I, pp. 54–55.
[2] *Ibid.*, p. 58.

Spencer shows, are not innately determined, but are the products of their social environment. He realizes that these do not constitute innate differences between primitive and civilized man, but are the same traits at different stages of evolution.

Primitive man is deficient in conceptions of general facts, and the provision of distant results is impossible to him. His beliefs are relatively rigid, he lacks abstract ideas, and is without notions of uniformity and definiteness ; the idea of truth is not clear to him, and hence he lacks scepticism and criticism. Finally, his imagination is small in range, is reminiscent but not constructive.

Primitive man is further characterized by the attention he gives to meaningless details, and by a small ability to select facts from which conclusions can be drawn. In general, he is unreflective and therefore very imitative. His mental action is chiefly determined by outer incidents and but little by thought, imagination and ideas. His grasp of thought is feeble, and hence he cannot formulate general notions, which implies the power of classing numerous things or events. Without a classified and systematized knowledge, the savage feels no incongruity between any absurd falsehood and some general truth which we believe established. For to him there is no established general truth. He is therefore credulous. Together with an absence of the idea of natural causation there goes an absence of rational surprise and an absence of curiosity. "He is commonly pictured as theorizing about surrounding appearances ; whereas, in fact, the need for explanation of them does not occur to him."[1]

---

[1] *Principles of Sociology*, Vol. I, p. 87.

Given these mental traits of primitive man " our postulate must be that primitive ideas are natural, and, under the conditions in which they occur, rational. In early life we have been taught that human nature is everywhere the same. Led thus to contemplate the beliefs of savages as beliefs entertained by minds like our own, we marvel at their strangeness, and ascribe perversity to those who hold them. This error we must replace by the truth that the laws of thought are everywhere the same ; and that given the data as known to him, the primitive man's inference is the reasonable inference."[1]

" The mind of the savage," he continues, " like the mind of the civilized proceeds by classing objects and relations with their likes in past experiences. In the absence of adequate mental power there result simple and vague classings of objects by conspicuous likenesses ; and hence come crude notions, too simple and too few in their kinds, to represent the facts. Further these crude notions are inevitably inconsistent to an extreme degree."[2]

This in brief is Spencer's account of the intrinsic factors of social change. He confines himself only to the physical emotional and intellectual traits of primitive man, though for completeness such an account would also be necessary for the separate divisions of modern man. A more detailed examination than he gives would also be required of man's psychological equipment and especially of his instinctive apparatus. In this respect the modern sociologist would have the advantage of being able

[1] *Principles of Sociology*, Vol. I, p. 98.
[2] *Ibid.*, p. 104–105.

to draw upon a more scientific social psychology than was available in Spencer's time.

In recent years a great deal of interest has been focussed on the problem of primitive mentality and a number of views in opposition to Spencer have been expressed. It is thought by modern sociologists that the conceptions of magic, religion, animism that we find among primitive peoples are so different in kind from our conceptions, that different mental processes must be postulated. It is even suggested that it is impossible for us to enter into the primitive man's mind, so different is it from ours.

Of this school of thought Lévy-Bruhl is the outstanding exponent. In a number of books[1] he developed Durkheim's thesis that collective representations are not the products of individual minds. He believes firstly, that primitive mentality is pre-logical, often disregarding logical processes. It compares objects and beings not from the standpoint of objective characteristics but from a standpoint which sees magical and supernatural bonds between them. Ordinary causal relationships do not exist for him. Secondly, he thinks that primitive mentality is a mystical mentality and is characterized by " a belief in forces, influences and activities that are real though imperceptible to our sense." It suffuses " representations " with emotional and motor elements, so that they become not merely objects which are real but things to be feared—things that can help or hinder by means of their active and magical emanations. Thus there is a *" participation mystique "* between man, beasts, objects and actions, a

---

[1] *Les fonctions mentales dans les sociétés inférieures*, 1910 ; *La mentalité primitive*, 1922 ; *L'âme primitive*, 1927.

mystical interpenetration that has nothing to do with objective form and substance but is based solely on supernatural connections.

This view has elements of truth in it, and it helps us to understand primitive ideas and practices. Lévy-Bruhl qualifies his own argument, however, when he admits that there are many prelogical elements in present-day Society, as, for instance, those numerous ideas which are confusing, non-objective and contradictory, and yet which are held tenaciously by a large number of people. Spencer had already seen this clearly when he maintained that the intellectual traits of primitive man may be seen in the lower classes and peasant women—" The united traits distinguishing them are—that they quickly form very positive beliefs which are difficult to change ; that their thoughts are full of special and mainly personal experiences, with but few general truths, and no truths of high generality ; that any abstract conception expressed to them they can never detach from a concrete case ; that they are inexact alike in processes and statements, and are even averse to precision ; that they go on doing things in the ways they were taught, never imagining better methods, however obvious ; that such a thing as the framing of an hypothesis, and reasoning upon it as an hypothesis, is incomprehenisble to them ; and that thus it is impossible for them deliberately to suspend judgments, and to balance evidence "[1] And even higher in the social scale—" they swallow with greediness the trivial details of table-talk, the personalities of fashionable life, the garbage of the

---

[1] *Principles of Psychology*, Vol. II, pp. 603–604.

police and divorce courts ; while their reading, in addition to trashy novels, includes memoirs of mediocrities, volumes of gossiping correspondence, with an occasional history from which they carry away a few facts about battles and the doings of conspicuous men. By such minds, this kind of intellectual provender is alone available ; and to feed them on a higher kind, would be as impracticable as to feed a cow on meat."[1]

To give up a rationalistic interpretation of the primitive mind does not imply, in the writer's opinion, that the intelligence of primitive man is inferior to that of modern man. He lives in a narrower world, with different interests and attitudes, whose emotional content is very high. Allier rightly argues that the retardation of intelligence is inevitable in a mind dominated by magical conceptions.[2]

Spencer's view as to the fundamental similarity of human traits at all stages of development, is upheld by sociologists like Tylor, Bastian, Ratzel, Wundt, Westermarck and Hobhouse. Forms of culture are in no way dependent upon race and Durkheim, Mauss and Lévy-Bruhl support the view that we should not judge primitive mentality by modern standards, and that we should always relate their thinking to their system of social organization.[3]

Spencer's extrinsic factors or the conditions under which the units of Society exist may now be enumerated. " We have climate ; hot, cold or temperate, moist or dry, constant or variable. We have surface ;

---

[1] *Principles of Sociology*, Vol. I, p. 79.
[2] Raoul Allier, *The Mind of the Savage*, 1929.
[3] Psycho-analytic methods of approach into primitive mentality are of recent application, and it is difficult to estimate their value at present.

much or little of which is available, and the available part of which is fertile in greater or less degree ; we have configuration of surface, as uniform or multiform. Next we have the vegetal productions ; here abundant in quantities and kinds, and there deficient in one or both. And besides the Flora of the region we have its Fauna, which is influential in many ways ; not only by the numbers of its species and individuals, but by the proportion between those that are useful and those that are injurious. On these sets of conditions, inorganic and organic, characterizing the environment, primarily depends the possibility of social evolution."[1]

The noteworthy points in his analysis are : the perpetual emigrations and immigrations caused by geological and meteorological changes, as well as by the consequent changes of Floras and Faunas ; the certain limits of temperature within which social evolution is possible at first ; the greater bodily activity in the people of hot and dry localities than in those of hot and humid ; the importance of configuration, social integration being easy in a territory which, while able to support a large population, affords facilities for coercing the units of that population ; the fitness of a habitat in respect of its Flora for supporting a large population ; the importance of its Fauna as leading to a hunting or pastoral mode of life, and the injurious effects of noxious animals and insects. All these points, it may be added, are now being comprehensively analysed in the growing science of human geography and have been treated at length by Vidal de la Blache, Jean Brunhes, and others.

---

[1] *Principles of Sociology*, Vol. I, p. 9.

Spencer emphasizes the fact that the "earlier stages of social evolution are far more dependent on local conditions than the later stages. Though societies, such as we are now most familiar with, highly organized, rich in appliances, advanced in knowledge, can by the help of various artifices, thrive in unfavourable habitats ; yet feeble, unorganized societies cannot do so. They are at the mercy of their surroundings."[1] The precise way in which environmental conditions have affected each society must be left to future investigators of what Spencer happily called "Special Sociology."

Spencer does not, like many investigators, exaggerate the effects of climate and environment on social evolution. He realizes that these are more in the nature of limiting conditions than initiating causal factors, that they set problems before man which he must solve if he is to survive. Some modern students have claimed without substantiating their conclusions that climate is the principal cause of the social structures of different peoples. Ellsworth Huntington[2] for instance, finds the pulse of progress in the climatic changes that have occurred throughout history, and correlates industrial and social progress with a temperate climate. This statement singles out one factor to the exclusion of others far more important, such as minerals, education, modes of production, political systems, etc. Profound changes in civilization and culture have occurred, without corresponding climatic changes, and the same climate can support varied cultures. It may be true also that many similar cultures can flourish in differing

---

[1] *Principles of Sociology*, Vol. I, p. 35.
[2] Ellsworth Huntington, *The Pulse of Progress*, 1926.

climates. Those correlations that have been established between climate, insanity, crime, and suicide may possibly be correct, but correlations are not explanations, and more careful investigation has revealed distinctive social factors. This is conclusively shown in Durkheim's study of suicide.

The present writer thinks that Spencer's scheme supports the following conclusions. The real importance of climate in the modern world is the indirect effect it has on the political and economic relationships of countries, in the way it limits the production of certain essential commodities to different areas. The United States, for instance, is the largest consumer of rubber and yet it is dependent on other areas for its supply. Russia has to import most of the products grown in tropical countries. Thus climate sets problems that require solution. In conjunction with other conditions, it may seriously limit or retard social progress. Malaria, for instance, which is a common disease throughout the warmer parts of the world, is estimated to be the direct or indirect cause of over one-half of the entire mortality of the human race. Its influence on the decline of Greek civilization is even now the subject of enquiry. But its limiting nature is only too clear when we realize that human ingenuity has overcome its terrors to some extent, and confined its geographical incidence. The same may be said of hookworm disease, another tropical disease whose ravages upon the health of millions of people is well known.

What applies to climate may also be applied in an even greater degree to the general physical environment. It has changed little throughout human history ; the seas are where they were, and the mountains stand where they stood, but social change has been rapid and enormous. Moreover, the significance of the physical environment alters with inventions and trade routes. The aeroplane, for instance, is bridging natural barriers, and is making almost every part of the earth accessible to man.

The effect of the physical environment before inventions and human ingenuity were operative have been investigated by Le Play[1] and others. They consider that its effect was all-pervasive, and that the different types of institutions of mankind are due to their different habitats. There are correlations between place and the form of the family, they argue—between the steppe and the patriarchal family, between fjords and the particularist family, between tundras and the weakened patriarchal family, between forest and the unstable family. Some of their correlations may be well founded, but their theory of the determination of institutions by the physical environment is open to serious objections. If it determined them in the first place, why is it not effective later ? The patriarchal form of family may have been due to the pastoral organization of the steppe, and yet it persisted for thousands of years in agricultural countries like China and India. The individualistic type of family is found in different social systems and it continues to persist where the systems change. Where such correlations

---

[1] F. Le Play, *L'Organisation de la Famille selon le vrai modèle signalé par l'histoire de toutes les races*, 1871. E. Demolins, *Les grandes routes des peuples. Comment la voute cree le type social*, 1901.

apply, they support the view that there is a general consistency or confluency of all social institutions at any particular time, that they affect and modify each other to the extent of achieving a certain uniformity. Thus it will be seen that later investigations arrive at conclusions agreeing with those of Spencer.

An important problem in connection with the environment not considered by Spencer is that dealing with the adaptation of different races to different areas, the problem of acclimatization and racial immunity to certain diseases. It is said that the Negro enjoys immunity from yellow fever which the white man does not, but is more prone than the white man to tuberculosis, respiratory diseases and leprosy. But work on this subject, of scientific value, is still proceeding, and only when we possess more knowledge will it be possible to evaluate the importance of the physical environment, and of man's adaptation to it. Scientific and medical discoveries are making it less difficult for the white man to adapt himself to life in tropical countries, and it is quite possible that in the future this difficulty will no longer exist.

Since Spencer's time, a great deal of progress has been made in what is now called Ecology, the study of habits and habitats, of the inter-relations and interconnectedness between the organic world and the inorganic world. The well-known correlation between the number of cats and spinsters in the countryside is a study in Ecology. Red clover depends on its fertilization upon humble-bees. The more humble-bees the more clover, the more clover the more field mice to eat the clover, the more field mice the more cats, and the more cats the more spinsters. Fluctuations in one factor lead to fluctuations in the others, resulting sooner or later in an equilibrium.

The application to human society of plant and animal ecology, the beginnings of which subjects we owe to Spencer, is a question for further research. Human ecology seeks to explain the symbiotic relationships between human beings and their human institutions and the physical and biological environment. Here, of course, human culture becomes all important for it affects population and institutions. At the moment no more than a vocabulary of human ecology exists ; American sociologists are attempting to draw up and delimit natural territorial groupings and zones of communal influence, and to show how under differing conditions of density and mobility, different spacial arrangements of institutions will arise.

Spencer's secondary or derived sets of factors, which social evolution itself brings into operation, demand attention, as they are the sociological factors proper, brought into being as the result of the inter-relations and the co-operation of men in Society.

First he mentions the progressive modifications of the environment, inorganic and organic, brought about by the action of societies. This was discussed among the external factors, for no sharp division can be made between the two sets of factors, as man differs from the animal world in not remaining passive to the environment but in moulding and changing it. So soon as primitive man donned skins of animals or tree-leaves against the cold he was changing the environment. Instead of being clay in its hands, he was the potter who fashioned the clay. As civilization advanced alterations in the climate were made by clearing and drainage. Here a rainy region was made less rainy by cutting down forests, or a swampy surface was made more salubrious by carrying off water. There forests may have been destroyed and a region, already dry, made arid. Plants useful and necessary to societies would be cultivated where weeds formerly grew, and better plants or even new varieties would be introduced. Noxious animals would be destroyed, and useful animals fostered. These effects Spencer saw clearly are not always beneficial in the long run, for the destruction of one species may bring other and greater evils as a result of the unchecked propagation of others. Here we come once more to ecology, and with greater knowledge we may be able to ward off such evils. "It needs but to think," Spencer writes, "of the immense contrast between a wolf-haunted forest or a boggy moor peopled with wild birds, and the fields covered with crops and flocks which eventually occupy the same area, to be reminded that the environment inorganic and organic of a society, undergoes a continuous transformation during the progress of the society; and that this transformation becomes an all-important secondary factory in social evolution."[1]

A second factor, and one to which Spencer attaches considerable importance, is the increasing size of the social aggregate. In his *Theory of Population,*

---

[1] *Principles of Sociology*, Vol. I, pp. 10–11.

1852, Spencer had already adopted a Malthusian attitude and argued that "from the beginning pressure of population has been the proximate cause of progress. It produced the original diffusion of the race. It compelled men to abandon predatory habits and take to agriculture. It led to the clearing of the earth's surface. It forced men into the social state ; made social organization inevitable ; and has developed the social sentiments. It has stimulated to progressive improvements in production, and to increased skill and intelligence. It is daily pressing us into closer contact and more mutually dependent relationships."[1] It has stocked the globe with people and made habitable almost every part, perfected processes for the satisfaction of human wants, and has developed the intellect and feelings. "Manifestly," he writes, "the wants of their redundant numbers constitute the only stimulus mankind have, to obtain more necessaries of life. Were not the demand beyond the supply, there would be no motive to increase the supply. And, manifestly, this excess of demand over supply is perennial : this pressure of population of which it is the index cannot be eluded."[2]

A consequence of increasing population is increasing density and a growing division of labour—"mass is both a condition to and a result of organization." Spencer, and Durkheim after him, makes division of labour an integral part of his sociological theory. He writes, "This constant increase of people beyond the means of subsistence causes, then, a never-ceasing requirement for skill, intelligence

---

[1] *Theory of Population*, 1852, p. 35.
[2] *Principles of Biology*, Vol. II, p. 526

and self-control—involves, therefore, a constant exercise of these and gradual growth of them."[1]

It is not certain that all migrations of early history were caused by the pressure of population. Some have been due purely to economic reasons such as the desire of plundering wealthy neighbours, and others to religious persecution. Moreover, the tendency towards over-population is denied by many authorities, who think that this tendency is to reach an optimum density, and that changes in the economic structure of society then occur and a new equilibrium is established. Over-population, therefore, may not be primary, but a consequence of other changes, generally of an economic nature. Like the physical environment, it is in the nature of a limiting condition, but much more elastic and variable. It is also conceivable that in the near future the problem will not be over-population, but under-population, if the prognostications of Bowley, Gini and Kuczynski are correct. Whether, when this phase of the population cycle is upon us, it will be possible to reverse the situation it is impossible to tell ; for the modern pattern of behaviour relating to the limitation of families has become so widespread and ingrained that it will be difficult to alter it.

Spencer himself inclined to such a view. He argued that if the excess of fertility was the cause of man's progress, only decline in fertility will now ensure further progress, which will be accompanied by an enhanced cost of Individuation, until the amount of life shall be the greatest possible and the

---

[1] *Principles of Biology*, Vol. II, pp. 526–527.

births and deaths the fewest possible. Ultimately, however, there must be a perfect equilibrium, and the pressure of population as it gradually finishes its work, must gradually bring itself to an end in the extinction of the total species.

Spencer developed a theory that an increase in fertility is caused by nutrition greatly in excess of expenditure of energy, and that a relative increase of expenditure, leaving a diminished surplus, reduces fertility. Mental labour, he points out, carried to excess, reduces fertility, and is shown in the fact that "most of the flat-chested girls who survive the pressure of their education are incompetent to bear a well-developed infant."[1] Modern peoples, since they are more complex and active, are less prolific than ancient peoples. The problem of differential fertility seems much more complex than was thought in Spencer's time owing to the researches that have been undertaken during the last half century, and that are still in progress. As regards the relationship between diet and fertility, recent discoveries go to show that certain vitamins are necessary in diet, and that a shortage of calcium in foods may lead to sterility. It may be necessary in the light of these discoveries to question Spencer's assumption that the fertility of modern man should be lower than that of primitive man.

A third factor is the reciprocal influence of the society and its units—the influence of the whole on the parts, and of the parts on the whole. " As soon as a combination of men acquires permanence, there begin actions and reactions between the community and each member of it, such that either affects the

---

[1] *Principles of Biology*, Vol. II, p. 513.

other in nature. The control exercised by the aggregate over its units tends ever to mould their activities and sentiments and ideas into congruity with social requirements ; and these activities, sentiments and ideas, in so far as they are changed by changing circumstances, tend to re-mould the society into a congruity with themselves. In addition therefore, to the original nature of the individuals and the original nature of the society they form we have to take into account the induced natures of the two. Eventually, mutual modification becomes a potent cause of the transformation in both."[1]

Spencer then pursues his usual course of giving physical analogies to illuminate this point : " Thus given the natures of the units, and the nature of the aggregate they compose is pre-determined. I say the nature—meaning, of course, the essential traits and not including the incidental. By the characters of the units are necessitated certain limits within which the characters of the aggregate must fall. The circumstances attending aggregation greatly modify the results ; but the truth here to be recognized is that these circumstances—in some cases, perhaps, preventing aggregation altogether, in other cases impeding it, in other cases facilitating it more or less—can never give to the aggregate characters that do not consist with the characters of the units. No favouring condition will enable the labourer to pile cannon-shot into a vertical wall ; no favouring conditions will make it possible for common salt, which crystallizes on the regular system, to crystallize like sulphate of soda, on the oblique prismatic system ; no favouring conditions will empower the

---

[1] *Principles of Sociology*, Vol. I, pp. 11–12.

fragment of a polype to take on the structure of a mollusk."[1]

This would imply that the original nature of man is fixed. But this he does not mean, for he writes, " If by altered circumstances such as those which continuous war or prolonged peace involve, some social structures are rendered inactive and dwindle, while others are brought into greater activity and grow, the natures of citizens are modified into congruity with them. While conversely, if changed modes of life change the characters of the citizens, their changed characters presently cause responsive changes in their institutions."[2] His discussion, therefore, relates to the different types of acquired responses that will result from different social environments.

Spencer's conception of the unit and of Society is thought by modern sociologists to need revision and revaluation. Spencer makes Society a mechanical collocation of units. Why do people concentrate at a certain place, or migrate ? Because of the law of least resistance. Do we wish to know the nature of law ? It is the consensus of individual interests. Do we seek to find the character of a Society ? It is the average of the moral character of its units. In addition to being a social organism, Society is also the sum of its parts.

Durkheim goes to the other extreme in postulating a social mind, and criticizes from his own point of view Spencer's conception of Society. De Greef has also pointed out that "if the social aggregates are only the larger and more complex images of the units

---

[1] *Study of Sociology*, p. 406.
[2] *Principles of Sociology*, Vol. I, p. 12.

that compose them, if social science is concerned only with the morphological or functional relations between the series of units and the resulting aggregates, it evidently follows that, although there are social phenomena, these are not markedly distinct from biological or psychological phenomena."[1] It should be added that on Spencer's theory of Society as a collocation of units, a crowd psychology such as has been developed by Tarde and Le Bon would be incomprehensible.

The fourth factor is the accumulation of superorganic products " which we commonly distinguish as artificial, but which, philosophically speaking, are no less natural than all other products of evolution."[2] These are the material products beginning with roughly shaped flints and ending in the complex automatic tools of an engine-factory driven by steam, which from huts of branches grow to towering skyscrapers. Then there is language developed to the point of expressing complicated ideas with precision. There must also be added writing and printing and knowledge comprised in the various sciences ; custom growing into law, ceremony and conduct, and established social sentiments ; the æsthetic products—" from necklaces of fish-bones we advance to dresses elaborate, gorgeous and infinitely varied ; out of discordant war-chants come symphonies and operas ; cairns develop into magnificent temples ; in place of caves with rude markings there arise at length galleries of paintings ; and the recital of a chief's deeds with mimetic accompaniments gives origin to epics, dramas, lyrics,

---

[1] Guillaume de la Greef, *Introduction à la Sociologie*, Pt. I, p. 19 2nd Ed. 1911.

[2] *Principles of Sociology*, Vol. I, p. 12.

and the vast mass of poetry, fiction, biography and history."[1]

Fifthly, should be mentioned the struggle between groups, a factor that is examined in some detail (see page 134 ff.) in dealing with political institutions. This factor of the struggle for existence between groups rather than between individuals, of natural selection and survival of the fittest groups, dominates Spencer's sociology. War, to him, is originally and almost exclusively an integrating force of the greatest social importance. Political development is determined by the struggle of group against group. Economic development is determined by man's struggle against nature.

All these factors, together with the primary and secondary factors, combine in variously complicated ways to bring about the process of social evolution. " The pre-established environing influences, inorganic and organic, which are at first almost unalterable become more and more altered by the actions of the evolving society. Simple growth of population brings into play fresh causes of transformation that are increasingly important. The influences which the society exerts on the natures of its units, and those which the units exert on the nature of the society incessantly co-operate in creating new elements. As societies progress in size and structure, they work on one another, now by their war struggles, and now by their industrial intercourse, profound metamorphoses. And the ever-accumulating, ever-complicating super-organic products, material and mental, constitute a further set of factors which become more and more influential causes of change. So that involved as the

---

[1] *Principles of Sociology*, Vol. I, p. 13.

factors are at the beginning, each step in advance increases the involution by adding factors which themselves grow more complex while they grow more powerful."[1]

A scientific sociology, Spencer realized, will not only disentangle the complexity of social causation and discover social uniformities and laws, but it will also attempt to predict and control the course of events. He saw that prevision is a necessary part of such a sociology. He writes: " In Geology, in Biology, in Psychology, most of the previsions are qualitative only ; and where they are quantitative their quantitativeness, never quite definite, is mostly very indefinite. Nevertheless, we unhesitatingly class these previsions as scientific. It is thus with Sociology. The phenomena it presents, involved in a higher degree than all others, are less than all others capable of precise treatment. Such of them as can be generalized, can be generalized only within wide limits of variation as to time and amount ; and there remain many that cannot be generalized. But so far as there can be generalization, and so far as there can be interpretation based on it, so far there can be science."[2] Spencer's view is endorsed by all modern sociologists. "Sociology, like all other natural sciences, aims at prediction and control based on an investigation of the nature of man and Society, and nature means here as elsewhere in science, just those aspects of life that are determined and predicted."[3]

The difficulties in the way of prediction and control must not, however, be minimized. Indeed, a scien-

[1] *Principles of Sociology*, Vol. I, p. 14.
[2] *Study of Sociology*, p. 45.
[3] R. E. Park and E. W. Burgess, *Introduction to the Science of Sociology*, p. 339.

tific sociology, an applied sociology, recall in this connection Spencer's well-known passage which it is worth quoting in full, although it was used by him in another connection. ("Against State interference.")—

"You see that this wrought iron plate is not quite flat: it sticks up a little here towards the left—'Cockles' as we say. How shall we flatten it? Obviously, you reply, by hitting down on the part that is prominent. Well here is a hammer, and I give the plate a blow as you advise. Harder you say. Still no effect. Another stroke? Well, there is one, and another and another. The prominence remains you see : the evil is as great as ever—greater indeed. But this is not all. Look at the warp which the plate has got near the opposite edge. Where it was flat before it is now curved. A pretty bungle we have made of it. Instead of curing the original defect, we have produced a second. Had we asked an artisan practised in planishing as it is called, he would have told us that no good was to be done, but only mischief by pitting down on the projecting part. He would have taught us how to give variously directed and specially adjusted blows with a hammer elsewhere : so attacking the evil not by direct but by indirect actions. The required process is less simple than you thought. Even a sheet of metal is not to be successfully dealt with after those common-sense methods in which you have so much confidence. What then shall we say about a society? 'Do you think I am easier to be played on than a pipe?' asks Hamlet. Is humanity more readily straightened than an iron plate?"[1]

---

[1] *Study of Sociology*, pp. 266–267.

BIBLIOGRAPHY. CHAPTER VIII.

ALLEE, W. E. *Animal Aggregations: A Study in General Sociology.* 1931.

ALLIER, RAOUL. *The Mind of the Savage.* 1929.

ALVERDES, F. *Social Life in the Animal World.* 1927.

BARTLETT, F. C. *Psychology and Primitive Culture.* 1928.

BOAS, F. *Mind of the Primitive Man.* 1912.

BOAS, FRANZ. *Anthropology and Modern Life.* 1929.

BRUHL, L. LÉVY-. *La mentalité primitive.* 1922.

BRUHL, L. LÉVY-. *L'âme primitive.* 1927.

BRUHL, L. LÉVY-. *Les fonctions mentales des sociétés inférieures.* 1910.

BRUNHÈS, JEAN. *Human Geography.* 1920.

BURGESS, E. W. *The Urban Community.* *See* papers on the Ecology of the City.

CASSIRER, E. *Philosophie der symbolischen Formen.* 2 vols. 1923–1925.

CLEMENT, F. E. *Plant Succession: An Analysis of the Development of Vegetation.* 1916.

DE LA BLACHE, VIDAL. *Le principes de géographie humaine.* 1922.

ELTON, C. S., Article: Ecology, in *Encyclopædia Britannica*, 14th ed.

GARTH, F. R. *Race Psychology.* 1931.

LEEUW, G. VAN DER. *La structure de la mentalité primitive.* 1928.

LEROY, O. *La raison primitive.* 1927.

MACKENZIE, R. D. Article: Ecology, in *Encyclopædia of Social Sciences.*

PREUSS, K. TH. *Die Geistige kultur der Naturvolker.* 1923.

PREUSS, K. TH. *Glauben und Mystik.* 1926.

RADIN, PAUL. *Social Anthropology.* 1932.

READ, CARVETH. *Origin of Man and His Superstitions.* 1930.

TARDE, G. *Laws of Imitation.* 1911.

THOMSON, SIR J. ARTHUR. *Darwinism and Human Life.* 1909.

TYLOR, SIR E. B. *Researches into the Early History of Mankind.* 1878.

VIERKANDT, A. *Naturvolker und Kulturvolker.* 1896.

WERNER, HANS. *Einfuhrung in die Entwicklungspsychologie.* 1926.

WUNDT, W. *Volkerpsychologie.* 10 vols. New ed. 1911–1920.

CHAPTER IX.

SOCIAL EVOLUTION.
(Integration and Differentiation.)

EARLY in the history of human speculation, the meaning of the eternal flux of things occupied the attention of philosophers, and systems of philosophy such as those of Democritus and Lucretius arose that attempted to explain phenomena by the unceasing motion of minute bodies or atoms, ever assembling, breaking up, and re-assuming innumerable forms and combinations. Sometimes emphasis was on the eternal forms of things, although the things themselves pass away, sometimes on the new things that arise in their stead, and sometimes on the origin of the things that have grown or come to be. The three main meanings of evolution thus trace back to early thought; it may mean persistence despite change, it may refer to the emergence of newness or novelty, and finally it may indicate an inquiry into origins.

The flux of things may also be regarded as irregular, chaotic and meaningless; it may be regarded as recurrent and cyclical in which life and death, youth and age, growth and decay perpetually succeed one another[1]; and lastly, it may be regarded as

---

[1] Spencer's law of rhythm is receiving much attention from those modern sociologists, such as Sorokin, who are attempting to discover cycles in social life and history. Spencer himself in his *First Principles* (pp. 240–242) points out that there are

exhibiting a definite trend in one direction. This meaning of a perpetual unilinear trend was in the 19th century new to human thought and was closely linked to the idea of progress. It received its full expression in Victorian times in the words of Tennyson :

> " For I doubt not through the ages an increasing
>   purpose runs,
> And the thoughts of men are widened with
>   the process of the suns."

Spencer belonged to the same optimistic era and change was to him definitely in one direction conforming to the universal law of evolution which governed the transition from the indefinite to the definite. In 1864 he conceived the great truth " that integration is a primary process and differentiation a secondary process ; and that thus while the formation of a coherent aggregate is the universal law of Evolution, the increase of heterogeneity, necessarily subsequent is but an almost universal trait, the one being unconditional the other conditional." " Evolution is an integration of matter, and concomitant dissipation of motion ; during which the matter passes from an indefinite, incoherent homogeneity to a definite coherent heterogeneity ; and during which the retained motion undergoes a parallel transformation."[1]

---

not wanting " evidences of mental undulations greater in length than any of these " (which he had just been considering). We continually hear of moods which recur at intervals. Many persons have their days of vivacity and days of depression. Others have periods of industry following periods of idleness ; and times at which particular subjects or tastes are cultivated with zeal, alternating with times at which they are neglected.

[1] *First Principles*, p. 396.

Ignoring for the present the metaphysical implications of the Spencerian conception of evolution,
let us consider its applicability to Sociology. The
problem is essentially the discovery of continuous
and causally connected changes both of a qualitative
and quantitative kind. In the first place, several
things become one, and one becomes several. In
the second place, there is a transition of the total
unconsolidated mass to a consolidated state. In
the third place, there is a similar transformation
in every portion of it so that each comes to have
a distinguishable individuality. And, finally, there
occurs a simultaneous increase of combination
among the parts. Bearing these four points in mind,
it will be well to examine Spencer's theory of social
evolution.

Societies like all other evolving aggregates " show
integration, both by simple increase of mass and by
coalescence and re-coalescence of *masses*. The
change from *homogeneity* to *heterogeneity* is multi-
tudinously exemplified ; up from the simple tribe,
alike in all parts, to the civilized nation full of
structural and functional unlikenesses. With progressing integration and heterogeneity goes increasing
coherence. We see the wandering group dispersing,
dividing, held together by no bonds ; the tribe with
parts made more coherent by subordination to a
dominant man ; the cluster of tribes united in a
political nexus under a chief with sub-chiefs and so
on up to the civilized nation, consolidated enough to
hold together for a thousand years or more. Simultaneously comes increasing *definiteness*. Social organization is at first vague ; advance brings settled
arrangements which grow slowly more precise ;

customs pass into laws, which while gaining fixity, also become more specific in their applications to varieties of actions ; and all institutions, at first confusedly intermingled, slowly separate at the same time that each within itself marks off more distinctly its component structures. Thus in all respects is fulfilled the formula of evolution. There is progress towards greater size, coherence, multiformity and definiteness."[1]

A number of points arise in this connection. Societies may pass from a state of incoherence to coherence, but what is important to know is the cause of this change. To Gumplowicz it was war, to Tarde imitation, to Durkheim division of labour. Societies show increasing definiteness and arrangements of parts, although Spencer does not include in his argument the possible effects of inventions, migrations or culture contacts which may be of such a nature as to disturb these arrangements. Again, societies not only become heterogeneous, but also homogeneous, especially when one language, one religion and similar customs come to prevail. It is interesting to note that while the individuals of Society become more and more differentiated as producers, they become more and more imitative as consumers. Social and technical inventions to which these results may be traced do not always introduce a greater degree of complexity. Sometimes they have a reverse and simplifying effect. Witness the social effects of " multiple " tea shops and stores and ready-made tailoring.

Spencer, considers that his evolutionary formula

---

[1] *Principles of Sociology*, Vol. I., p. 585.

in terms of integration and differentiation applies not only to societies, but to any social systems within societies. Political integration follows an increase of mass as a result of war, and the bodily and territorial annexation of conquered tribes. Political integration as it advances obliterates the original divisions among the united parts. Kinship ties disappear, local groups lose their separate organizations, and the old topographical boundaries are replaced by new administrative boundaries of a common organization. The subjugation of weak tribes by strong ones also involves the subjugation of their chiefs to a conquering chief. Combinations formed in this way are relatively permanent, and as we approach our own time, on a larger scale and more stable. Classes arise, and vassals become bound to their respective lords, groups of whom become subjected to higher ranks of lords, and these in turn to a king under whom there is an increase in consolidations. Within the state or nation a similar consolidating process occurs. " A civilized society is made unlike a savage tribe by the establishment of regulative classes—governmental, administrative, military, ecclesiastical, legal, etc., which, while they severally have their bonds of union, constituting them subclasses, are also held together as a general class by a certain community of privileges, of blood, of education, of intercourse. In some societies fully developed after their particular types, this consolidation into castes, and this union among the upper castes by separation from the lower, eventually grow very decided : to be afterwards rendered less decided only in cases of social metamorphosis caused by the industrial regime."[1] There is, further, a tendency to form alliances between groups, and for one government to exercise a restraining influence over another. " In the system of settling international arrangements by congresses, as well as in the weakening of commercial barriers and the increasing facilities of communication, we see the beginnings of a European federation, a still larger integration than any now established."[2]

As soon as there is some permanence of relation among the parts of the aggregate, political divisions arise. The first, Spencer teaches, was the division between the rulers and the ruled, that is, the men and the women. The next social differentiation is a slave class, and then a feudal class, with the military class at the apex of the social structure. A still greater superposition of ranks arises with militancy and conquest, and in time supreme power tends to become hereditary in one family. At the same time there arises a parallel species of government, that of religion which, at first closely associated with the civil government, later diverges. Religious and civil law, closely intertwined, separate. Having a common root with these and gradually diverging from them there is another controlling agency, that of manners or ceremonial usages. Each of these kinds of government is itself subject to successive differentiations. A highly complex political organization includes monarch, ministers, lords and commons, courts of justice, revenue offices and different degrees of local government. Complicated religious and ceremonial organizations also develop. " Moreover, it

---

[1] *First Principles*, p. 290.
[2] *Ibid.*, p. 290.

has to be observed that this increasing heterogeneity in the governmental appliances of each nation, has been accompanied by an increasing heterogeneity in the governmental appliances of different nations. All peoples are more or less unlike in their political systems and legislation, in their creeds and religious institutions, in their customs and ceremonial usages.[1]"

Industrial institutions also evolve according to the processes of integration and differentiation. There is the integration consequent on the growth of associated parts performing like functions as, for instance, the junction of Manchester with its calico weaving suburbs. Another kind of integration arises when, out of several places producing a particular commodity, one becomes dominant and absorbs the business of the others—instance the growth of Yorkshire cloth districts at the expense of those in West England. Still another kind of integration is that relating to the concentration of similar businesses in a certain quarter of the city, so that corn merchants will concentrate round Mark Lane, diamond merchants in Hatton Garden, and so on. Instead of fusion of parts, there may be fusion of functions seen, for instance, in the establishment of the Bankers' Clearing House and the Railway Clearing House ; of similar nature are the fusions of individuals pursuing the same profession, as in the institutes of architects, engineers, etc.

Differentiation occurs as soon as the mass of the community has been segregated into distinct classes : orders of workers, slave and caste divisions, guilds and associations of employers and employed. The original homogeneity of community interest

---

[1] *First Principles*, p. 317.

becomes split up and a class war is waged for the protection of class interests.

Economic processes likewise follow the above formula. " Political economists have long since described the industrial progress which through increasing division of labour, ends with a civilized community whose members perform different actions for one another ; and they have further pointed out the changes through which the solitary producer of any one commodity, is transformed into a combination of producers who, united under a master, take separate parts in the manufacture of such commodity. But there are yet other and higher phases of this advance from the homogeneous to the heterogeneous in the industrial organization of Society. Long after considerable progress has been made in the division of labour among the different classes of workers, there is relatively little division of labour among the widely separated parts of the community : the nation continues comparatively homogeneous in the respect that in each district the same occupations are pursued. But when roads and other means of transit become numerous and good, the different districts begin to assume different functions and to become mutually dependent. The calico manufacture locates itself in this country, the woollen manufacture in that ; silks are produced here, lace there ; stockings in one place, shoes in another ; pottery, hardware, cutlery come to have their special towns ; and ultimately every locality grows more or less distinguished, from the rest by the leading occupation carried on in it. Nay, more, this subdivision of functions shows itself not only among the different parts of the same nation, but among different nations.

That exchange of commodities which free trade promises so greatly to increase, will ultimately have the effect of specializing in a greater or less degree, the industry of each people."[1]

Spencer sums up the whole process thus—" So that beginning with a primitive tribe, almost if not quite homogeneous in the functions of its members, the progress has been, and still is, towards an economic aggregation of the whole human race ; growing ever more heterogeneous in respect of the separate functions assumed by the local sections of each nation, the separate functions assumed by the many kinds of producers in each place, and the separate functions assumed by the workers united in growing or making each commodity. And then, lastly, has to be named the vast organization of distributors, wholesale and retail, forming so conspicuous an element in our town populations, which is becoming ever more specialized in its structure."[2] The professions, too, manifest this elaborate specialization and each profession becomes subdivided again and again. The net result, is to make the members of Society more integrated and interdependent and to dovetail the economic processes within it so closely, that the destruction of one will inevitably react on the smooth working of the others. In other words, the formula of change from homogeneity to heterogeneity and increasing coherence applies both to industrial and economic processes. It is evident, for instance, in the functional specialization that has gone on throughout history, and the greater extent to which it has been carried in the present techno-

---

[1] *First Principles*, pp. 317–18.
[2] *Ibid.*, p. 318.

logical era.   Schmoller gives some interesting figures
bearing on this point :—[1]

Place.	Date.	Number of distinct occupations.
Ancient Rome	Early period	10–20
	Later period	150
Greece	337 A.D.	35
Frankfurt, Germany	1387	148
	1440	191
	1500	300
Germany	1882	4758

For 1920, the United States Census records
20,000 occupations classified into no less than 572
groups.

If by evolution is meant no more than a process
of integration and differentiation in the sense that
there is an increasing specialization of the institutions
of society, Spencer's formula holds both in regard
to societies and to the institutions within them that
we have examined.   Of course, by societies Spencer
does not mean every particular society, but the whole
complex of societies that make up humanity and
whose institutions, developing to different points
in different parts of the world taken in the aggregate,
show increasing integration and differentiation.
At the same time it is right to state that Spencer
did not think his formula applicable to the history of
every people and culture-area, and that he recognized
that retrogression has been as frequent as progression,
and that evolution does not imply an intrinsic

---

[1] G. Schmoller, " Die Thathsacen der Arbeitsteilung," *Jahrbuch fur Gesetzgebung, Verwaltung und Volkswirtschaft*, Vol. XIII, 1889, p. 1045.

tendency to become something higher.[1] He writes, " though taking the entire assemblage of societies evolution may be held inevitable as an ultimate effect of the co-operating factors, intrinsic and extrinsic, acting on them all through indefinite periods ; yet it cannot be held inevitable in each particular society, or even probable. A social organism like an individual organism comes into equilibrium with environing conditions ; and thereupon continues without further change of structure. When the conditions are changed meteorologically, or geologically, or by alterations in the Flora and Fauna, or by migration consequent on pressure of population, or by flight before usurping races, some change of social structure results. But this change does not necessarily imply advance. Often it is towards neither a higher nor a lower structure. Where the habitat entails modes of life that are inferior, degradation follows. Only occasionally does the new combination of factors produce a change constituting a step in social evolution, and initiating a social type which spreads and supplants inferior social types. And with these super-organic aggregates as with the organic aggregates progression in some causes retrogression in others. The more evolved societies drive the less-evolved societies into unfavourable habitats, and so entail on them decrease of size, or decay of structure or both."[2] It also deserves mention that Spencer's formula with its original terminology (integration, homogeneity, heterogeneity, coherence, and definiteness), when applied in his sociology and supplemented with a

---

[1] *Principles of Sociology*, Vol. I, p. 93.
[2] *Ibid.*, pp. 94–5.

wealth of factual research, is more than sufficient for his purpose. In discussing the evolution of political institutions, Spencer points to the main factors involved in their process, such as war, language, religion, and considers the conditions that favoured or hindered social growth and consolidation. Indeed, as regards political evolution, its description in terms of integration and differentiation still stands unassailable.

It is well known that in primitive groups there is very little class or social differentiation. There is a headman with restricted power, which grows only with the union of many groups into a tribe and with the growth of war. The headman may become a permanent war chief, or even a king, and his followers high officials and deputy chiefs. Tribes at this stage will be larger, more organized and differentiated. This tendency towards consolidation continues throughout early civilizations. The area of government tends to grow and with it the power of the monarch and the nobility. Even where the basis of the State is not only force and compulsion, but also some degree of consent on the part of the governed, this same tendency is to be observed. Thus tribes grow into nations and nations into empires.

Within the State there begins to be observed an increase in the number and variety of functional associations and institutions, and a greater diversity in the instruments of social communication such as roads, travelling conveyances, language. Especially clear is the development of justice as we ascend the social scale. Division of labour, class differentiation and economic interdependence increase. Slave economy gives way to serf economy, and this to free labour and a capitalist economy. The household economy decays and village and town economy grow up and ultimately a national economy. All these are different phases of a process of integration and differentiation. Spencer shows how many of these changes are results of increasing division of labour and the interdependence of functions within the group. He claims that just as in the embryo the contrast of parts are consequent upon the contrasted circumstances to which such parts are exposed, in the same way " adaptation of constitution to conditions is the principle which determines their primary changes, and that possibly if we include under the formula hereditarily transmitted adaptations, all subsequent differentiations may be similarly determined."[1]

Development along the lines of integration and differentiation is obviously a correlated process. The growth of the State and its functions is paralleled by the growth of industry, changes in political institutions by changes in industrial institutions. With the evolution of Society, language, religion, the arts and the sciences also evolve, and reflect the complexity of the former. Spencer saw more clearly than any other leading sociologist of his time that one of the tasks of sociology is the tracing of sequences and the marking of regular and orderly phases in social development. With his general theory of evolution and his formula of integration and differentiation, he paved the way for more specific studies into the development of society and its institutions.

---

[1] *Transcendental Physiology.* Essays, Vol. I, p. 102.

In the opinion of the author, Spencer's formula and his whole conception of evolution, gain considerably in value if some qualifications, some of which Spencer himself saw, are borne in mind. In the first place the formula must exclude unilinear development. Although Spencer, in his analysis of domestic institutions, saw an orderly development from promiscuity to monogamy, he rejected completely the economic sequence of hunting, pastoral and agricultural stages. He also saw clearly that intermediate states can be skipped, as where one country or colony will take over full-fledged the political institutions of the mother country. It is unfortunate that Spencer's very logical manner of exposition tends to emphasize the mistaken view that a uniform repetition of sequences was applicable both in the case of any particular society or any institution.

In the second place, a limit must be set to every social process or line of development. They must not be regarded as Spencer sometimes regards them, as limitless and perpetual. Take, for instance, differentiation and the division of labour. Modern economists are agreed that, other things remaining equal, the division of labour beyond a certain point is uneconomical and unlikely to take place. " When I tried to interest him," writes Beatrice Webb, " in the law of increasing heterogeneity and definiteness in structure and function at work—so the philosopher demonstrated throughout the universe, my father answered in this wise : ' Words, my dear, mere words. Experience tells me that some businesses grow diverse and complicated, others get simpler and more uniform, others, again, go into the bankruptcy court. In the long run and over the whole field, there is no more reason for expecting one process than another."[1]

With such a limitless conception it was natural for Spencer to envisage world-wide free trade and perpetual peace, although his foreboding in this connexion must not be forgotten.

Thirdly, evolution in the sense of descent with modifications must not be confused with evolution connoting an inquiry into origins. Spencer traces genetic affinities where they do not appear to exist. The origin of government he finds in the original and universal subjugation of woman by man. Women were the ruled, men the rulers; the origin of religion he discovers in ghost worship, and from these foundations he derives elaborate sequences.

Fourthly, the formula must not be unduly widened, or else it loses its explanatory value. One sweeping formula that embraces Matter, Life, Mind and Man can hardly be a satisfactory one in the present state of knowledge. For what is there in common between the evolution of the solar system in terms of force and motion and the evolution of a social system, between the evolution of a biological process and an economic process. Spencer's apparently mechanical categories give a semblance of simplicity to his evolutionism, although it requires for its comprehension as much concentrated thought as he devoted to it.

Fifthly, the criteria of evolution as given by Spencer may not hold in all cases. Social development may take place on the basis of integration and differentiation, but there is no evidence that all

[1] *My Apprenticeship*, Beatrice Webb, 1926, p. 24.

social processes exhibit increasing complexity in the course of evolution. Indeed there is evidence of some simplification, as in language and possibly religion.

Sixthly, Spencer's exposition of evolution takes but little account of the human factor. Evolution in his hands is naturally mechanical and self-motivating, endowed with perpetual motion. Social processes in societies must, however, according to modern students, have some reference to the human needs of individuals. Political institutions are largely dependent on conscious planning and formulation, and to an increasing extent conscious purpose and control enter into social evolution.

Seventhly, Spencer's evolution is a matter of equilibration, rest and motion, a series of quantitative changes only. He ignores the qualitative aspects of evolution and its immanent movement. He does not recognize the inner activity of evolution ; he only sees outer forces working themselves out in mechanical formulæ as a result of conflict and collision.

And, finally, Spencer associates progress with evolution. People who have evolved a more elaborate and complex system of institutions are better fitted to survive than those who live in a primitive society. To Spencer everything that has evolved is to the good, and everything is to the good that has evolved. This point will be discussed in the next chapter, for the confusion or identification of evolution and progress has been a great obstacle to clear sociological thought.

With these qualifications in mind, let us now turn to Spencer's treatment of the evolution and development of the products of the human mind, of culture and its main divisions, religion, language, science and art.

Integration in religion, says Spencer, is seen in the increase of mass—here meaning ghosts—so that as Society grows there is a multiplication of supernatural beings. Along with this increase of mass there goes an increase in coherence, and the originally vague beliefs come to be elaborated into a well-knit system (mythology). At the same time this supernatural aggregate increases in heterogeneity. Ghosts become differentiated into good, bad, friendly and malicious, and afterwards become modelled on the hierarchy of social ranks on earth, each god or demon possessing its special function. Finally, there is a change from the indefinite to the definite, the different kinds of deities grow more defined in their forms, dispositions, powers, habitats, and their attributes become distinguishable, specific and precise, all in accordance with Spencer's well-known formula.

Of religion taken as a whole, such a description may be applied if we do not read into this development a sequence of simple and uniform stages. Spencer, as we saw in another chapter (see pp. 187-210), should not have attributed a genetic relationship to all the different elements of religion, or built his explanation of religion on a foundation of ghost-worship. But the process of religious integration was much more complicated. It is comparable to the confluence of many separate streams into a river whose course is winding and irregular. Its main feature is not coherence or complexity—in a sense, it is less complex now—but its continuity from dim and remote beginnings. It is continuous in the sense that mankind is continuous. And its unification is closely connected with the unification that goes on in politics, economic organization and intellectual progress.

An analogous process is seen in the evolution of language, and as Spencer points out, its integrations are reflections of other integrations going on in Society (*e.g.*, the study of semantics). He shows, that parallel to the formation of higher languages out of lower, there goes progressive integration which reduces the polysyllables to dissyllables and monosyllables (*e.g.*, the coalescence of God be with you into Goodbye). A similar process is true of all grammatical development—in the number of subordinate propositions which accompany the principal one in the various complements to subjects and predicates ; and in the numerous qualifying clauses, so that sentences in modern languages show a remarkable degree of integration. Differentiation takes place in the gradual multiplication of parts of speech from a few primary ones, in the differentiation of verbs into active and passive, of nouns into abstract and concrete, in the rise of mood, tense, person, of number and case, in the formation of auxiliary verbs, of adjectives, adverbs, pronouns, prepositions, articles. Words of allied meaning are likewise differentiated, and languages consisting of hundreds of thousands of distinct words come into existence. Moreover, the same differentiation over the earth's surface which led to the differentiation of the race, simultaneously led to a differentiation of their speech. Thus the progress of language conforms to the general law in the evolution of languages, of families of words, and of parts of speech.

Here is a good example of an evolving human product. Spencer's criterion of complexity in languages is not now accepted by modern students, as many simple languages are seen to be as complex as the languages of to-day. Most philologists, such as Sapir, Vendryes, Jespersen, Meillet and Delacroix are agreed that the varieties of language are descended from a few main groups, and that each language has a tendency to pass from a flexional construction to a non-flexional one. The processes of differentiation and integration are met with clearly here in the enormous number of dialects giving way to a uniform pronounciation or even being displaced by one language. Like religion, language must be related to the people who speak it, if its development is to be understood, and the various political and social changes that they are undergoing.

Spencer finally applies his formula to science and art. Science has become, Spencer shows, highly integrated not only in the sense that each division is made up of mutually dependent propositions, but in the sense that the several divisions are mutually dependent—cannot carry on their respective investigations without aid from one another. On its practical side there has been a great advance in inventions and in the construction of huge and ingenious machines.

As evidence of the development of art, Spencer believed we have but to contrast the mural decorations of the Egyptians and Assyrians with modern historical paintings, which he thought were superior. Integration may be seen in the development of simple music into the elaboration of the oratorio, and in comparing the simple tales of the East with our

modern romances. Art began to be differentiated when mural decorations developed in to painting
sculpture and writing; and from the rhythm in
sound, speech and motion there arose music, poetry
and dancing.   The development of Literature,
Science, Architecture, the Drama and Dress, all alike
show that "from the remotest past which Science can
fathom up to the novelties of yesterday, an essential
trait of Evolution has been the transformation of the
homogeneous into the heterogeneous."[1]

The trait of complexity would be extremely difficult to apply to art in general, though for science it
seems more applicable.   This does not seem to be
essential in this development.   What seems to be
essential is the continuity of growth.   But ups and
downs have occurred and as regards art Spencer's
theory of the rhythm of all motion and the consequent progress and retrogression, seems to be better
founded.   Rhythms or cycles of styles are said
to mark prehistoric art.   Should these cycles be
regarded as spiral in nature, development in the
Spencerian sense is probable.   Spencer was however,
inclined to think in terms of dissolution in antithesis
to evolution.   Integration and differentiation are
processes marking the ascending cycle of history.
Then the descent begins and dissolution and decay
break up what evolution had slowly consolidated.

To sum up : what may be said of Spencer's formula of evolution ?   It has been shown above
that many modifications of it are necessary if
this concept is to be retained in sociology.   And yet
that it should be retained can hardly be doubted.
Spencer's formula does describe, even when it does

---

[1] *First Principles*, p. 331.

not explain, social processes as modern sociologists view them developing historically. Its application, moreover, is supported by much inductive investigation and by careful analysis of the causes that tended towards social integration and differentiation. His formula must, therefore, be regarded as a construction into which social processes can be fitted. It does not, however, place any impediment in the way of a modern student carefully investigating and unravelling the set of causal factors that are operative in any particular case.

When we leave the field of sociology, and give Spencer's law a cosmic setting applicable to every thing and process within it, the formula cannot be applied to include within its compass the description of any process. Its explanatory value does not yield in advance guidance for the understanding of a process. Once a process is completed it is quite easy to fit it into a formula. But while a social process is continuing or has begun, how will the formula help us to understand it ? Can Spencer's formula be applied deductively to predict any case in detail. The measured opinion of Royce is that " Spencer's theory of evolution does not determine the relations of the essential processes of evolution to one another, does not define their inner unity and does not enable us to conceive a series of types of evolutionary processes in orderly relations to one another."[1] " Spencer," he goes on to say, " appears as a philosopher of beautiful logical naïveté. Generalization was an absolutely simple affair to him. If you find a bag big enough to hold all the facts, that was a unification of the

---

[1] Josiah Royce, *Herbert Spencer*, 1904, p. 116.

sciences."[1] " Spencer's formula," writes Bergson, " consists in cutting up present reality already evolved, into little bits no less evolved, and then recomposing it with these fragments, thus positing in advance everything that is to be explained."[2] Spencer, maintains Bowne, was apt to confuse logical classification with genetic order—a confusion that leaves its impress on his sociology. Competent authorities maintain that the implications of the second law of thermodynamics are in exact opposition to Spencer's theory of increasing heterogeneity. They imply diminishing heterogeneity and ultimate uniformity—a dead level in the universe.

Spencer's theory at the hands of biologists has fared no better. Thomson says that " a general criticism must be made that Spencer thought of the germ-cell much too simply. It is a microcosm full of intricacy ; the nucleus is often exceedingly definite and coherent ; the early cells are often from the first defined, with prospective values which do not change. The fertilized ovum has only apparent simplicity ; it has a complex individualized organization often visible. No one can doubt that development is progressive differentiation, but is rather a realization of complex inheritance of materialized potentialities than a change from an incoherent, indefinite homogeneity to a coherent, definite heterogeneity."[3] But, in justice to Spencer it should be pointed out that he had not the advantages of modern discovery enjoyed by Thomson.

To make this concept more fruitful in sociology,

---

[1] Josiah Royce, *Herbert Spencer*, 1904, p. 115.
[2] H. Bergson, *Creative Evolution*, 1911, p. xiv.
[3] J. A. Thomson. *Herbert Spencer*, 1906, pp. 114–115.

it is necessary that criteria other than those given by Spencer must be determined. Complexity is not a fundamental characteristic, for it does not apply to all social processes. It may apply to the money-economy of to-day, but it does not apply to language or religion. It is the same with heterogeneity. Nor does the concept necessarily imply a development from a lower to a higher phase, for what is lower and what is higher has to be defined. This is not necessarily a hopeless task—it is one that a comprehensive sociology must attempt. What it does seem to imply is something persisting yet changing, something the same yet containing within it seeds of emergence or novelty. In biology a like process occurs when a new species or variety is produced, and in chemistry when new entities are produced from a smaller number of entities.[1]

That human evolution has taken place, whether it occurs immanently or not, is no more to be doubted than that biological evolution has taken place. What remain in doubt are the causes of evolution. In biology a number of theories have been postulated such as Lamarckianism, Natural Selection, and the Mutation theory. The explanations offered in connection with social evolution are worthy of some enquiry.

To discuss these adequately is impossible within the scope of the present essay, but certain aspects may be touched upon. Spencer's standpoint is liable to alter in differing circumstances, and although he

---

[1] For an exhaustive analysis of the concept of evolution in Sociology the reader should turn to Morris Ginsberg's essay on The Concept of Evolution in *Studies in Sociology*. The analysis involves a consideration of immanent causality that cannot be adequately dealt with in this short sketch.

sharply criticized Comte for finding the key of social development in Ideas, he adopted a position not very dissimilar, and argued that feelings to which ideas serve only as guides are the prime movers of social life. He writes—"Practically the popular character and the social state determine what ideas shall be current ; instead of the current ideas determining the social state and the character. The modification of men's moral natures, caused by the continuous discipline of social life, which adapts them more and more to social relations, is therefore the chief proximate cause of social progress."[1] Spencer elsewhere emphasizes the material environment and adopts what almost approaches an economic interpretation of social life.

Both Spencer's and Comte's conceptions were, on the whole, static in so far as they regarded evolution as a process of change by inviolable laws. Spencer, who embraced the universe in his law of evolution, assumed that everyone would see and appreciate its novel and emergent qualities. All phases of development were subsumed by him under a mechanism which made identical the evolution of the universe, of the solar system, of societies and of man.

A notable advance on this conception of evolution was made by Hegel. To Hegel the conflict of opposites was evolution. He argued that the juxtaposition of thesis and antithesis in the mind necessarily produced an interpenetration of the two opposites and their resolution in the synthesis. Evolution was of this nature, and its function was to reveal the material embodiment, with which

---

[1] *Social Statics*, 1st Ed., Chap. XXX.

the Idea clothes itself in all development. In man it takes on its highest expression and achieves freedom and self-consciousness. Evolution thus proceeds according to an immutable law, and progress or a tendency to higher and still higher forms of life was an inherent tendency in it.

Such a tendency, immanent in nature, was rejected by Marx and Engels who, accepting and refining Hegel's doctrines, regarded development as a process resulting from the inherent contradictions not in ideas but in the material world. Development they did not regard as an automatic process as Spencer did, but as a process bound up with human beings, with social classes. The evolution of human society and of its institutions were not the result of changes in men's ideas, but were the result of the changes in material conditions under which men live, and of their property relationships ; and these changes were neither good nor bad, but were neces-sary consequences of the negation within the social system, which must sooner or later destroy and transform it. Development thus proceeds gradually until a certain point is reached, at which evolution becomes revolution.

Some of these conceptions will be found useful in discussing social progress. Spencer like many other great thinkers before and after him regarded history as a whole and as a process of change and impermanence ; he recognized that all the pheno-mena of nature, man and Society are interrelated, and he was the first to realize the importance of tracing connections among all those historic processes that constitute social evolution. He saw, as Hegel and Marx did also, the urgency of formulating stages and trends of social development. And that when such a formulation has been achieved, sociology will be able to indulge in social prevision, and make social control and guidance its main task. Sociology must not only explain Society—it must also change it.

BIBLIOGRAPHY. CHAPTER IX.

CONN, H. W.   *Social Heredity and Social Evolution.*   1914.

COOLEY, C. H.   *Social Process.*   1918.

COOLEY, C. H.   *Social Organization.*   1922.

GEDDES, P., and A. J. THOMSON.   *Evolution.*   1912.

KELLER, A. G.   *Societal Evolution.*   1918.

KIDD, B.   *Social Evolution.*   1895.

MORGAN, T. H.   *The Scientific Basis of Evolution.*   1932.

NORTH, C. S.   *Social Differentiation.*   1926.

PATTEN, W.   *The Grand Strategy of Evolution.*   1920.

ROYCE, J.   *Herbert Spencer.*   1904.

CHAPTER X.

SOCIAL PROGRESS.

THE identification of progress with evolution seems so palpable a confusion to a generation that has witnessed the terrors of a world war, and the anxieties of a world peace, that it seems difficult to understand how it ever arose. And yet we have only to think of the complacency of the early Victorian era, of the stupendous industrial changes, of the astounding scientific discoveries, of the rapid spread of popular education and of the striking social changes in every other department of life, to realize how natural this identification was. Science, whose promulgations were considered absolute, gave the sanction of its authority to the union of progress with evolution. It was forgotten that evolution was an ethically neutral concept, and that the transformation of science into social philosophy, of the evolution of ethics into the ethics of evolution, was fraught with great danger. And, in fact, an aftermath of disillusionment soon followed, and progress was dismissed as an illusion—a tragic illusion. Civilization itself, through immanent decay of the " Weltgeist " was rapidly passing to its doom—a doom that neither the will nor the energy of the people could prevent. Fatalism, mysticism, political quietism found their apotheosis in Oswald Spengler.[1]

The theory of evolution and Darwin's unravelling of its causal agencies and exposition of the way they operated, gave the stamp of scientific finality to evolution's claim that it was progress. Darwin himself, with all his caution and reserve, subscribed to this view. Was not evolution through natural selection ever tending to produce better-adapted organisms, was there not a survival of the fittest ? But to Spencer who coined the expression, "survival of the fittest," perhaps more than to anybody else, was due the wide acceptance of this belief. He made evolution, to him synonymous with progress, an integral element in the intellectual climate of his time. He gave evolution not merely a biological setting but a cosmic setting, and unfolded the vast panorama of universal evolution in so simple and lucid a manner that no more satisfactory an explanation could be imagined. Everything was henceforth to be explained in terms of evolution. But Spencer did more than this. He made evolution automatic and inherently progressive. Independent of men's volitions, evolution was tending to higher and still higher forms of life. Was there not at the beginning a vast chaos of dissipated motion and diffused matter, and had it not evolved a solar system, a terrestrial globe, plants, animals, and the crowning glory of all—man ? Who could dispute so convincing an argument ? It is true that philosophers like Schopenhauer and von Hartmann did not accept this valuation, but their philosophy was one of pessimism and therefore unpopular. Progress, advance,

---

[1] O. Spencer, *The Decline of the West*, 2 Vols., 1928.

betterment, optimism, all implied in evolution, harmonized with the material comforts and intellectual tendencies of the times, and were eagerly accepted as true. Moreover, the notion of evolution as a perpetual trend forward in time, was psychologically important because it is in the future that man projects his hopes and wishes, and it is from the future that he expects fulfilment. Fears lie with the future, but then they are never so vivid and urgent as our hopes and desires. Spencer's evolution with its ideal of ultimate perfection and happiness, became the embodiment of a universal wish-fulfilment.

" Progress " declared Spencer, " is not an accident, but a necessity. Instead of civilization being artificial, it is a part of nature ; all of a piece with the development of an embryo or the unfolding of a flower."[1] Progress " is not a thing within human control, but a beneficent necessity."[2] He is convinced that ultimately evil will disappear and that absolute perfectibility will be the lot of man. He envisages a mighty movement towards perfection, an inherent sufficiency in things that subordinates in its universality all petty irregularities and fallings-back, just as the curvature of the earth subordinates mountains and valleys.

But on no account, says Spencer, must this conception be regarded as teleological, thus forsaking his earlier teleological views. " Rightly to understand progress, we must learn the nature of these changes considered apart from our interests."[3]

---

[1] *Social Statics*, p. 30.
[2] *Progress, Its Law and Cause*. Essays, Vol. I, p. 60.
[3] *Ibid.*, p. 9.

The notion of progress as consisting in a greater quantity and variety of articles required for satisfying men's wants, in greater security of person and property, in widening freedom of action, Spencer does not accept as true. Progress consists rather in those changes of structure in the social organism which have entailed these consequences. We must leave out the concomitants and beneficial consequences, he says, and ask what progress is in itself.

What are those changes of structure in the social organism ? It was shown in the last chapter that they were broadly the processes of integration and differentiation involved in evolution, both of animate or inanimate nature. But progress has also another distinguishing feature—adaptation or the continuous adjustment of organisms to environment. Concerning this doctrine, a biological rather than a sociological conception, Spencer writes, " Continuous adaptation was insisted on as holding of all organisms and mental faculties as well as bodily. For this adaptation, the first cause assigned was the increase and decrease of structure consequent upon increase or decrease of function, and the second cause assigned was the killing off or dying out of individuals least adapted to the requirements of their lives. The ideally moral state was identified with complete adjustment of constitution to conditions, and the fundamental requirement, alike ethical and practical, was represented as being the rigorous maintenance of the conditions to harmonious social co-operation, with the certainty that human nature will gradually be moulded to fit them."[1] This process of adaptation can be subsumed under the processes of integration

---

[1] *Autobiography*, Vol. II, p. 8.

and differentiation, for it involves increasing complexity of structure.

Spencer's position involved a number of contradictions. If progress implies increasing complexity of structure, adaptation need not always be a necessary consequence. There may be a change of conditions such that the successful adaptation could only take place through simplification of structure. Again, both man and microbe are equally well adapted to their environments, but to a biochemist both will be equally complex structures. And finally it may be asked, is the best adapted type necessarily the "highest"? Biological adaptation, it is now believed, is not the simple matter Spencer assumed. It is true that organisms fit themselves to their environment, but the environment is as much fitted to the organisms as the organisms to the environment. The relationship is reciprocal.[1]

Social progress to Spencer is thus a question of complexity, adaptation and natural selection. These Spencer regards as only the concomitants of progress, but it must be admitted that he sometimes refers to them as factors of progress. That progress is automatic and inherent in the cosmos and in every part of it, is evident when we examine the products of social evolution. In all cases they are accompanied by these concomitants. Societies have increased in mass, size and heterogeneity; industrial institutions in division of labour and interdependence ; political institutions in coherence, definiteness, growing decentralization and industrialism. Mental operations have become

---

[1] L. J. Henderson, *The Fitness of the Environment*, 1927. See also L. M. Bristol, *Social Adaptation*, 1915.

more complex and are therefore indicative of mental progress. Increasing adjustment of actions to ends points to moral progress. Religious progress may be observed in the fact that religious institutions and functions have become more complex (although doctrine has become simplified). Lastly, the greater " aggregate of thought, feeling and action " and the finer adjustment to ever increasing complex social situations and conditions are eloquent proofs that the individual, too, has made progress.

All these are necessary consequences of the changes in the structure of the social organism, and in some way they all result from the primary cosmic process of equilibration. This conception of progress is not teleological, Spencer says, and yet it is remarkable how closely its concomitants fit in with Spencer's philosophical leanings. But what avails all this progress, for when societies are no more antagonistic to each other, and the individual is perfectly adjusted to society, evolution will cease, and with it progress, and the cycle of existence will have to begin anew.

In later years Spencer came to see more clearly the difficulties implied in his conception of progress. It suggested automatic, inevitable and continuous progress and a fatalistic belief that all was best in the best of all possible worlds, when left to the blind working out of cosmic and social processes. It implied laissez-faire, and intervention and interference whether by the individual or society were useless and harmful. Struggle, natural selection and ruthless competition in social life were the best guarantees of progress, so long as they did not interfere with those natural laws according to which man had evolved. And, finally, it implied inactivity, fatalism, mysticism.

" The Moving Finger writes and having writ
  Moves on ; nor all thy piety nor wit,
  Shall lure it back to cancel half a line
  Nor all they tears wash out a word of it."

These implications Spencer saw. But instead of rejecting his earlier views of progress, he tried to give it a different interpretation. He writes, " The conception of evolution at large, as it exists in those who are aware that evolution includes much more than ' natural selection,' involves the belief that from the beginning it goes on irresistibly and unconsciously . . . The conception of evolution at large, thus far correct, is by some extended to that highest form of evolution exhibited in societies. It is supposed that societies, too, passively evolve apart from any conscious agency ; and the inference is that according to the evolutionary doctrine, it is needless for individuals to have any care about progress, since progress will take care of itself." And Spencer goes on to say, " Now suppose that some one argued that since, in the order of nature, continuance of the species was thus provided for, no one need do anything towards furthering the process by marrying ? . . . Yet absurd as he would be, he could not be more absurd than the one who supposed that the higher phases of social evolution would come without the activity of those sympathetic feelings in men which are the factors of them—or rather, he would not be more absurd than one who supposed that this is implied by the doctrine of evolution."[1]

[1] *Social Evolution and Social Duty. Various Fragments*, pp. 119–122.

This example is not quite appropriate, for if the perpetuation of the species was " in the order of nature " there would be no need for marrying. In any case marriage is such a complex social institution that it cannot be equated with its biological analogue of mating. What becomes evident from Spencer's quotation is that social evolution cannot mean the same thing as biological evolution, and that it has little if anything in common with cosmic evolution. Social evolution must take into account human beings, endowed with intelligence and purpose, who may alter its course instead of being guided by it. Because of intelligence, human adaptation is not always so passive as Spencer imagined, but is also active. Man is not only modified by the environment ; he also modifies it.

Spencer's admission was however too late to check the widespread belief to which he had give currency that social progress meant automatic progress. The biological school of sociologists popularized this belief. Gumplowicz was opposed to all legislation that could hasten or retard social development, which according to him followed its own laws. Novicow criticized State interference as an attempt to defeat the law of the survival of the fittest. Sumner glorified the class struggle because it tended to eliminate the social defectives and assure victory to the middle class, the sound bulwark of every society. The economics of capitalism found full justification in these theories which showed that *laissez-faire* in social life is a necessary parallel of the struggle for existence in biological life.

It was left to a contemporary of Spencer to show how conflicting all these theories were. In 1893,

Huxley delivered a memorable address on " Evolution and Ethics " in which he argued " that social progress means a checking of the cosmic process at every step and a substitution for it of another, which may be called the ethical process ; the end of which is not the survival of those who happen to be the fittest in respect of the whole of the conditions which exist, but of those who are ethically the best."[1] " Let it be understood," he said, " once for all, that the ethical progress of Society depends not on imitating the cosmic process, still less in running away from it but in combating it."[2] He went on to show that the qualities needed for the maintenance of social life were not biological qualities which ensure survival in the biological world. " In place of ruthless self-assertion it demands self-restraint ; in place of thrusting aside or treading down all competitors it requires that the individual shall not merely respect but shall help his fellows : its influence is directed not so much to the survival of the fittest as to the fitting of as many as possible to survival. It repudiates the gladiatorial theory of existence. It demands that each man who enters into enjoyment of the advantages of a policy, shall be mindful of his debt to those who have laboriously constructed it : and shall take heed that no act of his weakens the fabric in which he has been permitted to live. Laws and moral precepts are directed to the end of curbing the cosmic process and reminding the individual of his duty to the community, to the protection and

---

[1] T. H. Huxley, *Evolution and Ethics. The Romanes Lecture,* 1893, p. 33.
[2] *Ibid.,* pp. 31–34.

influence of which if not existence itself, at least the life of something better than a brutal savage."[1]

Huxley himself did not attempt to resolve this antithesis between cosmic and ethical evolution. But he made it perfectly clear that the principle of natural selection has no moral value whatever and that the cosmic process and the "horticultural process," cosmic evolution and social evolution are two different processes, in essence antagonistic to each other. Huxley's position is important, because he sowed seeds of dissension between progress and evolution that ultimately led to their divorce.

At this point, let us take up the idea of progress before it was united by Darwin and Spencer to evolution. This idea, as Bury has shown, is a comparative newcomer in human thought. It is closely bound up with the development of modern science, with the growth of rationalism, with the struggle for religious and political liberty, and with rapid economic and commercial transformation. To this last factor, Bury does not give sufficient weight. The idea of progress is intimately associated with the rise of modern capitalism, because for the first time in history, the possibility arose that man may become master over that nature which had so long tyrannized over him. By inventing machines to do his bidding and to satisfy all his requirements, man would be enabled to develop his higher potentialities, and escape the deadening drudgery of perpetual labour. In Bodin, Bacon and Descartes the idea of progress found

[1] T. H. Huxley, *Evolution and Ethics. The Romanes Lecture,* 1893, pp. 33–34.

[2] J. B. Bury, *The Idea of Progress,* 1920. *See* also W. R. Inge, *The Idea of Progress. The Romanes Lecture,* 1920.

eloquent expression. Fontenelle admitted intellectual progress but was sceptical as regards to moral progress. It was the Abbé de St. Pierre who gave it an unlimited and universal character and extended it to morals, man and Society, knowledge and science. The French encyclopædists, realizing the revolutionary significance of the idea, enthusiastically adopted it, and used it with deadly effect against the political and social evils of their time. Through Godwin and Shelley the idea became incorporated into philosophical anarchism, and through Charles Fourier, St. Simon and Robert Owen into utopian socialism. Comte made it a regulative principle in sociology and indeed it is pivotal in his writings, where progress meant the triumph of a scientific and positivistic over a theological and metaphysical outlook. Marx transformed the idea and showed that the control of nature, which was its pith and essence, and which was a reality for a few, could be made a reality for the many. History, he added, sets humanity only such tasks as it can achieve.

Man's control over nature, or at any rate the possibility of controlling nature is a common element in all these varied notions of progress, for it is evident that without this material basis the other desirable goals of life cannot be attained. What these are, may be left over for the moment. That such control has indeed increased since the beginning of history and that especially significant are the material achievements of the last few centuries can hardly be doubted. It is possible to trace a continuous development in technique from the crude pottery and iron of primitive times to the steamships, trains and aeroplanes, television, surgery and wireless of to-day. A like development probably holds of language, writing, printing and many other activities of human life, with the possible exception perhaps of some arts and some products of creative imagination, such as sculpture, painting, literature and oratory where consistent and continuous advance would be difficult to determine. Thus as regards control over nature, and if no more than that is claimed, an unanswerable case can be made out for progress.

This discussion has revealed, so far, two important principles that should be taken into account in building up a comprehensive theory of progress. The first principle is that progress cannot be something automatic but is something that is sustained by the efforts and volitions of men. The second principle is the possibility of man controlling and dominating nature.

A third and the most important principle arises when we go back to Huxley's distinction between cosmic and ethical evolution. It may be asked how far does material progress conform to the ethical standards man has set himself. The problem of ethical valuation arises, because in the final analysis progress is a question of ethics, of what people think there ought to be instead of what is. It cannot be denied that what people will consider good and right at any given moment will influence the course of social events at that moment, much in the same way as social events influence people's ethical conceptions. In so far therefore as an actual evolutionary trend is in accordance with certain ethical criteria, such a process will be progressive in the fullest sense of the word. So we are brought back to Spencer, whose wide generalizations gave rise to the subsequent studies of which the gist has been given.

These problems did not arise with Spencer, for evolution was to him inherently progressive and good. Whatever has evolved, he argued, was necessarily good. As Spencer grew older he reconciled himself to many institutions he disliked because he now recognized their beneficent necessity. Thus, in spite of his dislike of priesthoods and organized religion, Spencer writes—" Contemplating Ecclesiastical Institutions at large, apart from the particular cults associated with them, we have then, to recognize the fact that their presence in all societies which have made considerable progress, and their immense predominance in those early societies which reached relatively high stages of civilization, verify inductively the deductive conclusion, that they have been indispensable components of social structures from the beginning down to the present time : groups in which they did not arise having failed to develop.''[1]

Of the institution of slavery he writes—" Considered as a form of industrial regulation slavery has been natural to early stages of conflicts and consolidations. While all the native males in each society were devoted to war, there was great need for the labour of prisoners to supplement that of women. The institution became under such conditions, a necessity; for manifestly, other things being equal,

---

[1] *Principles of Sociology*, Vol. III : Ecclesiastical Institutions., pp. 148-149.

a people whose men were all warriors and who used their captives as producers, would have an advantage over a people who either killed their captives, or did not use them as producers. A society which had a slave-commissariat would, other things equal, survive in conflicts with a society which had no such commissariat."[1]

That the problem of ethical valuation has to be faced is evident when we recollect that the control man possesses over nature may be used for his own destruction, or for increasing human misery and unhappiness. Social life is so complex that the introduction of a partial good, let us say a motor-car, may have unforeseen bad effects upon the totality of social life. Their ultimate consequences and trend would have to be evaluated, and partial developments reconciled. It is probably true to say as a generalization, that all luxuries contain an element of danger. Freud is possibly right in his thesis that on the one hand " Love opposes the interests of culture, on the other hand culture menaces love with grievous restrictions."[2] If this conflict be inevitable or incapable of solution, and if it be true that *le genre humain n'est pas placé entre le bon et le mal, mais entre le mal et le pire*, there must be a weighing and balancing of partial goods, in so far as they contribute to the general good.

Progress thus seems to be a question which only a comparative sociology in conjunction with a social philosophy can answer. It is admittedly very difficult, but not necessarily impossible to determine whether progress has taken place.

---

[1] *Principles of Sociology*, Vol. II, p. 470.
[2] S. Freud, *Civilization and Its Discontents*, 1930, p. 12.

For while it is true that there is confusion and violent disagreement on mediate ends and on the means to be adapted to achieve ultimate ends, there is a large measure of agreement among thinkers on the matter. From this point of view, therefore, taking extensive periods of time, it may be possible to ascertain the trends of history. And for this reason the concept of progress, has a place in sociology. It is, in fact, possible to observe in many processes of history, the development of something of value for social life, which, however incomplete and partial, can be assimilated to the wider idea of progress.

This is in essence the meaning of the following conceptions of social progress gathered from sources contemporary with and subsequent to Spencer. Comte saw progress in the lessening superstition and increasing rationalism in life; Giddings in the amelioration of biological conflict between the individual and the race; Ratzenhofer in the substitution of co-operation for conflict; and Lester Ward in an increase of human happiness through the conquest of ignorance. Ward put emphasis on social telesis, on social purpose as characteristic of human societies, and developed a theory in which spontaneous progress gives way to telic progress, and individual telesis to social telesis. To Mackenzie social progress consists in : (1) The control of natural forces by human agency ; (2) the control of the individuals by the communal spirit ; (3) self-control.[1] J. A. Thomson defines

---

[1] See also G. Spiller, *The Origin and Nature of Man*, 1931, p. 240, for definitions of Progress. and A. J. Todd, *Theories of Social Progress*, 1918.

progress as " balanced movement of a social whole towards the fuller embodiment of the supreme values, and at the same time a more all-round realization of the physical and biological pre-conditions, namely, the health and wealth which secure stability." Fiske maintains that the " funda-mental characteristic of social progress is the con-tinuous weakening of selfishness and the continuous strengthening of sympathy."[1]

The most comprehensive account of the meaning, nature and conditions of social progress is to be found in the sociological teachings of Hobhouse, who realized that Spencer was right in premising that the first requisite was a social morphology, a classification of societies, institutions and beliefs, and these subjects occupied a large part of his life's work. The second, was to effect a transition from morphology to development. This necessitated the drawing up of certain criteria, of a non-ethical nature, and these were to Hobhouse : (1) scale ; (2) efficiency ; (3) freedom ; (4) mutuality.

By scale Hobhouse meant the number of popula-tion ; by efficiency the adequate co-ordination of means to an end, whatever the end may be ; by freedom, scope for thought, character and initiative ; and by mutuality, service of an end in which each who serves participates. Since it is obvious that the attainment by a community of one criterion may conflict for a while with the attain-ment of another, as when an increase in size may involve more subordination and less mutuality, all the criteria must be taken together if development

[1] J. A. Fiske, *Outlines of Cosmic Philosophy*, 1874, Vol. II, p. 92.

is to be complete and harmonious. He recognizes that in reality development has been partial and one-sided. " History on every side presents us not with a balanced movement towards the full development of communal life, but with a diverse multitude of partial advances and countervailing losses, which spell eventual arrests, retrogression and decay."[1] But taken broadly, Hobhouse concludes, communities may be said to exhibit a general advance as judged by these criteria, when we review their development from early times to the present day.

Hobhouse then establishes a parallel and broad correlation between social development as measured by these criteria and the growth of mind. Here too, morphology was succeeded by tracing of lines of development and the method adopted was to mark out certain phases in cultural development. These were : (1) stage of dependence upon nature where animistic and magic notions predominate ; (2) stage of proto-science ; (3) stage of reflection in the later east ; (4) stage of cultural reflection ; (5) stage of experiential reconstruction, where the nature of thought and the theory of knowledge are investigated. He arrived at the conclusion that there is orthogenic evolution consisting in the advance of mind.

Finally, Hobhouse seeks to determine the relation between development as thus measured and standards of ethical valuation, and to answer the question whether such development satisfies ethical criteria of value. He argues that it does, for " social

---

[1] *Social Development*, 1924, p. 84.

development thus conceived corresponds in its concrete entirety to the requirements of rational ethics. For a rational ethics starting with the web of human impulses is forced to discard those which are blind and contradictory."[1] and retain as reasonable those only which form a consistent whole.

" Thus social development," he continues, " and ethical development are in the end the same. They have a common goal. But it does not follow that they coincide all along the line of their advance, still less that the process of history can be treated as the continuous working out of an ethical idea. There is plenty and to spare in the historic process that cannot be regarded as development from either point of view, but merely as relapse, backsliding, disintegration or downfall. What is more serious the four conditions of social development which to satisfy ethical requirements must be united, may in actual operation fall apart, so that we may get what is undoubtedly a social development in one direction, along with arrest or even retrogression in another."[2] On the whole, however, the tendency is for these contradictions to be overcome. But they can only be overcome by conscious purpose directed to the common good. Progress to Hobhouse is not as it was to Spencer, something automatic, but something that depended upon human thought and will. Here again it will be seen that Hobhouse's later studies and conclusions owed an immense debt to Spencer, whose writings had led Hobhouse to draw inferences that would have

---

[1] *Social Development*, 1924, p. 88.
[2] *Ibid.*, p. 89.

seemed impossible to Spencer with his ideas of automatic evolution.

Hobhouse also avoided the fallacies of the early evolutionists, and saw clearly that social development does not proceed from one centre, but from many which converge and part and reconverge. He writes, " that it does not move with the assured sweep of a planet in its orbit on a mechanically determined curve. Neither does it resemble the inevitable unfolding of a germ through predetermined stages with harmonious correlation of parts to an assigned maturity of type. It more nearly resembles a series of efforts to grapple with an obstacle the nature of which is only half understood, and which in consequence when forced to yield at one point returns at another.[1]

But even in Hobhouse's scheme of correlation, valuable as it is, there are difficulties which weaken his conclusions. It may be asked, in the first place, whether his non-ethical criteria have completely avoided an ethical implication. Hobhouse derives these criteria from the nature of organic development, and as such they are ethically neutral. But can they be brought into social development without losing their neutrality ? Mutuality and freedom, for instance, refer to scope for thought, initiative, and character and are not these ethical in nature ? In the second place, there is the difficulty of obtaining a satisfactory morphology, a problem which as we saw elsewhere is not easy to solve (Chap. III). And, finally, there is the difficulty of passing from morphology to development. But these are difficulties

---

[1] *Social Development*, pp. 305-306.

that will beset any investigator in this field.   It is a striking fact that other sociologists from the time of Spencer, such as Ward and Oppenheimer, with opinions and social philosophies very different from Hobhouse's, arrive at conclusions not dissimilar from Spencer's.   All are agreed that social progress involves " a large area of peaceful relationship, a diversity of functions and organizations, which give more scope for the expression of a variety of human nature which increases the economy of effort, and in some degree liberates men from fixed irrational views of human destiny.'"[1]   And, once again, Spencer's original work in this respect, is shown to have been the basis of all enquiries and studies of the period that has elapsed since his death.

Hobhouse's treatment of social development is the most thoroughgoing that has been undertaken, and the reader should turn to his works.   Whatever validity attaches to his conclusions, it cannot be gainsaid, that as regards methodology he offers the hope that the problem of progress is not altogether beyond solution.   Hobhouse, in opposition to Spencer, shows that progress is not an automatic process, but rests on human energy and thought. He shows that the line of thought traced by Bury in his book on progress is significant in that it does envisage a self-directing humanity, capable of controlling the material foundations of life, and developing in accordance with clear-sighted purposes of its own choice.   " There can be no real test of the possibility of progress through conscious effort " he writes, " until the effort is made."[2]

---

[1] R. M. MacIver, *Society and Its Structure and Changes,*1931, p. 421.
[2] *Social Development*, 1924, p. 334.

And finally Hobhouse observes that although it is true that humanity is actually absorbed in partial and conflicting aims in " propounding to it an ideal as really good, we are at once stimulating the will and maintaining that because our ideal is valid it will be found in the long run to appeal to it. It will conquer all ideals, because they will at some point contradict themselves, while that which is valid will appeal to an infinity of points, and all of these will be found at least to lead to the same centre."[1] He does not ask for a different human nature, or new qualities in man. But he does ask that those very qualities, devotion, heroism, endurance, sacrifice and resolution, manifested in such a cataclysm as the world war, be applied not for destruction but for creation. And this is only possible with clear purpose and unified will, and in a social system in which these qualities will have full scope.

---

[1] *Ibid.*, p. 339.

BIBLIOGRAPHY. CHAPTER X.

BURY, J. B. *The Idea of Progress.* 1920.

DAVIS, JEROME. *Contemporary Social Movements.* 1930.

FREUD, S. *Civilization and Its Discontents.* 1930.

HERTZLER, J. O. *Social Progress.* 1928.

HOBHOUSE, L. T. *Social Development.* 1924.

INGE, W. R. *The Idea of Progress.* 1920.

TODD, A. J. *Theories of Social Progress.* 1930.

WILSON, W. D. *Culture and Progress.* 1930.

CONCLUSION.

THE more distinctive features of Spencer's sociology were well summarized by Giddings and approved by Spencer himself.[1] They were as follows :—

1. " Societies are organisms, or they are super-organic products.

2. " Between societies and environing bodies, as between other finite aggregates in nature, there is an equilibration of energy. There is equilibration between society and society, between one social group and another, between one social class and another.

3. " Equilibration between society and society, and between societies and their environment, takes the form of a struggle for existence among societies. Conflict becomes an habitual activity of Society.

4. " In this struggle for existence, fear of the living and of the dead arise. Fear of the living, supplementing conflict becomes the root of political control. Fear of the dead becomes the root of religious control.

5. " Organized and directed by political and religious control, habitual conflict becomes militarism. Militarism moulds character and conduct and social organization into fitness for habitual warfare.

---

[1] F. H. Giddings, *Studies in the Theory of Human Society*, 1922, pp. 113–114.

6. "Militarism combines small groups into larger ones, these into larger and yet larger ones. It achieves social integration. This process widens the area within which an increasingly large proportion of the population is habitually at peace and industrially employed.

7. "Habitual peace and industry moulds character, conduct and social organization into fitness for peaceful, friendly, and sympathetic life.

8. "In the peaceful type of Society, coercion diminishes, spontaneity and individual initiative increase. Social organization becomes plastic and individuals moving freely from place to place change their social relations without destroying social cohesion, the elements of which are sympathy and knowledge in place of primitive force.

9. "The change from militarism to industrialism depends upon the extent of the equilibrium of energy, between any given society and its neighbouring societies, and between the societies of any given race, and those of other races, between societies in general, and its physical environment. Peaceful industrialism cannot finally be established until the equilibrium of nations and races is established.

10. "In societies as in other finite aggregates the extent of differentiation, and the total complexity of all evolutionary processes depend upon the rate at which integration proceeds. The slower the rate the more complete and satisfactory is the evolution."

This summary must not be regarded as more than a bare statement, a scant framework of Spencer's sociological system. It is necessary to go to the completed building—to his own writing—to realize its architectural splendours and the skill with which it was constructed. Giddings mentions the struggle for existence, and the military and industrial types of society as Spencer's distinctive contributions to sociology. But as we have shown, it is to other aspects and elements of Spencer's thought that we must turn, if we wish to make a correct appraisement of his work, and of its value for contemporary sociology.

To sum up : throughout this brief sketch it has been our aim to give a balanced and adequate account of Spencer's sociology, emphasizing its permanent contributions and indicating some of the defects which later investigations have shown it to possess. It would have been miraculous indeed if any system of sociology were beyond improvement. We have criticized in the light of recent knowledge some of Spencer's miscalculations, but have also tried to show that these do not in any fundamental manner detract from his claim to have been the first in this country to present in broad outline a science of Society whose foundations still stand firm. Let us now consider in general terms both these aspects.

Spencer's high position as a sociologist was due to his realization of what a science of Society implied, although later developments show that his treatment of the subject did not cover the whole ground. Actually his sociology is mostly ethnology. In his search for origins, Spencer concentrated on primitive peoples because his scheme was to trace all developments (even those of the present day) back to origins. He does not appear to have studied very closely contemporary institutions and sociological problems, although he did issue volumes on

English and French civilizations in the *Descriptive Sociology* series. His sociology was descriptive rather than functional, and dealt more with structure than with process. He appears on occasion to have overlooked or acted in contradiction to his own methodological cautions, and found genetic affinities where none existed, and traced sequences of unilinear stages from data that did not permit it. He read little as a result of bad health, and had to depend on the results obtained by other investigators. Many of the doctrines which were the outcome of his deep meditations were to him original conceptions and discoveries, albeit they had already been deduced quite independently by other investigators. Nevertheless, they were genuinely original. He was compelled to rely on data gathered for him by the scholars he employed, and perhaps did not see the danger of abstracting facts from their context. Facts were just facts to him, and if they fitted into a theory so much the better. His emphasis on biology and the social organism, directed sociology for a generation into researches upon organismic speculations and socio-biological theories, and his spiritual heirs, Novicow, Lillienfeld, Schäffle and Worms, have not added any appreciable contribution to the results of Spencer's own conclusions. Two streams of thought derive from Spencer ; an individualism that saw in the struggle for existence its regulative principle for social life—and an absolutism and totalitarianism that found their justification in the theory of the social organism. But Spencer must not altogether be blamed for this heritage. It harmonized too well with the social and economic circumstances of his time and with the optimism of buoyant capitalism.

Spencer's theory of sociology was a distinct advance upon that of Comte. He exhibits a skilful application of ethnological data and the comparative method, and inspired both in his methods and results Durkheim in France, Hobhouse in England, Albion Small, Sumner and Giddings in the United States, and Wiese, Oppenheimer, Schmoller and Müller-Lyer in Germany. Spencer's outline of the scope and aims of sociology is marked by unity and coherence as indeed would be expected of a philosopher of Spencer's eminence as a thinker, and of what should truly constitute a science of Society. He emphasized the super-organic character of Society, but by his individualistic bias opposed the unit to the mass, the individual to Society. He saw clearly the close dependence of sociology on psychology, and also on history. He was one of the first, if not the very first, to point out the need for a comparative psychology, and drew up a very important syllabus of this subject. Unlike previous sociologists, he did not use that amorphous term Society, but spoke of societies, and framed a classification of societies and a social morphology, which is absolutely essential to a scientific sociology. His analysis of domestic, political, industrial and religious institutions abounds in apposite observations and illustrations. He showed the importance of the economic factor in shaping their development, and he sought correlations between institutions at any given time, and between them and types of Society. " He taught me to look upon all institutions exactly as if they were plants or animals—things that could be observed, classified and explained, and the action of which could to some extent be foretold if we knew enough about them," writes Beatrice Webb.[1] Spencer included in his investigation the psychological actions of Society upon individuals and of individuals upon Society, and revealed the psychological forces that maintain both family authority and state authority. He stressed the infinite variety and complexity of manners and customs, and urged further investigation into customs, morals, ceremony and law. The complexity of social causation and of the factors entering into social processes were analysed. His discussions of social evolution and social progress may, in the light of later studies, need qualification and modification, but they constitute a starting point for more comprehensive studies than he was able within the limits of his enquiries to devote to them. And, finally, Spencer outlined laws of social development, for without them he recognized that prevision is impossible.

Spencer's place in sociology remains unassailed in spite of recent developments in philosophic thought, although it should be borne in mind that the conclusions now deemed to be final may quite possibly be much modified by future philosophers. He saw sociology as a whole—a science encompassing every phase of human thought and activity. He combined encyclopædic knowledge with powers of synthesis and analysis that are unrivalled, and a great ability for clear and lucid exposition. His abilities were recognized by his greatest opponents, and the literature of sociology abounds in generous tributes to his genius. Marshall the English economist, and Ferri the Italian sociologist praise

---

[1] Beatrice Webb, *My Apprenticeship*, 1926, p. 38.

his universal scope ; René Worms the French sociologist regarded the *Principles* as the greatest synthesis sociological thought had produced ; Koval- evsky and Mikhailovsky, the Russian sociologists, acknowledge his seminal influence on human thought ; and Schäffle praises his colossal scientific knowledge and consistent mechanistic interpretation of the universe.   Philosophers also join in tribute to him. Höffding writes of him that " even if old problems reappear in new forms after they have passed through the purging fire of the evolutionary philo- sophy, his extension of the psychological horizon, and the proof which he adduces that the concept of evolution is the leading concept in all specialized investigation does not lose its significance."[1]   Pringle- Pattison declares that " it was much to hold aloft in an age of specialism the banner of completely unified knowledge . . . the idea of knowledge as a coherent whole, worked out on purely natural (though not therefore naturalistic) principles, a whole in which all the facts of human experience should be included—this was a great idea with which to familiarize the minds of his contemporaries. It is the living germ of philosophy itself."[2]

To this task Spencer devoted himself and aban- doned in early life a promising career as an engineer in order to pursue his ideal.   When he had completed his System of Synthetic Philosophy after 50 years of concentration, he wrote—" though along with other deterrents, many relapses, now lasting for

---

[1] H. Höffding, *The History of Modern Philosophy*, Vol. II, 1900, p. 456.

[2] A. S. Pringle-Pattison, *The Life and Philosophy of Herbert Spencer*, *The Quarterly Review*, Vol. 200, 1904. pp. 240-267.

many weeks, now for months and once for years, often made me despair of reaching the end, yet at length the end is reached. Doubtless in earlier days some exultation would have resulted ; but as age creeps on feelings weaken, and now my chief pleasure is my emancipation. Still there is satisfaction in the consciousness that losses, discouragements and shattered health have not prevented me from fulfilling the purpose of my life."[1] Noble, modest and brave words amply justified.

It is remarkable that although Spencer had a tremendous influence in Germany, France, Russia, Japan and the United States, and his works were translated into almost every language in the world, his influence in England was never, during his lifetime properly appreciated. This is probably due to the fact that Spencer was not a university man and never held an academic position. The universities in general were hostile to him and to his teaching, which they regarded as naturalistic and materialistic—a dangerous solvent to the rigidity of ancient beliefs, tradition and religion. Only late in life did the universities offer him recognition—honours and degrees which, by that time, meant nothing to him. The effect upon the development of sociology in this country was unfortunate, for had his merit been recognized as it deserved, the study of this science would be much more widespread than it is. It is largely due to Hobhouse, in direct line of descent from Spencer, that sociology is once again coming to its own, although in this connection the attitude of the older univer-

---

[1] *Principles of Sociology*, Vol. III, Preface.

sities is still to be deplored.[1]   Rarely is a man a prophet in his own country, and it is on the Continent and in the United States that his memory and his pioneer work in sociology are honoured and perpetuated.

At the beginning of this brief sketch and throughout this essay Spencer's sociology has been compared to an imposing edifice advisedly, in order to indicate partly its mechanical construction, and partly its solidity, power and strength. We have now examined its general architecture, penetrated into some of its splendid halls, glanced here and there at some of its furniture and attempted to climb some of the tortuous and winding staircases that led from his sociology to his other elaborate structures. We have seen that although not every room was habitable, the building has stood well the test of time, and many of its features deserve to be re-explored and re-embodied in present-day Sociology. The analogy at this point breaks down. Buildings are sooner or later demolished. But it is not so with the buildings of the mind. They are reconstructed but never destroyed. Sociology will build wisely if it continues to work on the foundations and framework devised by Spencer.

---

[1] Although the first chair in Sociology in England held by Hobhouse, was instituted in 1906, Spencer had urged its establishment as early as 1880. He writes " I had an interview with Lord Derby for the purpose of enlisting his sympathies in favour of a professorship of Sociology which I want to get established at Liverpool . . . . It seems, however, he has settled that it is to have a chair for Natural History so that my hope that he would at my instigation establish a chair of Sociology is balked . . ." (David Duncan, *Life and Letters of Herbert Spencer.* 1908, p. 211.)

APPENDIX.

PROSPECTUS OF A SYSTEM OF PHILOSOPHY ISSUED BY HERBERT SPENCER IN 1858.

FIRST PRINCIPLES.

PART I. *The Unknowable.*—Carrying a step further the doctrine put into shape by Hamilton and Mansel; pointing out the various directions in which Science leads to the same conclusions; and showing that in this united belief in an Absolute that transcends not only human knowledge but human conception, lies the only possible reconciliation of Science and Religion.

II. *Laws of the Knowable.*—A statement of the ultimate principles discernible throughout all manifestations of the Absolute—those highest generalizations now being disclosed by Science which are severally true not of one class of phenomena but of *all* classes of phenomena; and which are thus the keys to all classes of phenomena.

In logical order should here come the application of these First Principles to Inorganic Nature. But this great division it is proposed to pass over: partly because, even without it, the scheme is too extensive; and partly because the interpretation of Organic Nature after the proposed method, is of more immediate importance. The second work of the series will therefore be :—

THE PRINCIPLES OF BIOLOGY.

VOL. I.

PART I. *The Data of Biology.*—Including those general truths of Physics and Chemistry with which rational Biology must set out.

II. *The Inductions of Biology.*—A statement of the leading generalizations which Naturalists, Physiologists, and Comparative Anatomists, have established.

III. *The Evolution of Life.*—Concerning the speculation commonly known as " The Development Hypothesis "—its *à priori* and *à posteriori* evidences.

VOL. II.

IV. *Morphological Development.*—Pointing out the relations that are everywhere traceable between organic forms and the average of the various forces to which they are subject ; and seeking in the cumulative effects of such forces a theory of the forms.

V. *Physiological Development.*—The progressive differentiation of functions similarly traced ; and similarly interpreted as consequent upon the exposure of different parts of organisms to different sets of conditions.

VI. *The Laws of Multiplication.*—Generalizations respecting the rates of reproduction of the various classes of plants and animals ; followed by an attempt to show the dependence of these variations upon certain necessary causes.

THE PRINCIPLES OF PSYCHOLOGY.

Vol. I.

PART I. *The Data of Psychology.*—Treating of the general connections of Mind and Life and their relations to other modes of the Unknowable.

II. *The Inductions of Psychology.*—A digest of such generalizations respecting mental phenomena as have already been empirically established.

III. *General Synthesis.*—A republication, with additional chapters, of the same part in the already-published Principles of Psychology.

IV. *Special Synthesis.*—A republication, with extensive revisions and additions, of the same part, etc., etc.

V. *Physical Synthesis.*—An attempt to show the manner in which the succession of states of consciousness conforms to a certain fundamental law of nervous action that follows from the First Principles laid down at the outset.

Vol. II.

VI. *Special Analysis.*—As at present published, but further elaborated by some additional chapters.

VII. *General Analysis.*—As at present published, with several explanations and additions.

VIII. *Corollaries.*—Consisting in part of a number of derivative principles which form a necessary introduction to Sociology.

THE PRINCIPLES OF SOCIOLOGY.

Vol. I.

PART I. *The Data of Sociology.*—A statement of the several sets of factors entering into social phenomena—human ideas and feelings considered in their necessary order of evolution ; surrounding natural conditions ; and those ever complicating conditions to which Society itself gives origin.

II. *The Inductions of Sociology.*—General facts, structural and functional, as gathered from a survey of Societies and their changes : in other words, the empirical generalizations that are arrived at by comparing, different societies, and successive phases of the same society.

III. *Political Organization.*—The evolution of governments, general and local, as determined by natural causes ; their several types and metamorphoses ; their increasing complexity and specialization ; and the progressive limitation of their functions.

Vol. II

IV. *Ecclesiastical Organization.*—Tracing the differentiation of religious government from secular ; its successive complications and the multiplication of sects ; the growth and continued modification of religious ideas, as caused by advancing knowledge and changing moral character ; and the gradual reconciliation of these ideas with the truths of abstract science.

V. *Ceremonial Organization.*—The natural history of that third kind of government which, having a common root with the others, and slowly becoming separate from and supplementary to them, serves to regulate the minor actions of life.

VI. *Industrial Organization.*—The development of productive and distributive agencies, considered, like the foregoing, in its necessary causes : comprehending not only the progressive division of labour, and the increasing complexity of each industrial agency, but also the successive forms of industrial government as passing through like phases with political government.

VOL. III.

VII. *Lingual Progress.*—The evolution of Languages regarded as a psychological process deter mined by social conditions.

VIII. *Intellectual Progress.*—Treated from the same point of view : including the growth of classifications ; the evolution of science out of common knowledge ; the advance from qualitative to quantitative prevision, from the indefinite to the definite, and from the concrete to the abstract.

IX. *Æsthetic Progress.*—The Fine Arts similarly dealt with : tracing their gradual differentiation from primitive institutions and from each other ; their increasing varieties of development ; and their advance in reality of expression and superiority of aim.

X. *Moral Progress.*—Exhibiting the genesis of the slow emotional modifications which human nature undergoes in its adaptation to the social state.

XI. *The Consensus.*—Treating of the necessary interdependence of structures and of functions in each type of society, and in the successive phases of social development.

THE PRINCIPLES OF MORALITY.

VOL. I.

PART I. *The Data of Morality.*—Generalizations furnished by Biology, Psychology, and Sociology, which underlie a true theory of right living : in other words, the elements of that equilibrium between constitution and conditions of existence which is at once the moral ideal and the limit towards which we are progressing.

II. *The Inductions of Morality.*—Those empirically-established rules of human action which are registered as essential laws by all civilized nations : that is to say—the generalizations of expediency.

III. *Personal Morals.*—The principles of private conduct—physical, intellectual, moral, and religious —that follow from the conditions to complete individual life : or, what is the same thing—those modes of private action which must result from the eventual equilibration of internal desires and external needs.

VOL. II.

IV. *Justice.*—The mutual limitations of men's actions necessitated by their co-existence as units of a society—limitations, the perfect observance of which constitutes that state of equilibrium forming the goal of political progress.

V. *Negative Beneficence.*—Those secondary limitations, similarly necessitated, which, though less important and not cognizable by law, are yet requisite to prevent mutual destruction of happiness in various indirect ways : in other words—those minor self-restraints dictated by what may be called passive sympathy.

VI. *Positive Beneficence.*—Comprehending all modes of conduct, dictated by active sympathy, which imply pleasure in giving pleasure—modes of conduct that social adaptation has induced and must render ever more general ; and which, in becoming universal, must fill to the full the possible measure of human happiness.

BIBLIOGRAPHY OF HERBERT SPENCER.

Introductory Note.

The compilation of an exhaustive bibliography on Spencer and his writings would involve laborious research in almost every language and in every famous national library—in China, Japan and South America as well as in Europe and in the United States. For Spencer impressed not only his age, but different peoples and cultures, and his philosophy radiated beyond his own country and became incorporated into the thought of other lands.

If one may judge by books on Spencer and his philosophy—books which are legion—and by the numerous translations of his works, a detailed study of the influence of Spencer on the intellectual outlook of his time would disclose an astonishing chapter in the history of culture and thought. Astonishing, because there is no parallel case of a philospher who became so integral a part of his period, and whose teaching became so widely diffused. Spencer's influence on literature alone is a topic that would well repay investigation. Is not Jack London, in American literature, a striking example of Spencerian thought ? And is not the Russian literature of the time dominated by Spencer's philosophy ?

There were present, it is clear, certain conditions that facilitated the rapid diffusion of Spencer's philosophy. Not only did Spencer's philosophy harmonize with the buoyant economic individualism of his period, but it grew up in a soil that was fertile with the achievements of democracy—with widespread reading, writing and discussion. For the first time since the philosophical synthesis of ancient Greece, there was presented to a public anxious and eager to understand it a clear and consistent explanation of the universe. Spencer's theory of evolution, which explained the Cosmos and everything in it so convincingly and so simply, won widespread recognition. To Spencer and to Darwin more than to anyone else of that period are due the present scientific and naturalistic interpretation of the universe.

One indication of Spencer's growing influence was to be seen in the numerous translations of his works that began to appear as early as 1865, and in the many books that were written attacking, defending or modifying Spencer's views. Russia, it seems, was the first country to translate Spencer—and with a thoroughness that did not omit even the " Descriptive Sociology." Such translations were no easy task, for in Russia the authorities looked with suspicion on Spencer's doctrines. As late as 1903 we are told of a student who, " on being examined for admission to the University, was charged with being a Socialist on the ground that he had been seen in the street at the age of 15 with Spencer's Sociology under his arm." France, Germany, Italy, Spain and the rest of Europe quickly followed. Then came translations into Chinese and Japanese and into the chief Indian languages. " Education," one of Spencer's most popular works, was even translated into Arabic and Mohawk. In Japan, Spencer's influence was very pronounced and in 1873 and in 1891, Spencer was consulted by eminent Japanese personages on the reorganization of Japanese institutions. An Indian, it is to be noted, founded the Herbert Spencer lectureship at Oxford.

Another indication of Spencer's influence, especially in Europe, may be seen from the academic and scientific honours that were conferred upon Spencer, most of which were declined. In 1876, he was elected to membership of the Reale Academia dei Lincei, Rome ; in 1880, a correspondent of the Royal Academy of Science, Turin ; and in 1882, of the Royal Society of Naples. In 1888, the University of Bologna conferred upon him the degree of Doctor of Philosophy and Letters ; in 1895 the Royal Lombardian Institute, Milan, elected him a member, and in 1896 the Associazione Educativa Spenceriana, Rome, Honorary President.

France followed Italy, and in 1883 the Institut de France made him a correspondent ; and in 1885 the Society of Physiological Psychology in Paris. Spain showed her appreciation by electing him to an honorary Professorship of the Institucion Libre de Enzeñanza in Madrid in 1883, and in 1895, Germany honoured him with the Royal Order " Pour le mérite."

Many other countries too elected Spencer to membership or Fellowship—in 1883 the American Philosophical Society, Philadelphia ; in 1889 the Royal Danish Academy ; in 1891 the Royal Academy of Belgium ; in 1892 the Scientific Society of

Athens ; in 1895 the Imperial Academy of Vienna ; in 1897 the Psychological Society of Moscow. In 1896 the University of Buda-Pesth conferred upon him a doctorate.

This bibliography does not pretend to be exhaustive ; indeed, the time allowed to the compiler has been much too short to enable him to indicate every important book and article that has been published in every language. It is, nevertheless, the first bibliography on Spencer and is comprehensive both in the languages represented and in subject-matter, and should be of great service to the student who wishes to pursue more intensively Spencer's works.

In English alone there is a vast Spencer literature, and it is believed that every book of importance in this language and in French, German, Italian, Spanish and some of the minor European languages has been included. Unfortunately, the compiler could not trace many Russian books, and Japanese and Chinese are not represented at all. Not every book mentioned in the bibliography is important, but it has been thought desirable to include some books not of outstanding value, but still interesting, as showing how wide was Spencer's appeal. There have also been included books which, though not strictly on Spencer, are useful for the understanding of his thought.

So far as possible, full details of each book (name of author, date and place of publication, pagination, etc.) are given. For the convenience of the student the books are classified under the following headings :—

1. Bibliography of Spencer's own writings. 2. Some important Spencer translations. 3. Biographical and General. 4. Biology. 5. Psychology. 6. Sociology (including Politics, Economics and Education). 7. Ethics and Religion. 8. Philosophy. 9. Periodical Literature.

It cannot be insisted too often that the original work of an original thinker should always be read before commentaries are opened and in no instance does this apply so emphatically as in the case of Herbert Spencer. Commentaries are illuminating, but the most illuminating commentaries are nearly valueless unless the original work is thoroughly known. If this principle is adhered to in the present instance, the compiler feels confident that this bibliography will be of real service to the student of philosophy.

HERBERT SPENCER BIBLIOGRAPHY.

1.—BIBLIOGRAPHIES OF SPENCER'S WORKS.

DUNCAN, D. *The Life and Letters of Herbert Spencer*, 1908.

EDMONDS, J. *Reading Notes in Mercantile Library of Philadelphia Bulletin.* Jan., 1883, pp. 31–32.

ELLIOTT, H. S. In *Dictionary of National Biography.* Second Supplement. Vol. III, pp. 368–369.

HUDSON, W. H. *Introduction to the Philosophy of Herbert Spencer.* 1904.

TURNBULL, H. G. In *English Illustrated Magazine.* April, 1903. Vol. XXXLX, pp. 88–90.

WILLIAMS and NORGATE (Publishers). *Herbert Spencer's Works.*

2.—LIST OF HERBERT SPENCER'S WRITINGS.

THE SYNTHETIC PHILOSOPHY.

First Principles. First edition, 1862 ; second edition, 1867 ; third edition, 1875 ; fourth edition, 1880 ; fifth edition, 1884 ; sixth edition, and finally revised, 1900. Reprinted with an additional appendix and a new index, 1904.

Principles of Biology. Vol. 1, 1864 ; vol. 2, 1867 ; revised and enlarged edition, vol. 1, 1898 ; vol. 2, 1899.

Principles of Psychology. First edition, 1855 ; second edition, vol. 1, 1870 ; vol. 2, 1872 ; third edition, 1880 ; fourth edition, 1899.

Principles of Sociology. Vol. 1, first edition, 1876 ; second edition, 1877 ; third and enlarged edition, 1885. Vol. 2, Part IV, 1879 ; Part V, 1882. Vol. 3, Part VI, 1885 ; Parts VII and VIII, 1896.

Principles of Ethics. Vol. 1, Part I, 1879 ; Parts II and III, 1892. Vol. 2, Part IV, 1891 ; Parts V and VI, 1893.

OTHER WORKS.

Social Statics.   First edition, 1855 ; abridged and revised edition, 1892.

Education.   First edition, 1861 ; cheap edition, 1878 ; sixpenny edition, published by the Rationalist Press Association, 1903. Reprinted 1905.

The Study of Sociology. International Scientific Series, first edition, 1873 ; second to seventh editions, 1873–1878 ; library edition, 1880.

The Man versus the State. First edition, 1884 ; reprinted with abridged and revised edition of Social Statics, 1892.

Essays. First series, 1857 ; second series, 1863 ; third series, 1874 ; revised edition in three volumes, 1890.

Various Fragments. First edition, 1897 ; enlarged edition, 1900.

Facts and Comments. 1902.

Autobiography. In two volumes, 1904.

Descriptive Sociology. (Classified and arranged by Herbert Spencer.) Division I.—Uncivilized Societies : Lowest Races, Negrito Races and Malayo-Polynesian Races, by Dr. David Duncan (1874) ; African Races (other than Arab), by Dr. David Duncan (1876) ; American Races, by Dr. David Duncan (1878). Division II.—Civilized Societies, extinct or decayed : Mexicans, Central Americans, Chibchas and Peruvians, by Dr. Richard Scheppig (1874) ; Hebrews and Phœnicians, by Dr. Richard Scheppig (1880). Division III.—Civilized Societies, recent or still flourishing : English, by James Collier (1873) ; French, by James Collier (1881). *Issued by the Herbert Spencer Trustees :*—Division I.— Uncivilized Societies : Lowest Races, a new edition brought up to date by the original compiler, Dr. Duncan (1925) ; African Races, a new edition, practically re-written and greatly enlarged, by Emil Torday (1930) ; The Heritage of

Solomon. Division II.—Civilized Societies, extinct or decayed : Greeks, Hellenic Period, by Sir J. P. Mahaffy and Prof. W. A. Goligher, LL.D. (1910) ; Ancient Egyptians, by Sir W. Flinders Petrie (1925) ; Greeks, Hellenistic Period, by Prof. W. A. Goligher, LL.D. (1928) ; Mesopotamia by Reuben Levy, Litt.D. (1929) ; Ancient Rome (issued in incomplete form). Division III.—Civilized Societies, recent or still flourishing : Chinese, by E. T. C. Warner (1910) ; Islam, by Reuben Levy, 2 vols. (1933). Division I.—Uncivilized Societies : The Heritage of Solomon (Ancient Palestine), by Prof. John Garstang, LL.D. Division II.—Civilized Societies, extinct or decayed : Ancient Romans, by Dr. E. H. Alton and Prof. W. A. Goligher.

ESSAYS, ARTICLES, AND LETTERS PUBLISHED IN MAGAZINES AND NEWSPAPERS.

" Crystallization." *Bath and West of England Magazine* for January.

" The Poor Laws." *Bath and West of England Magazine* for March.

1839.

" Skew Arches." *Civil Engineer and Architect's Journal* for May. (*Autobiography* 1, p. 517.)

1840.

" A Geometrical Theorem." *Civil Engineer and Architect's Journal* for July. (*Autobiography* 1, p. 520.)

1841.

" A New Form of Viaduct." *Civil Engineer and Architect's Journal* for July.

" The Transverse Strain of Beams." *Civil Engineer and Architect's Journal* for September.

" Scale of Equivalents." Written for the *Civil Engineer and Architect's Journal*, but not published. (*Autobiography* 1, p. 525.)

1842.

" Architectural Precedent." *Civil Engineer and Architect's Journal* for January.

Letter on above. *Civil Engineer and Architect's Journal* for March.

" Velocimeter." *Civil Engineer and Architect's Journal* for July. (*Autobiography* 1, p. 522.)

Letters " On the Proper Sphere of Government." *Nonconformist*, 15, 22 June ; 13, 27 July ; 10 August ; 7, 21, September, 19, 26 October ; 23 November ; 14 December.

1843.

" Effervescence—Rebecca and her Daughters." *Nonconformist*
28 June.
" Mr. Hume and National Education." *Nonconformist*, 2 August.
" The Non-Intrusion Riots." *Nonconformist*, 11 October.
Letter about the Derby flood of April, 1842. *Architect, Engineer
and Surveyor* for October.

1844.

" Imitation and Benevolence." *Zoist* for January.
" Remarks on the Theory of Reciprocal Dependence in the
Animal and Vegetable Creations, as regards its bearing on
Palæontology." *Philosophical Magazine* for February.
(*Autobiography* 1, p. 533.)
" Situation of the Organ of Amativeness." *Zoist* for July.
" The Organ of Wonder." *Zoist* for October.
Various Articles. *Birmingham Pilot*, September to December.

1846.

" The Form of the Earth no Proof of Original Fluidity."
Philosophical Magazine for March. (*Autobiography* 1, p.
546.)

1848.

Article on " Political Smashers." *Standard of Freedom*, June or
July.

1851.

" A Solution of the Water Question." *Economist*, 20 December.
(*Various Fragments*, p. 229.)

1852.

" Use and Beauty." *Leader*, 3 January. (*Essays* ii, p. 370.)
" The Development Hypothesis." *Leader*, 20 March. (*Essays* i,
p. 1.)
" A Theory of Population." *Westminster Review* for April.
(*Principles of Biology*, i, p. 577.)
" The Bookselling Question." *The Times*, 5 April. (*Various
Fragments*, p. 1.)
" A Theory of Tears and Laughter." *Leader*, 11 October.
" The Sources of Architectural Types." *Leader*, 23 October.
(*Essays*, ii, p. 375.)
" The Philosophy of Style." *Westminster Review* for October.
(*Essays* ii, p. 333.)
" Gracefulness." *Leader*, 25 December. (*Essays* ii, p. 381.)

1853.

" The Value of Physiology." *National Temperance Chronicle* for February.

" The Valuation of Evidence." *Leader*, 25 June. (*Essays* ii, p. 161.)

" Over-Legislation." *Westminster Review* for July. (*Essays* iii, p. 229.)

" The Universal Postulate." *Westminster Review* for October.

" The Use of Anthropomorphism." *Leader*, 5 November.

1854.

" Manners and Fashion." *Westminster Review* for April. (*Essays* iii, p. 1.)

" Personal Beauty." *Leader*, 15 April and 13 May. (*Essays* ii, p. 380.)

" The Art of Education." *North British Review* for May. (*Education*, chap. 2.)

" The Genesis of Science." *British Quarterly Review* for July. (*Essays* ii, p. 1.)

" Railway Morals and Railway Policy." *Edinburgh Review* for October. (*Essays* iii, p. 52.)

1855.

" An Element of Method." A chapter in *Principles of Psychology*. (*Various Fragments*, p. 3.)

1856.

Letter to Editor on charge of Atheism. *Nonconformist*, 23 January.

1857.

" Progress : its Law and Cause." *Westminster Review* for April. (*Essays* i, p. 8.)

" The Ultimate Laws of Physiology." *National Review* for October. (*Essays* i, p. 63.)

" The Origin and Function of Music." *Fraser's Magazine* for October. (*Essays* ii, p. 400.)

" Representative Government : What is it good for ? " *Westminster Review* for October. (*Essays* iii, p. 283.)

1858.

" State Tamperings with Money and Banks." *Westminster Review* for January. (*Essays* iii, p. 326.)

" Moral Discipline of Children." *British Quarterly Review* for April. (*Education*, chap. iii.)

" Recent Astronomy and the Nebular Hypothesis." *Westminster Review* for July. (*Essays* i, p. 108.)

" A Criticism of Professor Owen's Theory of the Vertebrate Skeleton." *British and Foreign Medico-Chirurgical Review* for October. (*Principles of Biology*, second edition, ii, p. 548.)

1859.

" The Laws of Organic Form." *British and Foreign Medico-Chirurgical Review* for January.

" The Morals of Trade." *Westminster Review* for April. (*Essays* iii, p. 113.)

" Physical Training." *British Quarterly Review* for April. (*Education*, chap. IV.)

" What Knowledge is of most Worth." *Westminster Review* for July. (*Education*, chap. 1.)

" Illogical Geology." *Universal Review* for July. (*Essays* i, p. 192.)

Letter on Mr. J. P. Hennessey's Paper read at the meeting of the British Association. (*Athenæum*, 22 October.)

1860.

" Bain on the Emotions and the Will." *British and Foreign Medico-Chirurgical Review* for January. (*Essays* i, p. 241.)

" The Social Organism." *Westminster Review* for January. (*Essays* i, p. 265.)

" The Physiology of Laughter." *Macmillan's Magazine* for March. (*Essays* ii, p. 452.)

" Parliamentary Reform : the Dangers and the Safeguards." *Westminster Review* for April. (*Essays* iii, p. 358.)

" Prison Ethics." *British Quarterly Review* for July. (*Essays* iii, p. 152.)

1862.

" Theological Criticism." *Athenæum*, 8 and 22 November.

" On Laws in General and the Order of their Discovery." Part of the first edition of *First Principles*. (*Essays* ii, p. 145.)

1864.

" The Classification of the Sciences." Published as a brochure in April. (*Essays* ii, p. 74.)

" Reasons for Dissenting from the Philosophy of M. Comte." Appendix to the foregoing. (*Essays* ii, p. 118.)

" What is Electricity ? " *Reader*, 19 November. (*Essays* ii, p. 168.)

1865.

" The Constitution of the Sun." *Reader*, 25 February. (*Essays* i, p. 182.)

" The Collective Wisdom." *Reader*, 15 April. (*Essays* iii, p. 387.)

" Political Fetichism." *Reader*, 10 June. (*Essays* iii, p. 393.)

" Mill *versus* Hamilton—The Test of Truth." *Fortnightly Review* for July. (*Essays* ii, p. 188.)

1866.

" On Circulation and the Formation of Wood in Plants." *Transactions of the Linnæan Society*, vol. 25. (*Principles of Biology*, ii, p. 567.)

1870.

" The Origin of Animal Worship." *Fortnightly Review* for May. (*Essays* i, p. 308.)

1871.

" A New Fishing Rod." *Field*, 14 January. (*Autobiography*, ii, p. 504.)

" Morals and Moral Sentiments." *Fortnightly Review* for April. (*Essays* i, p. 331.)

" Mental Evolution." *Contemporary Review* for June.

" Specialized Administration." *Fortnightly Review* for December. (*Essays* iii, p. 401.)

1872.

" Survival of the Fittest." *Nature*, 1 February.

" Mr. Martineau on Evolution." *Contemporary Review* for June. (*Essays* i, p. 371.)

1873.

" Replies to Criticisms." *Fortnightly Review* for November and December. (*Essays* ii, p. 218.)

" Obituary Notice of J. S. Mill." *Examiner*, 11 May. (*Autobiography*, ii, p. 506.)

1874.

Correspondence relating to " Physical Axioms." *Nature*, March to June. (*Essays* ii, pp. 298–314.)

1875.

" Professor Cairnes's Criticisms." *Fortnightly Review* for February. (*Various Fragments*, p. 14.)

1876.

" The Comparative Psychology of Man." *Mind* for January. (*Essays* i, p. 352.)

1877.

" Views concerning Copyright." Evidence given before the Royal Commission. (*Various Fragments*, p. 18.)

" A Rejoinder to Mr. McLennan." *Fortnightly Review* for June. (*Various Fragments*, p. 63.)

" Mr. Taylor's Review of the Principles of Sociology." *Mind* for July.

1878.

Letter on the toast of " The Fraternity of the two Nations," proposed at a Dinner in Paris. *Standard*, 30 May.

" Consciousness under Chloroform." *Mind* for October. (*Principles of Psychology*, i, p. 636.)

1879.

Letter to M. Alglave about the " Lois Ferry." *Revue Scientifique* for July.

1880.

Letter on the feeling in England about the time of the outbreak of the Civil War in the United States—written in 1869, but not then published. *New York Tribune*, 28 June. (*Autobiography*, ii, p. 497.)

" Professor Tait on the Formula of Evolution." *Nature*, 2 and 16 December. (*Various Fragments*, p. 75.)

Letter disclaiming having had to do with " George Eliot's " education. *Standard*, 26 December.

1881.

" Replies to Criticisms on the Data of Ethics." *Mind* for January.

" Views concerning Copyright." Speech delivered at a meeting of the National Association for the Promotion of Social Science, held in May. (*Various Fragments*, p. 57.)

" Professor Green's Explanations." *Contemporary Review* for February. (*Essays* ii, p. 321.)

1882.

Letter on " The Anti-Aggression League." *Nonconformist and Independent*, 2 March.

" Professor Goldwin Smith as a Critic." *Contemporary Review* for March.

Pecuniary liberality of Mr. J. S. Mill. *Daily News*, 27 March.

" Concerning the Mis-statements of the Rev. T. Mozley." *Athenæum*, 22 July. (*Autobiography*, i, p. 549.)

" Ability *versus* Information." (*Various Fragments*, p. 91.)

" Book Distribution." (*Various Fragments*, p. 93.)

1883.

Letter on the Edinburgh Review and on the Land Question. *St. James' Gazette*, 14 February.

"The Americans." *Contemporary Review* for January. (*Essays* iii, p. 471.)

1884.

Political Articles. *Contemporary Review* for February, April, May, June and July.

Letter on a mis-quotation in the Duke of Argyll's "Unity of Nature." *Athenæum*, 16 February.

"Mental Evolution in Animals." *Athenæum*, 5 April.

"Retrogressive Religion." *Nineteenth Century* for July.

Letter repudiating the opinion attributed to him that we should be all the better in the absence of education. *Standard*, 8 August.

"Mr. Herbert Spencer and the Comtists." *The Times*, 9 September.

"Mr. Herbert Spencer and Comte." *The Times*, 15 September.

"Last words about Agnosticism and the Religion of Humanity." *Nineteenth Century* for November.

1885.

"A Rejoinder to M. de Laveleye." *Contemporary Review* for April. (*Various Fragments*, p. 98.)

Letters on the Spencer-Harrison Book. *The Times*, 1, 3, 4 and 6 June. *Standard*, 10 and 13 June.

"Government by Minority." *The Times*, 21 December. (*Various Fragments*, p. 110.)

1886.

"The Factors of Organic Evolution." *Nineteenth Century* for April and May. (*Essays* i, p. 389.)

1888.

"A Counter Criticism." *Nineteenth Century* for February. (*Essays* i, p. 467.)

Letter with reference to his Opinions on Painting. *Architect*, 24 February.

"The Ethics of Kant." *Fortnightly Review* for July. (*Essays* iii, p. 192.)

1889.

Rev. J. Wilson's Statements about articles on "Sociology" in the *Birmingham Pilot*. *Pall Mall Gazette*, 12 April.

Letters on the Land Question. *The Times*, 7, 11, 15, 19, 27 November.

1890.

"Absolute Political Ethics." *Nineteenth Century* for January. (*Essays* iii, p. 217.)

"Reasoned Savagery so-called." *Daily Telegraph*, 7 February.

"The Inheritance of Acquired Characters." *Nature*, 6 March.

"Panmixia." *Nature*, 3 April.

"Our Space Consciousness." *Mind* for July. (*Principles of Psychology*, ii, p. 717.)

"The Moral Motive." *Guardian*, 6 August. (*Principles of Ethics*, ii, p. 446.)

"The Origin of Music." *Mind* for October.

1891.

"From Freedom to Bondage." Introduction to A Plea for Liberty. (*Essays* iii, p. 445.)

"The Society for the Prevention of Cruelty to Children. *Pall Mall Gazette*, 16 and 28 May.

"The Origin of Music." A discussion. *Mind* for October.

1892.

Letter to Figaro about his unfamiliarity with M. Renan. *Pall Mall Gazette*, 20 October.

Letter on the sales of his books. *Daily Chronicle*, 3 December.

1893.

"Social Evolution and Social Duty." (*Various Fragments*, p. 119.)

"The Inadequacy of Natural Selection." *Contemporary Review* for February and March. (*Principles of Biology*, i, p. 602.)

"Professor Weismann's Theories." *Contemporary Review* for May. (*Principles of Biology*, i, p. 633.)

"A Rejoinder to Professor Weismann." *Contemporary Review* for December. (*Principles of Biology*, i, p. 650.)

"Evolutionary Ethics." *Athenæum*, 5 August. (*Various Fragments*, p. 111.)

1894.

"Obituary Notice of Professor Tyndall." *Fortnightly Review* for February.

"Parliamentary Georgites." *The Times*, 20 February. (*Various Fragments*, p. 122.)

Letters relating to the Land Question Controversy. *Daily Chronicle*, August to September.

"Weismannism Once More." *Contemporary Review* for October. (*Principles of Biology*, i, p. 167.)

"A Record of Legislation." *The Times*, 24 November. (*Various Fragments*, p. 125.)

" The Booksellers' Trade Union." *The Times,* 26 October.
(*Various Fragments,* p. 161.)
" The Book Trade." *The Times,* 30 October and 6 November.
(*Various Fragments,* pp. 163, 167.)
" The Bookselling Question." *The Times,* 21 November.
(*Various Fragments,* p. 169.)
" Publishers, Booksellers and the Public." *The Times,* 24
October. (*Various Fragments,* p. 156); *Athenæum,* 24
November. (*Various Fragments,* p. 171); 29 December.
(*Various Fragments,* p. 174); *The Author,* December. (*Various
Fragments,* p. 177.)
" Origin of Classes among the ' Parasol ' Ants." *Nature,* 6
December. (*Principles of Biology,* i, p. 687.)

1895.

" Herbert Spencer on the Land Question." (*Various Fragments,*
p. 196.)
" The Antiquity of the Medical Profession." *Nature,* 27 June.
" Mr. Balfour's Dialectics." *Fortnightly Review* for June.
" The Nomenclature of Colours." *Nature,* 29 August.
Note on the Ethical Motive. *Nineteenth Century Review* for
September.
" American Publishers." *The Times,* 21 September. (*Various
Fragments,* p. 236.)
" Heredity Once More." *Contemporary Review* for October.
Letter on Canadian Copyright. *The Times,* 21 October.
" Lord Salisbury on Evolution." *Nineteenth Century Review*
for November.
" The Board of Trade and Railway Station Boards." *The Times,*
2 December. (*Various Fragments,* p. 235.)
On Mr. Howard Collins' letter suggesting a portrait. *The Times,*
14 December.

1896.

" Dr. Bridget's Criticisms." *Positivist Review* for January.
" Anglo-American Arbitration." Letter read at a meeting in
Queen's Hall, 3 March. (*Various Fragments,* p. 128.)
" Against the Metric System." *The Times,* 4, 7, 9, 25 April.
(*Various Fragments,* p. 130.)
Letter on Mr. Bramwell Booth's charges of Inconsistency. *The
Times,* 17 December.

1897.

Clearing himself of seeming implication of " positive or negative
defect of quotation." *Fortnightly Review* for January.
" The Duke of Argyll's Criticisms." *Nineteenth Century* for May.

1898.

Letters on " Primitive Religious Ideas." *Literature*, 5 and 16 February. *Spectator*, 23 July.

" A State Burden on Authors." *The Times*, 9 and 16 February. (*Various, Fragments*, p. 220.)

Letter on " Mr. Mallock's Representation of his Views." *Literature*, 2 April.

The Times Art Critic on the Herkomer portrait. *The Times*, 5 May.

" Cell Life and Cell Multiplication." *Natural Science* for May.

" Stereo-Chemistry and Vitalism." *Nature*, 20 October.

" Asymmetry and Vitalism." *Nature*, 10 November.

" What is Social Evolution ? " *Nineteenth Century* for September. (*Various Fragments*, p. 181.)

1899.

" The Duke of Argyll and Mr. Herbert Spencer." *Nature*, 12 January.

" Prof. Meldola's Explanation." *Nature*, 26 January.

Mr. Crozier's Charge of Materialism. *Literature*, 21 January and 11 February.

" Publishing on Commission." *Literature*, 4 February. (*Various Fragments*, p. 217.)

" The Metric System Again." *The Times*, 28 March and 4, 8, 13 April. (*Various Fragments*, p. 205.)

" Professor Ward on ' Naturalism and Agnosticism.' " *Fortnightly Review* for December.

Letter on a misrepresentation of Spencer's Ethics. *Spectator*, 16 December.

Letter to Mr. Leonard Courtney on the South African War. (*Various Fragments*, p. 223.)

1900.

On the South African War. *Speaker*, 13 January ; *Morning Leader*, 5 February. (*Various Fragments*, p. 224.)

" Professor Ward's Rejoinder." *Fortnightly Review* for April.

" An Inhumanity." *The Times*, 25 July. (*Various Fragments*, p. 225.)

Genesis of the Vertebrate Column. *Nature*, 25 October.

1901.

Letter on Space Consciousness, with reference to Dr. Tolver Preston's Statement. *Mind* for January.

1902.

" The Spread of Small Pox." *Signed* " Observer," *Daily News*,
18 January.
" Ethical Lectureships." *Ethics*, 1 March.
The Education Bill. *Daily News*, 8 April.
Sir Michael Foster as M.P. for London University. *The Times*,
28 May.

3.—SELECTED TRANSLATIONS.

[Most of these books are in the British Museum Library.]

FRENCH.

Prémiers principes (2nd Eng. ed.). 1871 ; 1902.
Classification des sciences. 1871.
Introduction à la science sociale. 1874.
Principes de psychologie. 1875 ; 1898.
Principes de biologie. 1877.
Principes de sociologie. 1878–9 ; 1883–1887 ; 1898.
Essais de morale de science et d'ésthetique. 1877–79.
Principes de Morale. 1879–1896.
De l'éducation intellectuelle, morale et physique. 1885 ; 1897.
L'individu contre l'état. 1892.
Problêmes de morale et de sociologie. 1894.
Faits et commentaires. 1903.
Autobiographie. 1907.
Resumé de la philosophie de Herbert Spencer par Howard Collins.
1891.

GERMAN.

Erziehungslehre. 1874 ; 1905 ; 1927.
Einleitung in das Studium der Sociologie. 1875.
System der Synthetischen Philosophie von Herbert Spencer. 1875–
1902.
Grundlagen der Philosophie. 1875.
Prinzipien der Biologie. 1876–77.
Prinzipien der Psychologie. 1877–97.
Prinzipien der Ethik. 1892–1902.
Die Thatsachen der Ethik. 1879.
Prinzipien der Sociologie. 1877.
Von der Freiheit zur Gebundenheit. 1891.
Herbert Spencer. Eine Autobiographie. 1905.
Grundsätze einer synthetischen Auffassung der Dinge. (*First
Principles. 6th ed.* 1901.)

SPANISH.

Los primeros principios. 1879.
Educacion intellectual, moral y fisica. 1879 ; 1906.
Principios de sociologia. 1883.
L'Individuo e lo stato. 1886 ; 1904.
Instituciones sociales. 1894.
Beneficienza negativa e positiva. 1894.
Las instituciones ecclesiasticas. 1894.
La giustizia. 1893 ; 1897.
De las leges on general. 1895.
Etica de las prisiones. 1895.
Excesso de la legislacion (and other essays). 1895.
Hechos y explicaciones. 1903.
Créacion y evolution (and other essays). 1904.
Essayos cientificos. 1908.

ITALIAN.

La Basi della Morale. 1881 ; 1905.
Principios de Sociologia. 1884.
Scienza e religion (Pt. VI of Principles of Sociology). 1884.
Origine e funzione della musica. 1894.
La Basi della Vita. 1905.
La Basi del Pensiero. 1907.
Il diritto d'ignorare lo Stato. 1921.

RUSSIAN.

[By 1876 most of what Spencer had written was already translated, including part of the *Descriptive Sociology.*]
Principles of Psychology. 1876.
Principles of Sociology. 1876.
System of Synthetic Philosophy. (Abstract.) 1905.

DUTCH.

Rights of Children, etc. 1883.
The Man versus the State. 1886.
Education (Opvoeding). 1887.
System of Synthetic Philosophy (Eon system van synthetischen philosophie). 1898.

GREEK.

Education. 1876.
Principles of Sociology. 1876.
First Principles. 1896.

ROUMANIAN.

A Plea for Liberty (In contra socialismuliu). 1893.

YIDDISH.

Extracts. 1908.

4.—BIOGRAPHICAL AND GENERAL.

BONY L'ABBÉ IGNACE. *Herbert Spencer.* Paris, 1896.

BOURDEAU, JEAN. *Les Maîtres de la pensée contemporaine.* (Part of the Bibliothèque de Philosophie Contemporaine.) Paris, 1904, pp. 187.

BOWNE, BORDEN PARKER. *The Philosophy of Herbert Spencer : being an exposition of the " First Principles " of his system.* New York, 1874.

CLODD, EDWARD. *Pioneers of Evolution from Thales to Huxley : with an intermediate chapter on the causes of arrest of the movement.* London, 1897, pp. x, 250.

DARWIN, CHARLES. *Life and Letters,* edited by Sir Francis Darwin. London, 1887. 3 vols.

DIFEREE, HENDRIK C. *Herbert Spencer en zyn tyd.* Amsterdam, 1905.

DUNCAN, DAVID. *Life and Letters of Herbert Spencer.* (2 volumes.) London, 1908.

ELLIOT, HUGH SAMUEL ROGER. *Herbert Spencer.* London, 1917, pp. vi, 330.

FISKE, JOHN. *Essays, historial and literary.* New York, 1902. 2 vols.

GAUPP, OTTO. *Herbert Spencer.* (Frommans Klassiker der Philosophie, etc., No. 5.) Stuttgart, 1897, pp. vi, 160 ; 2nd edition. 1900, pp. viii, 180.

GEORGOV, IVAN A. *Herbert Spencer* (in Russian). Sofia, 1905, pp. 48.

GINGELL, JULIA RAYMOND. *Aphorisms from the writings of Herbert Spencer : selected and arranged by J. R. Gingell.* London, 1894, pp. xii, 170.

GOULD, GEORGE M. *The Origin of the ill-health of Spencer.* (In Biological Clinics, Vol. ii.) London, 1904, pp. 241, 249.

GRAVES, FRANK PIERPONT. *Great Educators of three centuries : their work and its influence on modern education.* New York, 1912, pp. ix, 289.

GROOT, JOANNES VINCENTIUS DE. *Denkers van onzen tijd. Em du Bois-Raymond, Louis Pasteur, Ferdinand Brunetière, John Henry Newman, and Herbert Spencer.* Amsterdam, 1910, pp. 328.

HARRISON, FREDERIC. *Herbert Spencer.* (The Herbert Spencer Lecture.) Oxford, 1905, pp. 30.

HEIDT, ALBERT. *Philosophische Beiträge aus Herbert Spencer's Autobiography.* Göttingen, 1908.

HUDSON, WILLIAM HENRY. *Herbert Spencer.* (Philosophers Ancient and Modern.) New York, 1908, pp. 89.

——— *An Introduction to the Philosophy of Herbert Spencer, with biographical sketch.* First edition. New York, 1894. Second edition. London, 1897, pp. ix, 234.

HUXLEY, T. H. *Life and Letters.* Edited by Leonard Huxley. London, 1903, 2 vols.

JAMES, WILLIAM. *Memories and Studies.* Edited by his son, Henry James. Cambridge (Mass.), 1911, pp. 411.

MACPHERSON, HECTOR. *Herbert Spencer. The Man and his Work.* London, 1900, pp. 227.

MELLONE, SIDNEY HERBERT. *Leaders of religious thought in the Nineteenth Century. Newman, Martineau, Comte, Spencer, Browning.* Edinburgh and London, 1902, pp. viii, 302.

NÖRREGAARD, JENS. *Studier over Spencer, Lotze og Grundtvig.* Copenhagen, 1890, pp. 276.

PARISOT, Edmond. *Herbert Spencer. Choix de Textes et étude du système philosophique.* (Les Grands Philosophes, français et étrangers.) Paris, 1912.

ROBERTSON, JOHN MACKINNON. *Modern Humanists. Sociological Studies of Carlyle, Mill, Emerson, Arnold, Ruskin and Spencer. With an Epilogue on Social Reconstruction.* London, 1891, pp. vi, 275.

———— *Pioneer Humanists (Machiavelli, Bacon, Hobbes, Spinoza, Shaftesbury, Mandeville, Gibbon, Mary Wollstoncraft).* London, 1907, pp. 399.

ROYCE, JOSIAH. *Herbert Spencer : An Estimate and a Review. Together with a Chapter of Personal Reminiscences by James Collier.* New York, 1904, pp. 234.

SACERDOTE, SALVATORE. *La vita di Herbert Spencer Ed.* " I Primi Principii." Turin, 1907, pp. 286.

SKARD, MATIAS. *Herbert Spencer. Opdrgelsestanker.* (Gjengwelse of Kritik). Holmstadt, 1891, pp. 40.

STRUVE, HENRYK. *Herbert Spencer i jego systemat filozofii synthetycznej obditka z. Biblioteki Warszawkiej, i testamencie Spencera.* (*Herbert Spencer and his Synthetic Philosophy.*) Warsaw, 1904, pp. 56.

TAYLOR, ALFRED EDWARD. *Herbert Spencer.* New York, 1928.

THOMSON, SIR J. ARTHUR. *Herbert Spencer. English Men of Science.* London, pp. ix, 284.

THOMPSON, DANIEL GREENLEAF. *Herbert Spencer.* (An essay on his philosophy.) Brooklyn Ethical Assoc., 1889. New York, 1889, pp. 22.

THOUVEREZ, ÉMILE. *Les Grands philosophes. Herbert Spencer.* Paris, 1905, pp. 59.

TWO. *Home Life with Herbert Spencer.* Bristol and London, 1906. Second edition, 1910, pp. 234.

UNDERWOOD, BENJAMIN FRANKLIN. *Herbert Spencer's Synthetic Philosophy.* Brooklyn Ethical Assoc., Evolution Series No. 4. New York, 1891.

WERNER, EDWARD THEODORE CHALMERS. *Herbert Spencer.* Shanghai, 1913, pp. 10, 13.

ZAMBONI. *Herbert Spencer.* Bologna, 1904.

ZUCCANTE, GIUSEPPI. *Herbert Spencer.* Vicenza, 1904.

5.—BIOLOGY.

BALL, WILLIAM PLATT. *Are the effects of Use and Disuse Inherited ? An examination of the view held by Spencer and Darwin.* (Nature Series, 1873, etc.) London, 1890, pp. xii, 156.

BATESON, WILLIAM. *Biological Fact and the Structure of Society.* (The Herbert Spencer Lecture.) Oxford, 1911, pp. 34.

BOURNE, GILBERT CHARLES. *Herbert Spencer and Animal Evolution.* (The Herbert Spencer Lecture.) Oxford, 1909, pp. 36.

FISHER, RONALD A. *The Social Selection of Human Fertility,* (The Herbert Spencer Lecture.) Oxford, 1932. pp. 31.

GALTON, FRANCIS. *Probability and the Foundation of Eugenics* (The Herbert Spencer Lecture.) Oxford, 1907, pp. 30.

MELDOLA, RAPHAEL. *Evolution, Darwinian and Spencerian.* (The Herbert Spencer Lecture.) Oxford, 1910, pp. 44.

MITCHELL, SIR PETER CHALMERS. *Materalism and Vitalism in Biology.* (The Herbert Spencer Lecture.) Oxford, 1930, pp. 30.

SEWALL, HENRY, Ph.D. *Herbert Spencer as a Biologist.* (University of Michigan Philosophical Papers. First Series, No. 4.) Ann Arbor, 1896, pp. 13.

THOMPSON, D'ARCY WENTWORTH (the younger). *On Aristotle as a Biologist, with a prooemion on Herbert Spencer.* (The Herbert Spencer Lecture.) Oxford, 1913, pp. 31.

TRALL, T. R. *A New Theory of Population.* (By Herbert Spencer. Republished from the *Westminster Review* for April, 1852.) With an introduction. New York, 1857.

WATTS, ROBERT, D.D. *An Examination of Spencer's biological hypothesis.* Belfast, 1875.

WEISMANN, AUGUST. *Die Allmacht der Naturzuchtung.* Eine Erwiderung an H. Spencer (*i.e.*, to his Articles in the *Contemporary Review*, Feb., Mar., May, 1893, entitled " The Inadequacy of Natural Selection " and " Prof. Weismann's Theories "). Jena, 1893, pp. iv, 96.

—————— *Neue Gedanken zur Vererbungsfrage.* Eine Antwort an H. Spencer (*i.e.*, to his article " Weismannism once more," in the *Contemporary Review*, October, 1894.) Jena, 1895, pp. iv, 72.

6.—PSYCHOLOGY.

ALLIEVO, GIUSEPPE. *La psicologia di Herbert Spencer. Studio espositivo-critico.* Torino, 1898, pp. 159. Second edition, 1913, pp. vii, 153.

BOLOGNA, VINCENZO. *I Processi Mentali nella Psicologia di Herbert Spencer. Studio critico.* Catania, 1921, pp. 231.

CHYREN, JOHAN. *Kritisk Grainställning af Herbert Spencer.* (Exposition critique des Principes de Psychologie de Herbert Spencer.) Lund, 1883.

FERRO, ANDREA ALBERTO. *La Critica della conoscenza in E. Kant e H. Spencer.* Savona, 1900, pp. 80.

HOLLANDER, BERNARD. *Herbert Spencer as a Phrenologist.* Re-printed from the *Westminster Review*, February, 1893 (1895 ?). London, 1893.

KHOKHRYAKOV P. *The psychological evolution of mankind and a criticism of Spencer's evolution of morals.* (In Russian.) Moscow, 1893.

LÉVY-BRUHL, LUCIEN. *La Mentalité primitive.* (The Herbert Spencer Lecture.) Oxford, 1931, pp. 27.

MYERS, CHARLES S. *Psychological Conceptions in other Sciences.* (The Herbert Spencer Lecture). Oxford, 1929, pp. 24.

PACE, EDWARD. *Das Relativitätsprinzip in Herbert Spencer's psychologischer Entwicklungslehre.* (W. Wundt's Philosophische Studien, Bd. vii, Heft 4.) Leipzig, 1892.

RIBOT, THÉODULE ARMAND. *La Psychologie anglaise contemporaine. École expérimentale.* Paris, 1870.

———— *English Psychology : Hartley, James Mill, Herbert Spencer, A. Bain, G. H. Lewes, Samuel Bailey.* London, 1873.

THURM, LÉON. *Les principes de psychologie et l'education intellectuelle de Herbert Spencer.* Paris, 1920, pp. ii, 85.

WARBECKE, JOHN MARTYN. *Das Homogenitäts Prinzip.* (Le principe d'homogenité dans la psychologie de Spencer et ses rapports avec la theorie de la connaissance de " First Principles. ") Leipzig, 1907.

7.—SOCIOLOGY

(including Politics, Economics and Education).

ADLER, I. *Die Organistische Gesellschaftsbegriff mit besonderer Berucksichtigung Herbert Spencer, Paul v. Lillienfeld und Albert v. Schäffle.* Bern, 1925.

ALEXANDER, SAMUEL. *Art and Instinct.* (The Herbert Spencer Lecture.) Oxford, 1927, pp. 23.

ANTÆUS, R. (*pseud.*), *i.e.*, William Joseph Ibbett. *Imaginary Conversation between Mr. Herbert Spencer and a Poet in a Railway Carriage.* Epsom, 1889, pp. 4.

BALDWIN, JAMES N. *The Super-State and the " Eternal Values."* (The Herbert Spencer Lecture.) London, 1916, pp. 38.

BEARD, GEORGE MILLER. *American Nervousness : its causes and consequences. A supplement to Nervous Exhaustion.* (*Ibid.*, Herbert Spencer on American Nervousness. Herbert Spencer on the Americans and the Americans on Herbert Spencer.) New York, 1881, pp. xxii, 352.

BENSO, MARIA GIUSEPPI. *L'Educazione secondo E Spencer, A. Bain, R. Ardigò.* Biella, 1919, pp. 117.

BLACH, S. *Herbert Spencer's Erziehungslehre-Programm.* Berlin, 1913.

BORSDORF, A. T. WILLIAMS. *The Science of Literature. On the literary Theories of Taine and Herbert Spencer.* (Two lectures.) London, 1903, pp. 69.

BREITENSTEIN, M. (?). *Essai sur la théorie de progrès dans la Sociologie de Herbert Spencer.* Génève, 1896.

BUSSE, CURT. *Herbert Spencer's Philosophie der Geschichte. Ein Beitrag zur Lösung Sociologischer Probleme.* Leipzig, 1894, pp. 114.

CARRASCO, ARENAL DE GARCIA. *La Instruccion del Pueblo.* (Observaciones sobre la educación fiscia, intelectual y moral, de Herbert Spencer. La instrucción del obero. La educación de la mujer.) (Tome II of the author's " Obras Completas.") Madrid, 1929, pp. 365.

CARR-SAUNDERS, A. M. *Professions : their organization and place in society.* (The Herbert Spencer Lecture.) Oxford, 1928, pp. 31.

CAVENAGH, FRANCIS ALEXANDER (Ed.). *Herbert Spencer on Education.* (Landmarks in the History of Education.) Cambridge, 1932, pp. xxxiii, 233.

CHILESOTTI, OSCAR. *L'Evoluzione nella Musica. Appunti sulla teoria di H. Spencer.* (Part of the " Piccola Biblioteca di Scienze Moderne.") Torino, 1911, pp. vi, 168.

COMPAYRÉ, GABRIEL. *Herbert Spencer et l'éducation scientifique.* (Part of a series entitled " Les grandes Educateurs.") Paris, 1901, pp. 116, 12°.

———— *Herbert Spencer's Scientific Education.* (Translated by Maria E. Findlay.) New York, 1907, pp. ix, 119.

FAIRMAN, FRANK. *Herbert Spencer on Socialism.* (A Reply to the article entitled " The Coming Slavery," in the *Contemporary Review* for April, 1884.) London, 1884, pp. 16.

FERRI, ENRICO. *Socialismo e Scienza positiva (Darwin, Spencer, Marx).* Roma, 1894, pp. 168.

FERRI, ENRICO. *Socialism and Positive Science (Darwin, Spencer, Marx)*. (Translated by Edith C. Harvey from the French edition of 1896.) (Socialist Library, No. 1.) London, 1905, pp. xii, 174.

GEORGE, HENRY. *A perplexed philosopher : being an examination of Mr. H. Spencer's various utterances on the land question.* New York, 1892, pp. iv, 319.

HALPERIN, S. *The organic theory of development and the development of society.* An exposition and criticism of Spencer's teaching (in Russian). Moscow, 1900.

HERBERT, HON. AUBERON. *The Voluntaryist Creed (Mr. Herbert Spencer and the Great Machine).* (The Herbert Spencer Lecture.) Oxford, 1906, pp. 56.

HUSAIN, SYED ABID. *Die Bildungstheorie Herbert Spencer's in Rahmen seines philosopheschen Systems.* (Berlin Phil. Diss., 6 Aug., 1926.) Langensalza, 1926, pp. vi, 101.

HYNDMAN, HENRY MAYERS. *Socialism and Slavery : being an Answer to Mr. Herbert Spencer's attack upon the Democratic Federation.* Contemporary Review, April, 1884. London, 1884, pp. 24.

INGE, VERY REV. WILLIAM RALPH. *Liberty and Natural Rights.* (The Herbert Spencer Lecture.) Oxford, 1934, pp. 38.

KIDD, BENJAMIN. *Individualism and After.* (The Herbert Spencer Lecture.) Oxford, 1908, pp. 36.

KIMBALL, ELSA PEVERLEY. *Sociology and Education : an analysis of the Theories of Spencer and Ward.* New York, 1932, pp. 325.

KURZBACH, WALTER. *Die Wirtschaftlichen Lehren Herbert Spencers.* (Maschinenschrift. Breslau R. u. Staats Diss.) Breslau, 1923, pp. 120.

LACY, GEORGE. *Liberty and Law : being an attempt at the refutation of the individualism of Mr. Herbert Spencer.* London, 1888, pp. 377.

LEVY, JOSEPH HYAM. *A Symposium on the Land Question.* 1890.

LYTTLETON, HON. WILLIAM HENRY. *Sins of Trade and Business : a sermon (on Neh. v. 15) by the Hon. W. H. L., and the morals of Trade by H. Spencer.* London, 1874 (reprinted 1891), pp. 64.

MACKAY, THOMAS. *A Plea for Liberty : an argument against socialism and socialistic legislation, consisting of an introduction by Herbert Spencer and essays by various writers.* Edited by T. M. London, 1891, pp. xxii, 414 (revised edition, 1892).

MACKINTOSH, ROBERT. *From Comte to Benjamin Kidd. The appeal to biology or evolution for human guidance.* London, 1899, pp. xxii, 287.

MEYER, BERTHA. *Aids to family government ; or from the cradle to the school according to Froebel.* (Translated from the second German edition by M. L. Holbrook. To which has been added an essay on the rights of children and the true principles of Family Government, by Herbert Spencer.) New York, 1879, pp. 208.

MICHEL, HENRY. *La Philosophie politique de Herbert Spencer.* Paris, 1892.

MIKHAILOVSKY, NIKOLAI KONSTANTINOVICH. *Qu'est ce que le progrès ? Examen des idées de M. Herbert Spencer.* Traduction du russe, revue par Paul Louis. Paris, 1897, pp. 200.

MÜND, L. *Spencer's Erziehungslehre in Bezug zu seinem philosophischen system.* Halle, 1913.

NOSSIG-PROCHNIK, FELICIE. *Zur sociologischen Methodenlehre, mit besonderer Rucksicht aur Herbert Spencer.* (Berner Studien sur Philosophie und ihrer Geschichte, Bd. 23, 1896, etc.) Bern, 1900, pp. 107.

OWEN, W. C. *The Economics of Herbert Spencer.* (Social Science Library, No. 7.) New York, 1891, pp. vi, 246.

QUESADA, ERNESTO. *Herbert Spencer y sus doctrinas sociológicas.* De la " Revista de la Universidad de Buenos Aires," tomo vii. Buenos Aires, 1907, pp. 87.

QUICK, ROBERT HERBERT. *Essays on Educational Reformers,* *ibid., Herbert Spencer,* 439–469. London, 1894 (first edition, 1868), pp. xxviii, 560.

RITCHIE, DAVID GEORGE. *The Principles of State Interference : four essays on the political philosophy of Mr. Herbert Spencer, J. S. Mill and T. H. Green.* London, 1891 (fourth edition, 1902), pp. vi, 172.

ROBERTY, EUGÈNE DE. *August Comte et Herbert Spencer.* (Contribution à l'histoire des idées philosophiques au xixe siècle.) Paris, 1894, pp. x, 200.

ROMANO, MATTEO. *Hobbes e Spencer.* Ovvero esposizione della teoria giuridico-sociale di Hobbes. Rapporti e differenze colla dottrina di Spencer e dei moderne sociologie. Avola, 1902, pp. xi, 113.

SALVADORI, GUGLIEMO. *La Scienza economica e la teoria dell' evoluzione. Saggio sulle teorie economicosociali di Herbert Spencer.* Firenze, 1901, pp. 168.

SORLEY, WILLIAM RITCHIE. *Tradition.* (The Herbert Spencer Lecture). Oxford, 1926, pp. 24.

TAINE, HIPPOLYTE ADOLPH. *Derniers Essais de Critique et d'Histoire.* Paris, 1894, pp. viii, 263.

TILLETT, ALFRED WILLIAM. *Militancy versus Civilization.* An Introduction to, and epitome of, the teaching of Herbert Spencer concerning permanent peace as the first condition of progress. London, 1915, pp. 59.

WIESE, LEOPOLD VON. *Zur Grundlegung der Gesellschaftslehre. Eine kritische Untersuchung von Herbert Spencer's System der synthetischen Philosophie.* Jena, 1906, pp. iv, 139.

WRIGHT, T. H. *The Philosophy of Style by Herbert Spencer.* With an introduction by T. H. Wright. 1895.

ZÜFLE, ADOLF. *Spencer's Ansichten über Erziehung. Gesamtdarst. u. Krit.* (Köln Phil. Diss v). Köln, 1925, p. 74.

The following books may also be consulted, as they contain much knowledge bearing on the proper comprehension of Spencer's position as a Sociologist.

BARKER, ERNEST. *Political Thought in England.* 1848–1914. 2nd ed. London, 1928, pp. 256.

CLIFFORD, WILLIAM KINGTON. *Lectures and Essays.* London, 1879. 2 vols.

DONISTHORPE, WORDSWORTH. *Individualism. A system of politics.* London, 1889, pp. 383.

DUNNING, WILLIAM ARCHIBALD. *A History of Political Theories from Rousseau to Spencer.* New York, 1920, pp. ix, 446.

GETTEL, RAYMOND GARFIELD. *History of Political Thought.* New York, 1924, pp. xi, 511.

GIDDINGS, FRANKLIN HENRY. *Studies in the Theory of Human Society.* New York, 1922, pp. vi, 308.

HEARNSHAW, FOSSEY JOHN COBB. *The Social and Political Ideas of some representative Thinkers of the Victorian age : A series of lectures.* London, 1933, pp. 270.

HERBERT, HON. AUBERON. *Taxation and Anarchism : a discussion between the Hon. Auberon Herbert and J. H. Levy.* London, 1912, pp. xi, 67.

KIDD, BENJAMIN. *Social Evolution.* London, 1895, pp. x, 388.

LICHTENBERGER, JAMES P. *Development of Social Theory.* New York, 1924, pp. xiii, 482.

LEWIS, A. M. *Introduction to Sociology.* Chicago, 1913.

MILL, JOHN STUART. *August Comte and Positivism.* London, 1866.

MAITLAND, FREDERIC WILLIAM. *Collected Papers.* Cambridge, 1911. 3 vols.

ROSS, EDWARD ALSWORTH. *The Outlines of Sociology.* New York, 1923, pp. xiii, 474.

SMALL, ALBION W. *General Sociology.* Chicago, 1905, pp. xiii, 739.

STEPHEN, SIR LESLIE. *Science of Ethics.* London, 1882.

WARD, LESTER FRANK. *Dynamic Sociology.* New York, 1883. 2 vols.

WEBB, BEATRICE (LADY PASSFIELD). *My Apprenticeship.* London, 1926, pp. xiv, 458.

8.—ETHICS AND RELIGION.

ALVIELLA, COUNT GOBLET D'. *Harrison contre Spencer sur la valeur religieuse de L'Inconnaisable.* (See also below Religion : a retrospect and prospect ; and the Insuppressible Book.) Paris, 1885.

ARFRIDSSON, HENRIK DANIEL. *Religion och Vetenskap i deras ömsesidiga förhållande med särskild hänsyn till Herbert Spencer uppfattning af frågon. Akademisk afhandling, etc.* Lund, 1894, pp. 139.

ARTHUR, REV. WILLIAM (Wesleyan Minister). *Religion without God and God without Religion.* (Part 2. Agnosticism and Mr. Herbert Spencer.) London, 1885–1887.

BEARE, J. J. *Organic Morality or the Ethics of H. Spencer.* 1889.

BEEBY, CHARLES EVANS. *The woes of the Gospel. Mr. Herbert Spencer and the damnation of most men. A protest.* London, 1884, pp. 62.

BLANC, L'ABBÉ ELIE. *Les nouvelles bases de la morale d'après Mr. Herbert Spencer. Exposition et Réfutation.* (Bibliothèque de la " Controverse.") Lyon, 1881, pp. 127, 12°.

BÖSCH, J. M. *Die Entwicklungstheoretische Idee sozialer Gerechtigkeit. Eine Kritik und Erganzung der Sozialtheorie Herbert Spencer.* Zurich, 1896, pp. iv, 247.

BOUTREUX, ÉMILE. *Religion according to Herbert Spencer. A Lecture.* Translated by A. S. Mores. Edinburgh, 1907, pp. 48.

BRIDEL, PHILIPPE SYRIACH. *Les bases de la morale évolutioniste d'après Spencer.* (Petite Bibliotheque du Chercheur.) Lausanne, 1886, pp. 77.

CATHRIEN, VICTOR. *Die Sittenlehre des Darwininismus.* (Eine Kritik der Ethik Herbert Spencer. See periodical publications Friburg in the Bressgan. Stimmen aus Maria-Laach Ergunzungshafte No. 29.) Friburg in Bresgan, 1888, pp. x, 146.

[A CLERGYMAN.] *God in Creation and in Worship.* Part first. The Answer of History to Herbert Spencer's Theories of the Evolution of ecclesiastical institutions. Second edition. New York, 1887, pp. 120, 12°.

DREY, SYLVAN. *Herbert Spencer's theory of Religion and Morality.* London, 1887, pp. 17.

DUBOIS, JULES. *Spencer et le principe de la morale.* Paris, 1899, pp. xiii, 329.

EVERETT, CHARLES CARROLL. *Psychological elements of Religious Faith.* New York, 1912.

FERRO, ANDREA ALBERTO. *La Critica della Conoscenza in E. Kant e Herbert Spencer.* Savona, 1900, pp. 80.

FISCHER, ENGELBERT LORENZ. *Über das Gesetz der Entwicklung auf psychischem Gebiete. Auf naturwissenschaftlicher Grundlage mit Rücksicht auf C. Darwin, H. Spencer und T. Buckle.* Warzbürg, 1875.

FISCHER, KARL HENRICH OTTO. *Die Objektive Methode der Moralphilosophie bei Wundt und Spencer.* Leipzig, 1909.

FOUILLÉE, ALFRED. *Critique des Systèmes de Morale contemporains.* Paris, 1883, pp. xv, 411.

GANEWA, ELENA. *Die moralische Verpflichtung.* (L'Obligation morale chez Darwin et Spencer.) Rustchuk, 1903.

GERASKOFF, MICHAEL. *Die Sittliche Erziehung nach Spencer unt. Berucks. sr. Moralphilos. u. Entwicklungslehre.* Zurich, 1912.

GONZALEZ, RAFAEL. *La idea racioal, Reflexiones sobre la filosofia moral de Spencer.* Madrid, Seville, 1890, pp. 292.

GOUNELLE, ELIE. *L'Agnosticisme de M. Herbert Spencer.* Moutanban, 1889.

GROUND, WILLIAM DAVID. *An Examination of the structural principles of Spencer's philosophy; intended as a proof that Theism is the only theory of the universe that can satisfy reason.* Oxford, 1883, pp. xvi, 346.

GUTHMANN, JOHANNES. *Entwicklung und Selbstenfalung bei Herbert Spencer.* (Inaugural Dissertation.) Ochsenfürt, 1930, pp. 85.

HALLEUX, JEAN. *L'Evolutionisme en morale. Étude sur la philosophie de Herbert Spencer.* Paris, 1901, pp. 228.

HAMILTON, GAIL (*Pseud*). *The Insuppressible Book.* A controversy between Herbert Spencer and Frederic Harrison. From the *Nineteenth Century* and *Pall Mall Gazette*, with comments by Gail Hamilton (*Pseud*.), i.e., Miss Mary Abagail Dodge. Boston, Mass., pp. 278.

HARRISON, FREDERIC. *Realities and Ideals : social, political, literary and artistic.* London, 1908, pp. xiii, 483.

JAEGER, MAX. *Herbert Spencer's Prinzipien der Ethik, ihre gedankliche Zergliederung und Beurteilung.* Hamburg, 1922, pp. xiv, 99.

LENZ, W. *Der Agnostikismus Herbert Spencers mit Rucksicht auf August Comte und Fredrich Nietzche.* Griefswald, 1902.

LOVELL, H. TASMAN. *Der Utilitarismus (l'utilisme dans l'education des droits possible et ses limites d'après Herbert Spencer).* Weida. i. Th., 1909.

LOWELL, J. *Der Utilitarismus in der Erziehung.* Jena, 1919.

LUCAS, GEORGE J. *Agnosticism and Religion.* Being an examination of Spencer's Religion of the Unknowable. Preceded by a history of Agnosticism (Dissertation for the doctorate of Theology at the Catholic University of America). Baltimore, 1895, pp. 136.

McCosh, James. *Herbert Spencer. Philosophy as culminated in his Ethics.* (Philosophy Series viii.) New York, 1886.

Maguire, Thomas. *Agnosticism. Herbert Spencer, Frederic Harrison.* (A Lecture.) Dublin, 1884, pp. 15.

Mironescu, Al. *Etica evolutionistă si etica crestină. Studiu vitíc asupra eticeĭluĭ. H. Spencer.* Estras din Revista. " Bis. Ort. Română. Bucharest, pp. xi, 176.

Müller, E. A. *Spencer's Versöhnung der Egoismus und Altruismus.* Berlin, 1899.

Mund, L. *Spencer's Erziehungslehre in Bezug su seinem philosophischen System.* Halle, 1913.

Nicholson, J. A. *The Immorality of Naturalism. A Sermon on A. J. Balfour's " Foundation of Belief," with remarks on the Ethics of Spencer.* Birmingham, 1896, pp. 12.

Nostrom, Vitalis. *Grunddragen af Herbert Spencers sedeläva. Kritik framstallning.* (Uppsala Universitets Årsskrift.) Uppsala, 1889, pp. 68.

Pagnone, Annibale. *Le intuizioni morali d l'eredita nello Spencer.* Torino, 1897, pp. 79.

Porter, Josias Leslie. *Science and Revelation ; their distinctive provinces.* (With a review of the theories of Tyndall, Huxley, Darwin and Herbert Spencer.) Belfast, 1874.

Religion. *A retrospect and prospect. The Nature and Reality of Religion. A controversy between Frederic Harrison and Herbert Spencer.* With an introduction, notes and an appendix on the religious value of the Unknowable by Count d'Alviella. (With a preface by E. L. Y[oumans]. London, 1885, pp. 218.

Röder, A. *Der Weg Zum Glück.* Leipzig, 1888.

Rüfner Vinzenz. *Die Naturalistisch-darwinistische Ethik Englands entwicklungsgeschichte betrachtet. u. auf ihr Hoh. p. bei Herbert Spencer Krit.-analysiert.* (Würzburg Phil. Diss v. 1924.) Würzburg, 1924, pp. 150.

Saint-André, L. *Simple Notes sur la Moral e de Spencer, de Littré, de A. Fouillée.* Paris, 1892, pp. 65.

Salvadori, Guglielmo. *L'Etica evoluzionista : Studio sulla filosofia morale di Herbert Spencer.* Torino, 1903, pp. xv, 476.

Savage Minot Judson. *Herbert Spencer : his influence on religion and morality.* Liverpool, 1887, pp. 15.

Schwarze, K. *Die Ethik Herbert Spencer.* Altenburg, 1907.

Shirreff, Emily A. E. *Moral Training : Froebel and Herbert Spencer.* London, 1892, pp. 20.

Simmon, A. *Agnostic First Principles.* London.

SIDGWICK, HENRY. *Lectures on the Ethics of T. H. Green, Herbert Spencer and J. Martineau.* London, 1902, pp. 374.

SINCLAIR, A. G. *Die Utilitarismus bei Sidgwick und Spencer.* Heidelberg, 1907.

SORLEY, WILLIAM RITCHIE. *The Ethics of Naturalism: a criticism.* Second edition. Edinburgh, 1904, pp xiv, 338.

SPICKER GIDEON. *Spencer's Ansicht über das Verhältnis der Religion zur Wissenschaft.* Münster, 1889, pp. 42.

STADLER, DR. AUGUST. *Herbert Spencer's Ethic. Schopenhauer. Herausgegeben von J. Platter.* Leipzig, 1913, pp. 211.

STAMULIS, S. P. *Gibt es kein Naturrecht. Versuch einer Kritik der über das Naturrecht herrschenden Theorien: Herbert Spencer's Rechtslehre.* Jena, 1906.

STOLL, OSWALD. *The grand survival. A theory of immortality by natural law, founded upon a variation of Herbert Spencer's definition of evolution.* London, 1904, pp. 202.

TEGEN, EINAR J. *Moderne Willenstheorien. Eine Darstellung und Kritik.* Uppsala Universitets Årsskrift 1924. (Translated from the Swedish by Gerda Harms.) Uppsala, 1924, pp. 309.

TILLETT, ALFRED WILLIAM. *Spencer's Synthetic Philosophy: What it is all about. An introduction to Justice—" the most important part.* London, 1914, pp. xx, 177.

TORCEOMA, J. R. *Die Grundlagen der Spenscherschen Ethik.* Erlangen, 1900.

TRAINA, TOMASSO. *La Morale di Herbert Spencer. Studio preceduto da una introduzione.* Turin, 1881, pp. 162.

TROILO, ERMMIO. *La dottrina della conoscenza nei moderni precursori de Kant.* Torino, 1904, pp. x, 304.

VANNI, ICILIO. *Il sistema etico-giurdico di H. Spencer. Prefazione alla Giustizia.* Castello, 1893.

VARRENKAMP, A. *Agnosticism van Herbert Spencer.* Groningue, 1897.

VIDARI, GIOVANNI. *Rosimini e Spencer: Studio espositivo-critico di filosofia morale.* Milano, 1899, pp. xvi, 297.

WARD, JAMES. *Naturalism and Agnosticism.* 4th ed. London, 1915, pp. xvi, 623.

WATSON, ROBERT A. *Gospels of Yesterday. Drummond, Spencer, Arnold.* London, 1888.

———— *Hedonistic Theories from Aristippus to Spencer.* Being a criticism of the theories of Aristippus, Epicusus, Hobbes, Locke and Herbert Spencer. Glasgow, 1895, pp. xiii, 248.

WIESENHUTTER, ALFRED. *Die Prinzipien der evolutionistischen Ethik nach Herbert Spencer und W. Wundt.* (Abhandlungen zur Philosophie und ihrer Geschichte 16.) Leipzig, 1910, pp. vii, 40.

WILLIAMS, C. M. *A Review of the Systems of Ethics founded on the Theory of Evolution.* London, 1893, pp. xv, 581.

[WYKEHAMIST.] *A short examination of Mr. Spencer's article entitled "Religion, Retrospect and Prospect."* London, 1884, pp. 15.

ZUCCANTE, GUISEPPE. *La Dottrina della coscienza morale nello Spencer.* Lonigo, 1896, pp. 197.

9.—PHILOSOPHY.

ALBERT, F. *Das Verhältniss H. Spencer's zu D. Hume in das Erkenntnisstheorie.* Leipzig, 1914.

ALLARA, GIOVANNI. *Studio critico sopra " I Primi Principii " de H. Spencer. Con un breve raffronto tra " I Primii Principii " de H. Spencer e " La Formazione naturale nel fatto del sistema solare " de R. Archigo.* Casale, 1891, pp. 86.

[ANON.] *Free notes on Herbert Spencer's First Principles with suggestions regarding Space, Time and Force. Also theories of Life, being a summary of recent discussions thereon, including the questions of the origin of the species and of intelligence.* Edinburgh, 1878, pp. 90.

ARDIGO, ROBERTO. *Opere filesofiche v–viii Padova. viii, L'Inconsocible de Herbert Spencer e il Noumeno di E. Kant. Vol. iii. Spencer e Kant. Il Meccanismo dell intelligenza e l'Ispriazione geniale. L'Indistinto et it Distinto nella formazione naturale. Cingue note etico-sociologiche. Articoli pedagogigci Il Pensiero ie la Cosa.* Padove, 1901.

———— *La Dottina Spenceriana dell inconoscible.* Roma, 1899, pp. 138.

BAUR, KARL. *Das Raumproblem.* (Le problem de l'éspace chez Herbert Spencer.) Tubingen, 1908, pp. 80.

BIRKS, THOMAS RAWSON. *Modern Physical Fatalism and the Doctrine of Evolution, including an examination of Herbert Spencer's first Principles.* London, 1876. (Second edition, with a preface in reply to the strictures of Mr. Herbert Spencer, by C. Pritchard.) 1882.

BONNART, E. *La Critique de M. Renouvier et l'évolutionisme.* Lausanne, 1880.

BOUTREUX, EMILE. *The Relation between Thought and Action from the German and from the Classical point of view.* (The Herbert Spencer Lecture, 1917.) Oxford, 1918, pp. 32.

BOWNE, BORDEN PARKER. *Kant and Spencer: A critical exposition.* New York, 1912, pp. xi, 439.

CARUS, PAUL. *Kant and Spencer.* Chicago, 1904, pp. 107.

CESCA, GIOVANNI. *L'Evolutinismo di Erberto Spencer: exposizione critica.* Verona, 1883, pp. 196.

COLLINS, F. HOWARD. *An Epitome of the Synthetic Philosophy*. With a Preface by Herbert Spencer. Fifth edition. [An authoritative work written with the approval of Spencer.] London, 1889, pp. xviii, 639 ; 1901, pp. xlx, 692.

CRESPI, ACHILLE. *Meditazione Spenceriane*. Alba, 1913, p. 286.

EINSTEIN, ALBERT. *On the Method of Theoretical Physics*. (The Herbert Spencer Lecture for 1933.) Oxford, 1933, pp. 15.

FISCHER, E. L. *Über das Gesetz der Entwicklung mit Rücksicht auf Herbert Spencer*. Würzburg, 1875.

FISKE, JOHN. *Outlines of Cosmic Philosophy, based on the Doctrine of Evolution*. London, 1874. 2 vols.

FONTANA, BARTOLOMMEO (Professor of Imola). *Del sistema filosofico di Herbert Spencer, e della inesattezza di alcuni suà precetti didattici*. Imola, 1879, pp. 47.

GAQUOIN, KARL. *Die Grundlage der Spencerschen Philosophie insebesondere als Basis für die Versöhnung von Religion und Wissenschaft kritisch beleuchtet. Nebst einem Anhange : Zur Kritik des Laaschen Positivismus*. Darmstadt, 1888, pp. 68.

GAUPP, OTTO. *Die Erkenntnislehre Herbert Spencer*. Berlin, 1890.

GREENE, WILLIAM BATCHELDER. *The Facts of Consciousness and the Philosophy of Mr. Herbert Spencer*. Boston, Mass., 1871.

GROSSE, ERNST DR. PHIL. *Herbert Spencer's Lehre von dem Unerkennbaren*. Leipzig, 1890, pp. vi, 119.

GUTHRIE, MALCOLM. *On Mr. Spencer's Formula of Evolution as an exhaustive statement of the changes of the universe, followed by a résumé of criticisms of Spencer's " First Principles."* London, 1879, pp. 267.

———— *On Mr. Spencer's unification of Knowledge*. London, 1882, pp. xvi, 476.

HÄBERLIN, DR. PAUL. *Herbert Spencer's Grundlagen die Philosophie. Eine kritische Studie*. Leipzig, 1908, pp. iv, 205.

HELLSTRÖM CARL FRANS AUGUST. *Om forhallandet emallanutvecking läran och etiten v. Herbert Spencers Syntetiska filosofi. En studie över den naturalistika utvecklingstoriens etiska konsekvenser. Uppsala Skrifter utg av K. Humanist Vetenskaps Samfunder Uppsala*. Leipzig, 1930, pp. 312.

HORN, E. F. B. *Perisdiatetens Belydning, for Herbert Spencer Philosophi*. (La périodicité dans la philosophie de Herbert Spencer.) Christiania, 1885.

IVERACH, JAMES. *The Philosophy of Mr. Herbert Spencer examined*. (Present Day Tracts, No. 29.) 1884, pp. 58.

JONES, JESSE H. *Know the Truth : a critique on the Hamiltonian Theory of Limitation, including some strictures upon the theories of Herbert L. Mansell and H. Spencer*. Cambridge (Mass.), 1865.

JOSEPH, HORACE W. B. *The Concept of Evolution.* (The Herbert Spencer Lecture, 1924.) Oxford, 1924, pp. 32.

LACY, M. W. *An Examination of the Philosophy of the Unknowable as expounded by Herbert Spencer.* Philadelphia, 1883.

LAMMINE JACQUES, PROF., BRUXELLES. *La théorie de L'Evolution. Étude critique sur les " Premiers Principes " de Herbert Spencer par le chanoine Jacques Lammine.* Bruxelles, 1907, pp. 488.

LAURENS, CH. *L'évolution et Mr. Herbert Spencer.* (Extract de la Controverse et le Contemporaire.) Lyon, 1899, pp. 33.

MARIUPOLSKY, L. *Die Philosophische Begrundung der Evolutionstheorie Herbert Spencer.* Jena, 1897 ; Helsingfors, 1904.

MARTINEAU, JAMES. *The Place of Mind in Nature.* London, 1872.

———— *Essays.* London, 1879.

MICHELET, CARL LUDWIG. *Herbert Spencer's System der Philosophie und sein Verhältnis zur deutschen Philosophie. Nebst den Entgegnungen des Lic. Dr. F. Kirchner und des Prof. Lasson. Philosophische Vorträge, herausgegeben von der Philosophischen Gesellschaft zu Berlin.* (*See* Berlin Philosophische Gesellschaft, Philosophische Vorträge, 1 serie, 1884 (1882), etc.) Halle A.S., 1882 ; Berlin, 1884.

———— *Spencer's Lehre von dem Unerkennbaren.* Leipzig, 1891.

MIGNARDI, G. *Herbert Spencer e la sua scuola condonnati nella Regia Università di Genova.* Macerata, 1881, pp. 32.

MORGAN, C. LLOYD. *Spencer's Philosophy of Science.* (The Herbert Spencer Lecture.) Oxford, 1913, pp. 53.

MORSELLI, EMILIO. *La teoria d'evoluzione secondo e Spencer.* Milan, 1896, pp. 84.

NAUMANN, A. *Spencer wieder Kant. Eine Erörterung der Gegensätze von Realismus und Kriticismus mit besonderer Rücksicht auf das egoistische Moral princip.* Hambourg, 1885, pp. 36.

PAINTER, L. S. H. *Spencer's Evolutionstheorie.* Jena, 1897.

PAPINI, GIOVANNI. *Il Crepusculo dei filosofi Kant Spencer.* 1906.

———— *Le Crépuscule des Philosophes (Kant, Hegel, Comte, Spencer, Nietszche). Precédé d'une étude de William James sur le pragmatisme de Papini.* Paris, 1922.

PAYLOT, JULES. *Quid Apud Millium Spencerum que de Exteris rebus disserentes sit reprehendum.* Thèse latine presentée à la Faculté des Lettres de Paris. Avec une préface sur l'inutilité de la thèse latine. Aureliani.

PEARSON, KARL. *The Grammar of Science.* Second edition. London, 1900, pp. xviii, 548.

[Psychosis.] *On Modern Philosophers: Darwin, Bain and Spencer. Or the Descent of Man, Mind and Body. A rhyme (on Darwin's " Descent of Man," Bain's " Mind and Body," and Herbert Spencer's " Data of Ethics ") with Reasons, Essays, Notes and Quotations.* London, 1884, pp. xix, 215.

RASCH, P. *Untersuchungen über die Grundlagen der Philosophie von Herbert Spencer.* Magdeburg, 1908.

RENOUVIER, CHARLES BERNARD. *Examen des Premiers Principes de Herbert Spencer.* Paris, 1886.

RÓTH, LÁZÁR. *Schelling und Spencer. Eine logische Kontinuität, Berner Studien zur Philosophie und ihrer geschichte.* Bd. 29. Bern, 1901, xxix, 38.

ROYCE, JOSIAH. *Herbert Spencer. An estimate and a review. Together with a chapter of personal reminiscences by James Collier.* New York, 1904, pp. 234.

RUSSELL, BERTRAND [now EARL RUSSELL]. *Scientific Method in Philosophy.* (The Herbert Spencer Lecture.) Oxford, 1914, pp. 30.

SALEEBY, CALEB WILLIAMS. *Evolution the Master Key : a discussion of the principle of Evolution as illustrated in atoms, stars, organic species, mind, society and morals.* London, 1906, pp. viii, 363.

SALVADOR, GUGLIELMO. *Herbert Spencer e l'operea sua.* Firenze, 1900, pp. 80.

SANTAYANA, GEORGE. *The Unknowable.* (The Herbert Spencer Lecture.) Oxford, 1923, pp. 62.

SELLE, CARL FREDERIC. *Herbert Spencer und Fr. Nietzche. Vereinigung der Gegensätze auf Grund einer neuen These.* Leipzig, 1902.

SHEPPERSON, M. F. *Comparative Study of St. Thomas Aquinas and Herbert Spencer.* Pennsylvania, 1925.

SIDGWICK, HENRY. *The Philosophy of Mr. Herbert Spencer in " The Philosophy of Kant and other lectures."* London, 1905, pp. 475.

SULLY, JAMES. *Evolution article in Encyc. Brit.* Ninth edition. 1879.

TILLETT, A. W. *Herbert Spencer refutes recent misrepresentations. Prof. Bourne's Defamatory Attacks met by excerpts culled from the Philosopher's Works.* London, 1910, pp. 15.

TSIMBOURASKY, ALEX. I. *Essai d'un plan de métaphysique,* 2nd ed. ; *Appendix to the Epitome of First Principles of Herbert Spencer* (in Greek). Athens, 1896, pp. 12.

VILLARI, PASQUALA. *Il pensiero filosofico di Spencer.* Torino, 1905.

WAITE, CHARLES BURLINGAME. *Herbert Spencer and his Critics.* Chicago, 1900, pp. 184.

WATSON, JOHN. *Comte, Mill and Spencer. An Outline of Philosophy.* Glasgow, 1895, pp. x, 302.

WEBER, REINHARD H. *Die Philosophie von Herbet Spencer.* Darmstadt, 1892, pp. v, 44.

WECHESSER, WILHELM. *Kants Teleologie. La teleologie de Kant et la philosophie sympathetique de Spencer.* Weinsdorf, 1913.

WEIR, J. *Der Monismus.* Jena, 1895.

WIESNER, Julius van. *Bemerkungen zu Spencers Evolutionsphilosophie (im Jahr. d. Philos. Ges. an. d. Universität Wien, 1914–1915).* Vienna, 1916, pp. iv, 165.

YOUMANS, EDWARD LIVINGSTON. *Herbert Spencer and the Doctrine of Evolution* in *Life and Letters of Edward Livingston Youmans* by John Fiske. And "*Outline of the Evolution Philosophy*," by E. Cazelles. London, 1894, pp. 502–551.

YOUNG, GEORGE A. *Whatever is, was (A philosophical treatise). Also a critical examination into the philosophy of Herbert Spencer and the theories of Charles Darwin.* San Francisco, 1887, pp. xv, 481.

10.—PERIODICAL LITERATURE.

To 1880.

" Spencer's Reconciliation of Religion and Science," by E. L. Youmans. *Christian Examiner*, May, 1862.

" The Positive Philosophy of Mr. Herbert Spencer," by James Hinton. *The Christian Spectator*, May, 1863.

" Herbert Spencer et les études philosophiques en Angleterre," by A. Langel. *Revue de deux Mondes*, February, 1864.

" Naturalism and Agnosticism," by James Ward. *British Quarterly Review*, October, 1873, and January, 1874.

" Biographical sketch of Herbert Spencer," by E. L. Youmans. *Popular Science Monthly*, March, 1876.

" Les Naturalistes philosophes ; Herbert Spencer," by Proost. *Revue des Questions Scientifiques*, January and April, 1878.

" Essays on Herbert Spencer." *Popular Science Monthly*, November, 1874. *North American Review*, October, 1879.

" La Philosophe naturelle en Angleterre," by Proost. *Revue Génève*, July, 1879.

" Herbert Spencer's Data of Ethics," by A. Bain. *Mind*, 4, p. 561. By H. Calderwood. *Contemporary Review*, 37, p. 64. By H. Wace. *Contemporary Review*, 38, p. 254, By A. W. Gundry. *Canadian Monthly*, 16, p. 646. By H. Sidgwick. *Mind*, 5, p. 216. By A. W. Benn. *Mind*. 5, p. 489. By W. James. *Nation*, 29, p. 178. By J. McCosh. *Princeton Review*, 4, p. 607.

" Herbert Spencer." *Quarterly Review*, London, 135, p. 509.

" Herbert Spencer," by W. T. Harris. *Journal of Speculative Philosophy*, St. Louis. 1, p. 6.

" Herbert Spencer and Evolution," by E. L. Youmans. *Popular Science Monthly*, New York, 6, p. 20.

" Herbert Spencer and his Critics," by W. D. L. Sueur. *Canadian Monthly*, Toronto, 17, p. 413.

" Herbert Spencer and his Philosophy," by E. L. Youmans. *Appleton's Journal*, New York, 5, p. 732.

" Atheism, Pantheism and Materialism," by L. H. Atwater. *Princeton Review*, Princeton, 37, p. 243.

" Definition of Mind," by W. James. *Journal of Speculative Philosophy*, St. Louis, 12, p. 1.

" Evolutionary Philosophy of Herbert Spencer," by E. L. Youmans. *North American Review*, Boston and New York, 129, p. 389.

" Green on Spencer," by R. Hodgson, Jr. *Contemporary Review*, 38, p. 898.

" Laws of the Knowable," by B. P. Bourne. *New Englander*, New Haven, 33, p. 1.

" Laws of the Unknowable," by B. P. Bourne. *New Englander*, New Haven, 31, p. 86.

" Spencer and the Basis of Religion," by J. S. Patterson. *Radical Review*, New Bedford, 1, p. 419.

" Spencer on Evolution and Thought," by T. H. Green. *Contemporary Review*, 31, p. 25 ; 32, p. 88.

" Spencer on Relativity of Knowledge," by J. Watson. *Journal of Speculative Philosophy*, St. Louis, 11, .p. 19.

" Spencer on Matter and Force." *British Quarterly Review*, 58, p. 472.

" Philosophy of Herbert Spencer," by J. Watson. *Journal of Speculative Philosophy*, St. Louis, 12, p. 113.

" Philosophy of Herbert Spencer," by St. G. Mivart. *Dublin Review*, 86, p. 26.

" The Philosophy of Herbert Spencer," by C. Wright. *North American Review*, 100, p. 423.

" Herbert Spencer and the Philosophy of Religion," by A. M. Fairbairn. *Contemporary Review*, 40, p. 74.

" Empirical Dissent from Herbert Spencer," by L. Adams. *New Englander*, 35, p. 47.

" Herbert Spencer's Principles of Psychology," by B. P. Bourne. *New Englander*, 32, p. 468. By L. Adams. *New Englander*, 34, p. 419. *Dublin Review*, 75, p. 476.

" Psychological Congruities of Herbert Spencer," by A. Bain. *Mind*, 6, p. 266.

" Refutation of Herbert Spencer," by H. Holt. *Nation*, New York, 8, p. 394. By J. Fiske, *Nation*, 8, p. 434.

" Herbert Spencer's Descriptive Sociology," by E. B. Taylor, *Nature*, 8, p. 544. By N. Porter. *Princeton Review*, 6. p. 268. By E. L. Godkin. *Nation*, 19, p. 288. By A. Bain. *Mind*, 1, p. 128. By E. B. Taylor. *Mind*, 2, p. 141. By A. V. Dicey. *Nation*, 18, p. 63.

" Herbert Spencer on Biology," by F. E. Abbott. *North American Review*, 107, p. 377. By C. Wright. *Nation*, 2, p. 724.

1880–1900.

" The Unknowable and the Unknown," by Stephen Fitzjames. *Nineteenth Century*, June, 1884.

" Herbert Spencer's Soziologischeswerk," by F. Tönnies. *Philosophische Monatshefte*, 1885.

" The Relations of the Individual to the State from Herbert Spencer's point of view " (in Russian), by V. Yarotsky. *The Northern News*, 1885.

" The Gospel according to Herbert Spencer," by Grant Allen. *Pall Mall Gazette*, 28 April, 1890.

" Herbert Spencer." Article by W. H. R. Sorley. *Chambers's Encyclopædia*, 1892.

" Herbert Spencer's Soziologie," by K. Vorländer. *Zeitschrift für Philosophie*, 1893.

" Kritik der Grundanschaungen der Sociologie Herbert Spencer," by F. Barth. *Vierteljahrschrift für Philosophie*, 1893.

" Herbert Spencer's Autobiography," by W. H. Hudson. *Independent Review*, July, 1894.

" Herbert Spencer et l'Evolutionisme Mécaniste," by L. Rouse. *Études Religiques*, March, 1895.

" Herbert Spencer et l'Idée Religieuse," by L. Rouse. *Études Religiques*, August, 1895.

" Herbert Spencer," by A. Lynch. *Free Review*, 1895.

" Herbert Spencer et l'Évolutionisme," by Veloardita. *Revista Italiani di Filosofia*, 1897.

" La Philosophie de Herbert Spencer," by D. Mercier. *Revue Néo-Scholastique*, February, 1898.

" Herbert Spencer's Biology," by Morgan C. Lloyd. *Natural Science Review*, xiii, 1898.

" Comparison of Some Views of Herbert Spencer and Kant," by S. T. Preston. *Mind*, April, 1900.

" Herbert Spencer and F. Harrison." Suppressed book by E. L. Youmans. *Popular Science Monthly*, 27, p. 433.

" Herbert Spencer and the Clothes of Religion," by W. Ward. *Nation*, 3, p. 553.

" Herbert Spencer," by R. A. Proctor. *The Edinburgh Review*,
5, p. 167.

" Herbert Spencer and the French Academy." *Popular Science
Monthly*, 23, p. 554.

" Classifications of Cognitions," by C. Mercier. *Mind*, 8, p. 260.

" Data of Ethics," by A. C. Sewell. *New Englander*, 42, p. 103.
By H. Calderwood. *Contemporary Review*, 37, p. 64. By
H. Wace. *Contemporary Review*, 38, p. 254.

" German View of Herbert Spencer," by F. von Baerenbach.
Popular Science Monthly, 23, p. 195.

" Goldwin Smith on Herbert Spencer," by W. D. le Sueur.
Popular Science Monthly, 22, p. 145.

" Ethics of Herbert Spencer," by A. C. Armstrong. *Journal
Christian Philosophy*, 3, p. 105.

" Few words with Herbert Spencer," by P. Lafargue. *To-day*,
1, p. 416.

" Spencer, Harrison and Arnold," by S. R. Bennett. *Contemporary Review*, 48, p. 700.

" Spencer's Man *versus* The State," by E. de Laveleye. *Contemporary Review*, 47, p. 485.

" Herbert Spencer on American Civilisation," by E. L. Godkin
and A. G. Sedgwick. *Nation*, 35, p. 348.

" Political Philosophy of Herbert Spencer," by W. R. Barnes.
Dial, Chicago, 3, p. 85.

" L. Rice's Criticism of Herbert Spencer," by E. L. Youmans.
North American Review, 139, p. 492.

" Agnosticism of Herbert Spencer," by W. Bussy. *Dublin
Review*, 102, p. 311.

" Herbert Spencer as a Moralist," by W. S. Lilly. *Fortnightly
Review*, 49, p. 427.

" Critics of Herbert Spencer," by C. H. Henderson. *Education*,
Boston, 10, p. 297.

" Our Great Philosophers," by W. S. Lilly. *Contemporary
Review*, 55, p. 752 ; 56, p. 536.

" Collins Epitome of Herbert Spencer," by W. S. Lilly. *Nineteenth Century*, 27, p. 662.

" Herbert Spencer's Reconciliation of Science and Religion," by
J. M. Greenwood. *Education*, Boston, 10, p. 145.

" Herbert Spencer and the Synthetic Philosophy," by W. H.
Hudson. *Popular Science Monthly*, 41, p. 1.

" Herbert Spencer as a Phrenologist," by B. Hollander. *Westminster Review*, 139, p. 142.

" Herbert Spencer as a Thinker," by R. A. Proctor. *Open
Court*, Chicago, 1, p. 145.

" Ethical System of Herbert Spencer," by Van Buren Denslow.
Social Economist, 8, p. 96.

" Guiding Principles of Herbert Spencer," by G. H. Hudson. *Educational Review*, 16, p. 78.

" Metaphysics of Herbert Spencer," by T. C. Laws. *Open Court*, 8, p. 4039.

" Herbert Spencer on the Ethics of Kant." *Open Court*, 2, p. 1155.

" Herbert Spencer on Justice," by J. Iverach. *Contemporary Review*, 2, p. 75.

" Political Ethics of Herbert Spencer," by L. F. Ward. *Annals of the American Academy of Political Science*, vol. 4, January, 1894.

" Herbert Spencer *versus* Balfour," by St. Geo. Mivart. *Nineteenth Century*, 38, p. 261.

" Herbert Spencer and Darwin," by Grant Allen. *Fortnightly Review*, 67, p. 251.

" Herbert Spencer's Views of Kant," by S. T. Preston. *Mind*, 25, p. 234.

" Herbert Spencer's Principles of Biology." *Natural Science Review*, 13, p. 377.

" Herbert Spencer, Buckle and Comte," by L. Gambetta. *North American Review*, 171, p. 55.

" Herbert Spencer's Principles of Psychology," by J. M. Baldwin. *American Naturalist*, 31, p. 553.

" German Appreciation of Herbert Spencer," by R. Didden. *Westminster*, 148, p. 604.

" Herbert Spencer's Principles of Sociology." *Guntons Magazine*, 12, p. 291.

" Reply to Herbert Spencer's Psychology," by J. Ward. *Fortnightly Review*, 73, p. 464.

1900–1930.

" Principles of Biology." Review. *Dial*, 22, 1 January, 1900.

Ward on " Naturalism and Agnosticism." *Popular Science Monthly*, January, 1900.

" Consideration of the Essay on Education," by D. S. Jordan. *Cosmopolitan Review*, July, 1900.

" Four Synthensists ; Cross-sections from Comte, Spencer, Lillienfeld and Schäffle," by B. H. Meyer. *American Journal of Sociology*, July, 1900.

" Herbert Spencer's Life," by H. McPherson. *Athenæum*, 12 May, 1900.

" Spencer's Spencerism," by H. McPherson. *Westminster*, July, 1900.

" Spencer as a Novelist." *Atlantic*. May, 1900.

"Spencer's Synthetic Philosophy," by J. Ward. *Fortnightly Review*, March, 1900.

"Spencer, the Man and the Philosopher," by W. Knight. *Bookman*, October, 1901.

"Facts and Comments." Review in *Athenæum*, June, 1902, by W. Rice. *Dial*, June, 1902. *Nation*, 17 July, 1902.

"Gloom of Herbert Spencer," by S. W. Boardman. *Independent Review*, New York, August, 1902.

"Musical Heresies," *Nation*, 29 May, 1902.

"Spencer and What to Study," by W. F. Harris. *Education*, September, 1902.

"Spencer's Definition of Evolution," by J. B. Nichols. *Monist*, 1 October, 1902.

"Autobiography" reviewed by F. H. Giddings. *Independent Review*, New York, 56, p. 9638, 28 April, 1903. By J. W. Chadwick. *Current Literature*, 1 May, 1903. *Blackwoods*, May, 1903. *Athenæum*, 7 May, 1904. *Living Age*, 28 May, 1903. By W. James. *Atlantic Quarterly*, July, 1903.

"Character Sketch," by G. Iles. *World's Works*, February, 1903. By G. Iles. *Review of Reviews*, February, 1903.

"Greatness of Herbert Spencer," by F. H. Giddings. *Independent Review*, 17 December, 1903.

"Herbert Spencer's Influence on Religious Thought." *Outlook*, 19 December, 1903.

"Herbert Spencer's Life and Teachings," by M. W. Collins. *Outlook*, December, 1903.

"Spencer–George Controversy," by T. Scanlon. *Independent Review*, 30 June, 1903.

"Spencer, the Man," by G. E. Vincent. *American Journal of Sociology*, March, 1903.

"Twilight of the Gods." *Independent Review*, 17 December, 1903.

"L'inconnaisable de Spencer et de Comte," by R. Grulier et M. Brunetière. *Revue Philosophique*, February, 1903.

"Unpublished Letters." *Independent Review*, 5, 26 May, 30 June, 1904.

"What Knowledge is most Worth." *Popular Science Monthly*, January, 1904.

"Breadth of Herbert Spencer's Teaching," by L. G. McPherson. *Cosmopolitan*, February, 1904.

"Character Study," by W. H. Hudson. *North American Review*, January, 1904.

"Dangers of Specialism," by J. B. Crozier. *Fortnightly Review*, January, 1904.

"Defects in the Work of Herbert Spencer," by J. J. Fox. *Catholic World*, February, 1904.

" Herbert Spencer and his Contribution to the Concept of Evolution," by R. Joyce. *International Review*, June, 1904.

" Herbert Spencer and Social Statics," by J. C. Cox. *Athenæum*, 9 January, 1904.

" Herbert Spencer, his Autobiography and his Philosophy," by F. Gribble. *Fortnightly Review*, June, 1904.

" Herbert Spencer on Dreams," by P. F. Bucknell. *Dial*, 16 September, 1904.

" Herbert Spencer's Sociology," by L. F. Ward. *The Independent Review*, New York, 31 March, 1904.

" Liberalism and Divergent Types of Genius," by P. E. Roberts. *Westminster*, November, 1904.

" Personal Reminiscences of Herbert Spencer," by G. Allen. *Forum*, April, 1904.

" Prophet of Evolution," by G. Iles. *World's Work*, January, 1904.

" Spencer and Hîs Critics," by M. von Bulow. *Westminster*, October, 1904.

" Spencer's Japanese Blunder." *Independent Review*, February, 1904.

" Spencer's Nescience," by B. P. Bourne. *Independent Review*, 14 January, 1904.

" Work of Spencer." *Athenæum*, 12 December, 1903. By W. James. *Critic*, January, 1903. *Popular Science Monthly*, January, 1903. *Living Age*, 2 January, 1903. A. M. Fairbairn, *Contemporary Review*, January, 1903. *Westminster*, January, 1904. By S. T. Wood. *Canadian Monthly*, February, 1904. By I. Zangwill. *Reader*, June, 1904.

" Herbert Spencer und A. Schäffle," by P. Barth. *Vierteljahrschrift für Philosophie*, 1904.

" Herbert Spencer—a Character Study," by W. Hudson. *Fortnightly Review*, January, 1904.

" Mr. Herbert Spencer and the Dangers of Specialism," by J. B. Crozier. *Fortnightly Review*, 1904.

" Herbert Spencer's Autobiography," by L. F. Ward. *Science*, 10 June, 1904.

" The Philosophy of Herbert Spencer," by F. Aveling. *Dublin Review*, April, 1904.

" Herbert Spencer," by Ph. B. *Revue de Théologie et de Philosophie*, January, 1904.

" The Philosophical Work of Herbert Spencer," by J. Derwen. *Philosophical Review*, May, 1904.

" Spencer e i suo sytema filosofico," by A. Faggi. *Revista Filosofica*, January and February, 1904.

" La Philosophie de Herbert Spencer," by J. Halleux. *Revue Scholastique.* February and March, 1904.

" Thèse sur les origines de la Philosophie de Spencer," by Berthelot. *Bulletin de la Société française de Philosophie*, April, 1904.

" Herbert Spencer et Charles Renouvier," by Michel. *L'anée Psychologique*, 1904.

" La sintesi de Herbert Spencer," by G. Tarozzi. *Revista di filosofia*, January and February, 1904.

" La filosofia de Herbert Spencer," by Villa. *Revista italiana di Sociologia*, September and December, 1904.

" Herbert Spencer, la sua vita e le sue Opera," by Villa. *La Civilia Catholique*, January and February, 1904.

" Herbert Spencer, his Autobiography and his Philosophy," by Francis Gribble. *Fortnightly Review*, 1904.

" Spencer ; his Influence on Education," by W. T. Harris. *National Educational Association*, 1904, pp. 214–223.

" Spencer as an Educational Force," by A. E. Winship. *National Educational Association*, 1904, pp. 230–231.

" Spencer as a Philosopher," by W. Rose. *National Educational Association*, 1904, pp. 231–234.

" Herbert Spencer," by Th. Gollier. *Revue Générale*, October, November, December, 1905.

" La filosofica de Herbert Spencer," by G. Marchesini. *Revista di filosofia*, January and February, 1905.

" La Religion vella filisofia di Herbert Spencer," by A. Crespi. *Revista di filosofia*, January and February, 1905.

" Herbert Spencer and the Master Key," by J. B. Burke. *Contemporary Review*, June, 1906.

" Spencer and Socialism," Mill. *Independent Review*, 30 August, 1906.

" The Funeral Address of Leonard H. Courtney." Herbert Spencer Lectureship. Letters of Herbert Spencer on his connection with the Ethical movement. *Ethical Review*, No. 4, December, 1906. Herbert Spencer London Memorial Number, London. Reprint by Mark H. Judge, 1906.

" Spencer on Socialism," by W. Hogg. *Westminster*, October, 1907, pp. 367–380.

" The Sociology of Political Parties," by E. F. Ward. *American Journal of Sociology*, January, 1908.

" Herbert Spencer," by Grant Allen. *Edinburgh Review*, July, 1908.

" Spencer's Hedonism and Kant's Ethics of Duty," by P. Carus. *Monist*, April, 1908.

" The Career of Herbert Spencer," by L. F. Ward. *Popular Science Monthly*, January, 1909.

" Herbert Spencer as an Ethical Teacher ," by H. S. Shelton. *International Journal of Ethics*, July, 1910.

" Spencer's Formula of Evolution," by H. S. Shelton. *Philosophical Review*, May, 1910.

" Basis of Sociology," by J. T. Driscoll. *American Catholic Quarterly*, October, 1911.

" Spencerian Formula of Justice," by H. S. Shelton. *International Journal of Ethics*, April, 1911.

" Ethics of Punishment," by J. Crimlaw. March, 1911.

" Unknowable of Herbert Spencer," by E. Jordan. *Philosophical Review*, May, 1911.

" Reviving Old Political Teachers." *Nation*, 4 November, 1915.

" Spencer's Philosophy of Education," by G. R. Davies. *School and Society*, 20 February, 1915.

" State as a Fighting Savage ; Treitschke *versus* Spencer," by W. H. Mallock. *Fortnightly Review*, June, 1915.

" Religions of Comte and Spencer," by Charles E. Hooper. *Open Court*, October, 1915.

" Herbert Spencer's From Freedom to Bondage," with comments by A. P. Gardner. *Forum*, December, 1915.

" Herbert Spencer's Over Legislation," with comments by E. H. Gary. *Forum*, November, 1915.

" Herbert Spencer's The Coming Slavery," with comments by H. C. Lodge. *Forum*, October, 1915.

" Herbert Spencer's The New Toryism," with comments by E. Root. *Forum*, September, 1915.

" Did Spencer anticipate Darwin ? " by I. W. Howerth. *Science*, 31 April, 1916.

" The Sins of Legislators," with comments by H. F. Stone. *Open Court*, March, 1916.

" Herbert Spencer's Postscript to the Man *versus* the State," with comments by D. J. Hill. *Forum*, February, 1916.

" Herbert Spencer's Specialised Administration," with comments by C. W. Eliot. *Forum*, June, 1916.

" Herbert Spencer's The Duty of the State," with comments by W. H. Taft. *Forum*, August, 1916.

" Herbert Spencer's The Great Political Superstition," with comments by H. M. Butler. *Forum*, July, 1916.

" Frustrated Prophet of Pacifism," by J. Jastrow. *Dial*, 30 August, 1917.

" Has the War vindicated Herbert Spencer's Theory of the State ? " *Current Literature*, June, 1917.

" Spencer as a Philosopher," by H. Holt. *Unpartizan Rev.* No. 7. October, 1917.

" Pitfalls in Anthropology into which Spencer fell." *Current Opinion*, September, 1919.

" Herbert Spencer," by G. Sarton. *Scribners Monthly*, June, 1920.

" Physical Spencer," by J. F. Rogers. *Popular Science Monthly*, June, July, 1920.

" Philosophy of Herbert Spencer," by A. H. Lloyd. *Popular Science Monthly*, August, 1920.

" Reflections upon the Sociology of Herbert Spencer," by C. H. Cooley. *American Journal of Sociology*, September, 1920.

" Work and Play with Herbert Spencer," by J. H. Bridge. *Unpartizan Review*, July, 1920.

" Spencer's Philosophy," by A. H. Lloyd. *American Journal of Sociology*. September, 1920.

" Early Psychological Theories of Herbert Spencer," by C. B. Denton. *American Journal of Psychology*, January, 1921.

" Some Typical Contributors to English Sociology and Political Theory," by H. E. Barnes. *American Journal of Sociology*, November, 1921.

" Herbert Spencer on Immigration." *Literary Digest*, 14 August, 1921.

" Herbert Spencer," by D. Bernard. *Monist*, January, 1921.

Note on Double Personality of Herbert Spencer. *Social Research*, July, 1921.

" Herbert Spencer—the Man and his Age," by D. Bernard. *South Atlantic Quarterly*, July, 1922.

" Japanese Craze for Herbert Spencer." *Current Opinion*, January, 1922.

" Great Friendships—George Eliot and Herbert Spencer." *Canadian Monthly*, December, 1922.

" Prophecies and Fulfilment." Prefaces by well-known Americans to a volume of essays by Herbert Spencer. *Freeman*, 21 February, 1923.

" Spencer, Darwin and the Evolution Hypothesis." *Sociological Review*, January, 1925.

" Sources of Spencer's Education particularly Priestly," by H. G. Good. *Journal of Educational Research*, May, 1926.

" Mrs. Webb recalls Herbert Spencer's false Optimism." *Christian Century*, 18 February, 1926.

" My Apprenticeship," by B. Webb. *Survey*, February, 1926.

" Herbert Spencer's Electrical Apparatus," by F. Sherlock. *Nature*, 7 May, 1927.

" The Passing of Herbert Spencer," by W. Barry. *Bookman*, London, August, 1927.

" Darwin on Spencer," by B. J. Stern. *Popular Science Monthly*, February, 1928.

" Herbert Spencer and Music," by E. M. Grew. *Musical Quarterly*, January, 1928.

" Herbert Spencer and Music," by R. Hill. *Musical Opinion*. February, 1928.

" Herbert Spencer on Race Mixture." *Eugenics*. February, 1930.

" Sources of Herbert Spencer's Educational Ideas," by N. T. Walker. *Journal of Educational Research*, November, 1930.

" Herbert Spencer and Oscar Wilde." Extracts from the Diary of Michael Field. Edited by T. S. Moore. *Bookman*, August, 1932. *Cornhill*, May, 1932.

" Satire of Thorstein Veblen's Theory of the Leisure Class," by J. Dorfman. *Journal of Political Science Quarterly*, September, 1932.

" Herbert Spencer and his Work," by W. I. Cranford. *South Atlantic Quarterly*, 3, p. 123.

" Heart of Spencer's Ethics," by F. H. Giddings. *International Journal of Ethics*, 14, p. 496.

" Spencer's Philosophical Work," by J. Dewey. *Philosophical Review*, 13, p. 159.

" Life and Philosophy of Herbert Spencer," by A. S. Pringle Patterson. *Quarterly Review*, 200, p. 240.

" 40 Years of Scientific Friendship ; Herbert Spencer and Tyndall," by M. Shipley. *Open Court*, 24, pp. 252–255.

INDEX.

**Other Current
Atheling Books**